Awakening Consciousness

SELECTED LECTURES OF SIR GEORGE TREVELYAN

Awakening Consciousness

SELECTED LECTURES OF
SIR GEORGE TREVELYAN

COMPILED BY

Keith Armstrong

GODSTOW PRESS

First published 2008 by
Godstow Press
60 Godstow Road, Oxford OX2 8NY
www.godstowpress.co.uk

ISBN 978-0-9547367-8-1

Typeset in Garamond by Jean Desebrock of Alacrity
Cover design by Linda Smith

Printed by Hobbs the Printers, Totton, Hampshire

ACKNOWLEDGEMENTS

THE PUBLISHERS would like to thank the following who contributed so much to this book, giving so freely of their time and enthusiasm. It was Keith Armstrong who had the vision of publishing a selection of Sir George's lectures. He collected the material from various sources, turned it into electronic copy and has helped throughout with the editing process. Janice Dolley, Development Director of the Wrekin Trust, oversaw the whole project and gave generously of her time and advice. David Lorimer, Executive Vice-President of the Wrekin Trust, gave much helpful guidance and Ruth Nesfield-Cookson contributed the introduction.

We would also like to thank Sir George's great-nephew, the artist Jonathan Parker, for his permission to use the portrait of Sir George on the cover. *George on the Wrekin*, 1997, on permanent display in the National Trust Collection at Wallington in Northumberland, was inspired by a photo taken by the artist's father at Attingham in 1972, when Jonathan was four years old. 'The event was legendary - I remember cine films and photos of the people and light.'

Acknowledgements and thanks are made to the following for quotations appearing in the text:

'The Cage' by Martin Armstrong from *The Bird-Catcher* (© Martin Armstrong 1929) is reproduced by permission of PFD (www.pfd.co.uk) on behalf of The Estate of Martin Armstrong.

W.B. Yeats, extracts from 'Sailing to Byzantium' and 'The Second Coming', A.P. Watt Ltd. on behalf of Gráinne Yeats.

T.S. Eliot, extracts from 'The Four Quartets', *Collected Poems* 1909-1962, Faber & Faber Ltd.

Robert Frost, extracts from 'The Trial by Existence' from *The Poetry of Robert Frost*, edited by Edward Connery Lathem, published by Jonathan Cape. Reprinted by permission of The Random House Group Ltd.

Pierre Teilhard de Chardin, from *The Divine Milieu*, HarperCollins 1957, LE MILIEU DIVIN, Editions du Seuil 1957 and Sussex Academic Press; from *Hymn of the Universe*, HYMNE DE L'UNIVERS by Pierre Teilhard de Chardin © Editions du Seuil, 1961; from *The Future of Man*, HarperCollins 1964.

Sydney Carter, 'Nowhere and Never', reproduced by permission of Stainer & Bell Ltd., London, England.

Sri Aurobindo, extracts from 'Karmayogin', CWSA Vol. 8, p.168 and 'Essays in Philosophy and Yoga', CWSA Vol. 13, p.509-511, reproduced by kind permission of Sri Aurobindo Ashram Trust.

Every effort has been made to trace copyright holders and to obtain their permission for the use of copyright material. The publishers would gladly receive information enabling them to rectify any error or omission in subsequent editions.

CONTENTS

FOREWORD

EVERYONE WHO MET Sir George Trevelyan will have their own special memories of his dramatic and inspiring presence. I first met him at the Mystics and Scientists conference in 1981, when I was teaching at Winchester College, little realising how my own role would evolve into a long association with these conferences, with which I have been intimately connected for twenty years. A couple of years later, I invited him to give a guest lecture to the Toynbee Society, which I was running with a friend at the time. His delivery captivated even the sceptical and rational Wykehamists (shorthand for those attending Winchester College) with whom he entered into animated discussion at dinner in my house after the lecture.

After leaving Winchester in 1986, one of my first engagements was a joint seminar with George at Lorna St Aubyn's centre in the South of France on 'The New Gnostics'. In subsequent years, we also ran courses on 'The New Essenes' and 'The New Cathars'. These movements represent esoteric, gnostic and ecological streams within the Christian tradition, evoking strong resonances with the agenda of our era. One abiding memory of these hugely enjoyable courses was the adjective game we played at the end. George created a narrative about the course, leaving gaps for people to insert adjectives as we went round the room. The result was invariably hilarious and often synchronistically instructive. I also recall his immense physical courage and determination in struggling up some of the hills towards Cathar castles, particularly at Puylaurens, with the stalwart help of his companion Rhoda Cowen.

Looking back on these experiences and reading these lectures with the benefit of hindsight, it is clear that Sir George had a remarkable grasp of the underlying realities of our time. He was quick to appreciate the value of the Gaia hypothesis, realised the centrality of the evolution and expansion of consciousness, and was committed to a thorough-going holism in all his activities. He had internalised and integrated these insights into his own vision, which he articulated with the powerful help of inspirational poetry. Running through his lectures is a range of striking metaphors with perennial relevance.

Some readers will recall how he explained that the human soul was 'a droplet of Divinity' in the ocean of the Divine intelligence. Water metaphors appear elsewhere in his work: the Aquarian Age and that of the water-bearer. The process can be likened to a rising tide of consciousness leading to a flood of understanding. Alternatively, he might speak of an influx of light, with the understanding that God is quintessentially Life and Love, of which we ourselves can become the bearers.

Another key metaphor is that of awakening, especially, as he put it, spiritual awakening in our time. An awakening from what he called 'the sleep of the senses' in which we mistake our bodily identity for our ultimate essence. Indeed, one of his favourite poems was Christopher Fry's *The Sleep of Prisoners*, with its concluding lines 'Will you wake, for pity's sake?' In the wonderful book by Valentin Tomberg, *Meditations on the Tarot*, the author draws a parallel between sleeping and waking, forgetting and remembering, death and (re)birth. As Plotinus famously put it, 'remembering is for those who have forgotten'; likewise, awakening is for those who are asleep and rebirth for those who have died to the old in themselves. Sir George was fond of quoting the lines from Goethe, 'if you do not grasp this, *die and become*, then you are but a dismal guest on this dark earth.'

George was convinced that humanity is currently at a turning point of its evolution. His expectations were somewhat apocalyptic, and have not come about in the timescale he anticipated. Perhaps, however, the process is a slower one, even if it can be accelerated through the awareness created by major disasters. There is little doubt that we are moving towards an intensification of apocalyptic possibilities in all major spheres of life. This has both individual and collective aspects. We have less influence over the collective, but a great deal of influence on our own individual response, and even more so on in the inner attitude we adopt towards life. We can, as Sir George suggested, try out the power of living ideas.

George catalysed and supported many initiatives which are still flourishing today, apart from Wrekin Trust, which Janice Dolley describes in her afterword. For instance the Gatekeeper Trust, the Schools and Universities Network and the Wessex Research Group (with the late Nigel Blair), the Francis Bacon Research Trust with Peter Dawkins, where he often took part in Shakespeare weekends. He was a friend of Lady Eve Balfour and a number of early Soil Association conferences were held at Attingham. He spoke often at The Findhorn Foundation – again his connection goes back to the very early days when giant vegetables were being grown in poor soil. He was part of The Lamplighter Movement and supported the Institute for Outdoor Adventure – which is now the Stoneleigh Project. This reflected his passion for the outdoors manifest in the Northumbrian manhunt, cave exploration and mountaineering. Here he was following a great Trevelyan tradition – his uncle G.M. Trevelyan used to walk long distances with Bertrand Russell on the Cornish coast.

George had a special connection with Hawkwood College through Bernard and Ruth Nesfield-Cookson (Ruth writes about this in her introduction) and with the Columba Hotel on Iona, where Elinore Detiger arranged a remarkable week-long meeting in the autumn of 1987. Among the other organisations whose work he supported were the Centre for Alternative Technologies in Wales, the Richard Glyn Foundation at Gaunts House, The Essene Network, Wholistic World Vision, Tony Neate's School of Channelling and the Haus der Begegnung in Bad Pyrmont, Germany. All this reflects the range of his interests and enthusiasms. He was always ready to lend his support and encouragement to worthwhile activities, and also wrote forewords for quite a number of books.

However, all this activity did not imply a lesser intensity of inner life. Perhaps the central mystical and paradoxical question that can be posed on the spiritual path is Who Am I? In the Zen tradition, it might be seen as the ultimate koan. In Christianity, it is an affirmation of non-duality between human and divine, as Fr Bede Griffiths explained in his 1992 Mystics and Scientists lectures. A person's answer to this question indicates their current level of identity. As one opens to deeper levels, so the personal becomes suffused with the universal, with those principles of life, light and love already referred to. This was the path taken by Sir George. In his last years, he embodied and emanated light and love, with an undiminished energy and enthusiasm for life and its possibilities. Readers will sense this spirit of adventure as they read these pages by a modern Knight of the Round Table as he pursued his Grail Quest. May this encourage you to follow your own deepest aspirations.

DAVID LORIMER
January 2008

David Lorimer was Chair of the
Wrekin Trustees for many years and
is now Executive Vice-President.

INTRODUCTION

WHEN IN MARCH, 1960, I became secretary to Sir George
Trevelyan, my world was about to be transformed. I was to begin
to find real meaning and purpose in life. George was running
a short-term residential adult college (the Shropshire Adult
College), offering mainly two- or three-day courses in the
romantic setting of Attingham Park, a stately country home in
the heart of England. He had an infectious enthusiasm for every
subject he offered, but spiritual adult education was gradually
becoming the subject to which he would eventually dedicate
his life.

In 1960, George was a handsome, silver-haired man with
bright blue eyes in his early fifties, a man who could not but be
noticed when he entered a room, but who would always retain a
deep humility. As guests arrived, he escorted them to their rooms,
carrying their bags for them; returning to the office he dropped
down the stairs three at a time. Every weekend, after only
forty-eight hours at Attingham, people left looking so much more
awake – ready to re-think their habitual ideas and attitudes – than
they had looked on arrival. Stirring people by what he said was
something George could do to perfection. He would later
become an author, but it was in the spoken word that his
passion had the greatest power.

In the fifteen years I worked with George, I watched
him develop from being a man in the physical prime of life,
charming everybody he met, awakening people to a wide variety
of subjects, to a man who accepted that he had wider respons-
ibilities than had previously been thought. It would be his role
to teach that, at around the beginning of the new millennium,
people must begin to experience not a religious revival but a
spiritual awakening. He would warn that disasters, including the

results of climate change, earthquakes, terrorism, financial breakdown, mental illness, etc., would be hitting us. Humankind's consciousness had evolved through past civilisations. Now it would be up to humanity to accept that people were eternal spiritual beings, must develop brotherliness, must create a new age, believing in a spiritual world view, and must fit themselves to work in co-operation with angelic beings.

Now, in 2007, this is obvious to an ever-increasing number of people but George was talking about it when neither the immanence of a greatly increased number of disasters, nor the fact that we are spiritual beings dipping down to earth for a short educational period, were normally acknowledged. I believe that George takes his place as a leading figure in the current phase of the evolution of consciousness. He was seeing these things when they were revolutionary. It took enormous courage to speak out against orthodox thinking and a great wisdom and diplomacy to cause as little offence as possible.

George was born into an aristocratic and agnostic family and he took a degree in history at Cambridge. He had hoped to create an adult college at the family home at Wallington in Northumberland, but his father bequeathed the property to the National Trust. However, in 1947, to his surprise and delight, he was given the opportunity to create a college sponsored both by local authorities and Birmingham University, in the centre of England at Attingham Park. Here he could show his idea that adult education is an 'escape into reality', and here he was able to present spiritual knowledge amongst a wide variety of courses. The next twenty-three years gave him a wonderful launching pad for the work he was to do after leaving Attingham.

George's life was transformed during the Second World War when he attended a lecture by Dr Walter Johannes Stein, who had been a close associate of Rudolf Steiner, the Austrian philosopher and educationalist. Standing at the back of a crowded lecture hall, George was galvanised. To every idea presented by Stein he said 'Yes! Yes! Yes!'. For the first time he heard about the Cosmic Christ, the celestial hierarchies, karma and reincarnation, of man as an eternal spirit dipping down to earth for periods of 'education'. George knew then that he had been waiting for these thoughts and insights. He was later to acknowledge the validity of many movements and thinkers but always looked on Rudolf Steiner and Anthroposophy as his primary inspiration. I remember the occasion when he said to me as we left a conference we had been running on 'The Cosmic Christ': 'Ruth, it is the Cosmic Christ that we are primarily about.' He was totally committed to Christianity in his personal life but always acknowledged that all major religions had their destined roles in the evolution of consciousness.

It was in the 1950s that George had organised a course at Attingham on Rudolf Steiner's work. The speakers were intellectuals from Central Europe. Few attended the course and they understood little of what was presented. George realised that it was his role to absorb the main aspects of Steiner's work and to present it in a way more suitable for an English-speaking audience. This was the background of what some were to call his 'New Age Crusade'.

As the years went on, George explored the work of many other thinkers and made some of their ideas his own. However, Steiner's work always remained the principal influence on his thinking. He also gained his knowledge from the works of Shakespeare, Goethe, Blake, Hopkins, the romantic poets, etc., and also the works of more modern thinkers including Teilhard de Chardin, Wellesley Tudor Pole, Grace Cook and the White Eagle teachings, etc. His close link with Pierre Vilayat Inayat Khan, the leader of the Sufi movement in Britain, illustrated his awareness of the current significance of Eastern streams of spirituality. He knew there were many routes up the mountain and that no one route was right for everybody. George had the capacity to extract the core of the ideas of others and to bring them to life. He was never sensational and never attempted to force people to accept what he said. He asked people to re-think new ideas, to let them live within them and then decide whether they were true for them.

It was in June 1964 that George mounted a course at Attingham on 'Death and Becoming', sharing the lecturing with

Bernard Nesfield-Cookson, who is now my husband. When we were planning the course, George said to me, 'Never let me be so brave again' – fearful that he would draw a bad reaction by presenting a subject which, at that time, was simply not mentioned. However, for the first time in the history of the College, we ran a course which attracted one hundred and seventy participants. It was then that George realised that it was time to be increasingly courageous in what he offered. He was later to say to me that if he achieved no more in life than to transform attitudes towards death, then his life would have been well spent.

George believed earthly life to be a short interlude in the totality of our eternal life, a time for necessary adult education. This belief was an integral part of his being. In his personal life he accepted illness as part of the educational process. Having been able to run downhill at speed only months earlier, he described the onset of crippling arthritis in a knee as being a 'mild inconvenience'. He faced the ageing process with dignity, even with humour, never with complaint or fear of the future. He knew, without doubt, that he would be returning to a sphere where he would be reunited with friends and colleagues and other spiritual beings and that the life of development and service would continue.

George's cultural interests were wide. His great love was poetry – and his memory was phenomenal. To listen to him and his sister, Kitty, capping each other with poetry, ranging from Shakespeare and the Romantic poets to border ballads, was to feel yourself to be sharing in a cultural event typical of house parties in the time of their youth. He was a great orator and knew poetry to be a wonderful medium by which to fire the imagination with spiritual ideas. I remember a weekend course he gave on Gerard Manley Hopkins's 'The Wreck of the Deutschland'. Whilst talking, he saw that Hopkins had re-lived the nun's experience of Christ at the moment of her death. In turn, it seemed that George, and therefore his audience, also shared this moment. We had a hint of what is meant by an increased intensity of awareness.

George was a dramatic figure himself and I am sure he could have been a great Shakespearean actor … he played lead roles in amateur productions at Attingham and he used drama and ritual as teaching aids. In later years he could appear to be an old man when starting to talk … but the years seemed to quickly drop away as the ideas and words flowed. He was using his abilities to the full, yet never became dogmatic or sensational; he insisted that listeners have their freedom to accept or reject what he said. As a climax to the courses presenting some aspect of a spiritual world view, he invariably 'lifted' the whole audience by the use of poetry and other appropriate quotations, such as the Great Invocation, and music. An excerpt from Wagner's 'Lohengrin' was a regular favourite. On one occasion we concluded with an excerpt from Beethoven's Pastoral Symphony. Gradually we all became aware of a great mooing from the cows in the park. It appeared that they were joining in with our experience.

As part of summer schools or New Year or Epiphany celebrations, we often processed round the house bearing lighted candles – this being a serious and dedicated ritual for most of us. On one occasion a trumpet sounded from the pinnacle of the triangular arch above the colonnade at the front of the house, played by one lone trumpeter; we broke into 'Hark, the Herald Angels Sing'. On another occasion George and I were heading the procession at a time when he was very incapacitated with arthritis and we were about to start the Wrekin Trust with very limited financial support. We launched into 'We Shall Overcome' and a meaningful glance passing between us.

George had a great love of architecture and was passionately enthusiastic about the furniture created in tune with the ideals of the Arts and Crafts movement. He lectured on architecture and enjoyed escorting parties of enthusiasts around the country. In his youth he worked in the Gimson workshops in the Cotswolds, these being a part of the Arts and Crafts Movement. He personally designed and created some very fine pieces of furniture. He was also thrilled by heraldry. Here his aristocratic heritage, his love of the heroic and of the symbolism by which spiritual truths could be represented artistically, were united. At one time, heraldic shields, painted by students on 'Creative Leisure' courses, adorned the stairs at Attingham.

The world of nature was another of George's great interests. He presented annual courses on the study of birds, rousing the whole household at 3.30am on a May morning to escort us along the banks of the river to hear the dawn chorus. He often spoke about the metamorphoses of plants – presenting the ideas of Goethe and Steiner on the development of the flower and fruit from the original seed.

George supported and encouraged many people who were doing pioneering work. For instance, in the 1960s the annual Soil Association conferences were held at Attingham. At that time Lady Eve Balfour and her colleagues were fighting a lonely battle against the ridicule they received. The prevalent thinking of the time claimed that ideas about the value of organic husbandry were no more than the empty thoughts of a few cranks. George did all he could to support he Association and, in 1964, presented a course to the general public on 'Life Threatened' – this then being a somewhat revolutionary idea. Today, of course, support for agricultural methods which do not involve artificial fertilisers and pesticides is widespread.

Another organisation George supported from its infancy was the Findhorn Foundation, based in north-east Scotland. This was founded by Peter and Eileen Caddy and Dorothy Maclean in 1962. The Community began its existence in a single caravan in the corner of a park on the sand dunes, with three adults and three children. Eileen was receiving guidance form the spiritual worlds regarding the work they would do. This was to lead to the development of the Community that is now a Foundation and a Non-Governmental Organisation attached to the UN and has spread its influence worldwide. George gave the Findhorn Foundation and community a great deal of support in its early days.

In 1971, George, already crippled with arthritis, reached retirement age. He and I knew we could not but continue with his work. We therefore created the Wrekin Trust to enable us to run short courses in conference houses around Britain, spreading the work further afield. Initially, we were running an average of a course every two weeks, though George did not need to go to all of them. At the same time he was giving an ever-increasing number of single lectures around Britain and beyond. The Wrekin Trust came to a temporary closure in the early nineties, before its revitalisation before the end of the decade, but it had given him the next platform that he needed. He was receiving as many invitations as he could fulfil. He was seeing ever more clearly that the acceptance of changed attitudes to life and of personal transformation were essential if humanity was to survive the impending challenges. He was now known as a leading figure in the so-called 'New Age' movement throughout the English-speaking world and his books were being translated into other languages.

George was very aware that for his lectures to hold conviction, he must live out in his own life all that he believed in. His meditations were both an exploration of things spiritual and a personal training. When I first heard his lectures in the 60s they were idealistic. He often used the phrase 'there never was such a time to be alive'. He referred to the coming challenges as though we would enjoy them! By the 80s, whilst still retaining his positivity and enthusiasms, he was also showing a much greater understanding of people as psychological beings with challenges to meet, and he was seeing much more of the size of the disasters that would be confronting us. I shared a wonderful moment with him at Hawkwood College in 1986 at one of the events that was celebrating his eightieth birthday. He said to me 'I have fallen deeply in love', followed at length by, 'with everybody'. I believe this remark illustrated that he had reached a very high point in spiritual development. This was not lightly said. He had carried a great light for many years. Now he had also found a great love for all humanity. He had long been stressing that we were approaching a great turning-point for all mankind, but now he had a new conviction that a Rising Tide of Love was beginning to happen, that Christ is Love and becoming ever more available to us in the etheric worlds, if, in full freedom, we can

awaken to Him. The words he quoted so often from Christopher
Fry's *A Sleep of Prisoners* were an integral part of all that he was:

> Thank God our time is now when wrong
> Comes up to meet us everywhere,
> Never to leave us till we take
> The longest stride of soul men ever took.
> Affairs are now soul size.
> The enterprise
> Is exploration into God.
> Where are you making for? It takes
> So many thousand years to wake
> But will you wake for pity's sake?

George's long-term influence on many areas of spiritual
development, of thinking and activity involving service to
humanity and the planet is inestimable. Moreover, there is
no doubt that his courage in presenting what was in his time
revolutionary thinking, his inspiration and encouragement,
certainly made a considerable contribution towards mankind
taking 'the longest stride of soul men ever took', that
mankind has to take if our tenancy of the planet is to continue.

This little book cannot be more than an introduction to the work
of Sir George Trevelyan. It contains only a small selection of the
thousands of lectures he gave, most of them dating from
the 1970s. However, I sincerely hope it will encourage readers to
explore further, to read George's books (he felt *Exploration into
God* to be the culminating point of what he had to say) and the
biography, *Sir George Trevelyan and the New Spiritual Awakening* by
Frances Farrer. There is much material on George's website –
www.sirgeorgetrevelyan.org.uk, including his taped lectures. May
George's introduction lead you to further exploration, to the
work of other thinkers and to your own personal journey and
contribution to the next phase of humanity's life on earth.

RUTH NESFIELD-COOKSON

1

THE ALLEGORICAL JOURNEY

THE GREAT LEGENDS of mankind all enshrine truths which are of the utmost importance to us now. This is, broadly speaking a materialistic age, which may be defined as an outward-looking age in which the values are chiefly what we can get of things and possessions. The inward values, the inward vision, tends to get lost or overlaid. The great truths about the development of the human soul and of man's relation to the great 'whole' of life were taught in the mystery temples of the ancients. Over the gates of Eleusis was carved 'Man know thyself and thou shalt know the universe'. Only the candidate for initiation might hear the secrets and if he betrayed them, death was his reward. The secret knowledge however was hidden in the myths and legends. It is as if the higher beings poured knowledge in symbol form through those who could hear and record the great stories. From the great legends such as the Odyssey to the smallest fairy story, all these tales seem to enshrine vital truths which our modern psychological and spiritual understanding can learn to unravel. The knowledge is of deepest significance particularly for modern man. It is curious that in an age which tends to despise fairy tales and myths as mere fantasy, their content is rediscovered as holding the truths we most need to know.

For the healing impulses of our time this hidden knowledge needs to be recovered. The legends, in a thousand variants, all tell one tale. It is the picture of the eternal being of man, belonging to a timeless realm of light, descending into the plane of the earth to take to himself a body so that he may pass through adventures in dark forest or wild ocean. It undertakes the allegorical journey which is life on the earth plane and is put through ordeals and soul trials until he is worthy to win the love of his 'lady', symbolising his higher spiritual self. Then, the mystical marriage consummated, he returns to the realm from which he descended, a step in consciousness having been achieved through his experiences.

Once we see that in all our individual lives we are working out an allegorical journey whose end is the return to the Realm of Light, our whole attitude towards our apparent misadventures radically changes. We are prepared gladly to accept our personal destiny as part of a much larger pattern full of meaning. This gives us courage to accept all that comes to us and to say 'yes' to our experiences, however difficult or frustrating they may seem. All the myths include the experience of loneliness – of being cut off from the divine source.

> Alone alone, all all alone,
> Alone on a wide wide sea
> And never a saint took pity
> on my soul in agony.

We are each of us in some sense the 'ancient mariner'.

The hero legends concern the souls who are drawn into the task of exploring back into the realms of the eternal to bring down to benighted fellow men some elixir of life, some life-enhancing diadem which proves the reality of the higher worlds. This may be the golden fleece, or some heavenly jewel, or a magic sword or the Holy Grail itself.

The assurance of higher reality is what man needs today. There are doctrines abroad, notably in Marxism, which would have us believe that matter is the only reality, that all the marvellous framework of art, philosophy and religion is only a super-structure which human fantasy has built up for consolation. Man is then seen as nothing but an economic animal.

If this be so then it is quite valid to breed him like cattle and to condition him in concentration camps. What modern man desperately needs is the inner assurance that the core of the human soul is eternal and belongs to the realm of spiritual being. The logical intellect alone cannot prove this and indeed may flatter itself that it can disprove it. The raised Imagination, that most precious faculty of the soul can discover the radiant truth – true Imagination can enter into the secrets of life and discover the great truth which is spoken in the symbolical language of every myth. Once you see that each soul is an unrepeatable experiment of God, you cannot and dare not enslave and torture your fellow man. It is strange that the telling of fairy stories to children and of great legends to the young comes to be seen as one of the strongest answers to materialist communism. The inner being of the child knows subconsciously that it belongs to the eternal realms of light and is strengthened by these stories to face bravely the soul trials of this earth plane. This knowledge is part of a great healing process. In this age of so much separation, when the scientific intellect explores ever deeper into division, the Imagination comes to give us the conviction that life is a great unity and that the planet on which we tread is indeed a living organism. Our earth is to be seen as a huge living creature.

Nature is a mighty and complex whole of which man is integrally part. It is so easy for the modern mind to think that the earth is a dead speck of dust in a vast empty cosmos and that man is no more than a chance evolutionary accident to whom nature is quite indifferent. When this world-view is held we may appear justified in exploiting our planet for personal gain and greed.

The view which our enhanced imagination gives us is quite other. The great truth is born in on us that the Earth is a living creature, that nature is an incredibly complex whole of which the human kingdom is a vital part. Man is then seen as, so to speak, an organ of consciousness of this being of earth. He is that point where nature becomes aware of herself and is able to 'think' out into the yet greater organism of the cosmos. As we wake up to

3

the unity of life we see that so far from being merely a dead speck of matter the earth is a tiny seed carrying in it however a vast spiritual future. Why otherwise should the exalted Being of the Spiritual Sun have chosen to have descended into the stream of earth evolution? The task of man is to serve the Earth.

The world of matter in all its complexity and diversification is shot through with the world of spirit by which it has been formed. The higher worlds of which the legends speak are very near to us since spirit can be found within matter, impregnating it and giving it 'life'. Healing is the letting of the Light of the great Oneness pour through all aspects of our being. Healing, 'Whole-ing', is the achievement of the reality of that vision which the Imagination can grasp.

The higher worlds, the realms of Spirit, are not infinitely distant. In the sense of higher frequency they interpenetrate and indeed form our material plane and are to be found and explored by imaginative consciousness.

When man can really learn to co-operate with these planes of Being, vast new possibilities for human development in the New Age begin to open up. For our very intellectual minds one of the most valuable lines of approach is the re-interpretation of the great achievements of the human spirit in mythology, poetry and drama, rediscovering the eternal truths in a symbolic form which our modern minds can understand.

2

SPIRITUAL AWAKENING
IN OUR TIME

OUR THEME is spiritual awakening in our time. An extraordinary phenomenon seems to be happening in these years and months; it seems as if there is a new consciousness rising in people, bringing with it a deep sense of joy and of hope that change is afoot. Something is really happening, something that is exciting and full of prospects for the redemption of mankind. Let me stress immediately that I am not trying to force any form of dogma or belief. We all know that it brings up a resistance if we feel something is being put over on us. It is quite a different thing to invite thought. The mind has a faculty for apprehending an idea for its beauty. Do we not all have that experience? This may be a first step towards opening the faculties of higher knowledge. It could be the sign that we are beginning to be able to seize an idea immediately out of what we might call the reservoir of living ideas which fills the Cosmos. We take the idea and live with it as a concept. Think it, and if it is true it will draw to itself other ideas which support it, carrying certainty and enhancing the meaning of life.

As I said, there seems to be something comparable to a rising tide within our consciousness. What Teilhard de Chardin calls the 'noosphere', that layer of intelligence encircling the earth, seems to be shot through and lightened by a spiritual vision of what life and the universe is about, and this new light is available to all who have open minds.

What then is this spiritual world-view? There are those who are convinced that matter is the primary, if not the only, reality, and that by spiritual values we mean simply that superstructure of poetry and painting, architecture and music, and religion in the narrower sense. A materialistic outlook is, after all, concerned with outward looking and with the getting and control of things and the meeting of desires. On the other hand there are those who have the deep conviction that matter is derivative from the world of spirit, that behind all appearance is a vast universal realm of absolute being, of creative intelligence from which the forms in the relative world have been deposited. This is saying no more than that which we have so often said and read and heard; 'In the beginning was the Word and the Word was with God and the Word was God, by Him were all things made and without Him was not anything made that was made.'

Do we or do we not believe that? Dare we take that literally? First comes Divine Imagining, creative intelligence which divides itself into ideas, into exalted fixings, sub-dividing down into lesser levels of being, and gradually consolidating those ideas into matter. This planet is nothing but a reflection of the divine ideas which as living thoughts have worked down from this realm of creative thought. Space is not an empty dead mechanism but is shot through and through with thought, with being, with creative spirit. The whole of space is, in this sense, alive. It looks to us like empty space because we are looking at it merely with eyes that are tuned in to the vibratory rate of physical matter. Therefore the great astronomer of Napoleon's time, La Place, could say proudly, 'I have searched the heavens with my telescopes and I found no sign of God!' Of course, however great the telescope, you are still looking on the matter-bound frequency rate, but if we could tune in to a higher rate, other levels of being and consciousness would become apparent. It becomes clear that on earth we live in the lowest, slowest, darkest frequency band. If the earth is a reflection of the realms of absolute Being, must we not conceive that it is in truth a living creature, with its own organs, glands, sensitivity, breathing and thinking. We men are like corpuscles in its bloodstream, points in which evolution becomes conscious of itself and can think out towards the cosmos.

This thinking, if it be valid, reverses the tacit assumption held by so many that man is but an accident in evolution in a universe to which he is irrelevant, and which cares nothing at all about him. While we thought that the planet is merely a lump of mineral, a tiny speck of dust in a vast and indifferent Cosmos, then naturally enough we felt that we are perfectly free to exploit the minerals and the life of the animals of the planet to our own advantage, for our own pleasure or gain. But now we begin to come up against the vision that the earth is a great living being of which we are part, that we are therefore truly the stewards of life on this planet, and that we have a profound relation to all the kingdoms of nature. Man has something which none of the other kingdoms of nature have – he is the bearer of the spiritual being, a conscious 'ego'. The inner core of each of us, that which can say 'I', is a droplet of the divine source, a spark of the cosmic light. Life is inextinguishable. The outer sheath in which being is enshrouded can decay and fall away, but nothing can possibly kill the eternal spark. Each of us is on a long and endless journey through life on many levels of consciousness. If the spark were extinguishable it would make nonsense of the whole concept of a Creator. If you are drawn to this view then let's take it as a working thought that the droplets which take to themselves the sheath of a body are in fact imperishable. As the Bhagavad Gita says, 'you always are and you always will be. There is no time when you were not, and there will be no time when you are not.'

This is an awe-inspiring thought. It means that discussion of survival becomes irrelevant. Of course you will survive the change that is called death; how can you do any other? There are many levels of consciousness in which the spiritual being which is in each of us can have experience. 'In My father's house are many mansions,' said the Christ. Our souls have descended into this lowest density for a very good reason, and we are on a path back, through the aeons, to that divine source from which we came.

Why then are we down here? It looks as if the divine invention of gravity, on a planet like this, gives the setting into which the eternal core in each of us can incarnate in order to go through the experience of drastic limitation which entry into a body involves. It looks as if the descending soul has to accept something like a death in entering into the sarcophagus of the body, and that the function of the body is to slow down a spiritual being that can move at the pace of thought and can expand consciousness to the width of the Cosmos. Experiences in meditation sometimes lead us towards understanding that potentially we are able to unite in thought with the Creative Intelligence, with the thought field of the Universe, to draw directly and immediately from the great reservoir of creative ideas. The human mind can lift beyond brain-bound thinking, and unite with the whole thought structures and processes of the world.

This means the possibility of man drawing knowledge immediately, if he can but step up the voltage of his thinking to unite with Creative Intelligence on the higher levels. Some of the great seers of our time, following the achievement of Rudolf Steiner, have demonstrated the possibility of this development in human thinking, proving to us that ultimately there are no limits to knowledge. We are incarnated in an extraordinary mechanism, itself the work of the divine thinking and divinely-guided evolution, and so complex that it is able to carry self-consciousness and open itself towards cosmic consciousness and ultimately God-consciousness. But let us accept that our entry into the earth life is a powerful limitation. There is an admirable and brief poem by Martin Armstrong which he calls 'The Cage':

> Man, afraid to be alive
> Shuts his soul in senses five
> From fields of uncreated light
> Into the crystal tower of sight,
> And from the roaring songs of space
> Into the small flesh-carven place
> Of the ear whose cave impounds

Only small and broken sounds,
And to his narrow sense of touch
From strength that held the stars in clutch,
And from the warm ambrosial spice
Of flowers and fruits of paradise,
Into the frail and fitful power
Of scent and tasting, sweet and sour;
And toiling for a sordid wage
There in his self-created cage
Ah, how safely barred is he
From menace of Eternity.

There is the soul, shut inside the cage, filtering a little of cosmic experience through the limitations of the senses, which are tuned only to work in this world. Perhaps the legs are not so much to walk with but rather to slow us down to a pace at which we can carry on our social relationships effectively. If we were all moving at the pace of Ariel, business on this plane would be much more difficult!

We start with the premise that behind all is the great One-ness of living creative Being and creative thought, of which this world of separation is only a manifestation, and that we in our ordinary consciousness are living in the illusion that the world is a mass of millions of separate things and people. It is all one great living unity manifesting in infinite diversity of forms of expression and appearance. The droplet in each of us is part of the same great source and is eternal, though each of us has obviously been through immensely varied experiences.

Could we look back through corridors of time and memory, we should begin to see what we have been through. If this is the plane on which we experience being cut off from the divine source and developing egohood and self-consciousness, it is to be seen as the great training ground in which we can experience freewill and learn to become free moral beings and, like the Prodigal Son, come to ourselves and say, 'I will go back to my Father'. Every soul has to go through the experience of alone-ness before it can take the next step out of self-consciousness to be re-united with the One-ness.

We go, all of us, through the experience of the Ancient Mariner

> Alone, alone, all all alone, alone in a wide, wide sea,
> And never saint took pity on my soul in agony.

Each one of us is the Mariner. Coleridge's great ballad takes its place among the world's myths in giving a picture of the passage of the soul through earth life. These great allegories are speaking to us of the nature of the soul, and they all tell essentially the same story, namely that each soul is a droplet of the eternal and does come down on to this plane to go through all the trials and obstacles and difficulties of life in order to discover his higher, more spiritual principle, his higher self, to unite with it in the mystical marriage and so go back again to the worlds of light.

Now if this is the great training ground, it is hardly thinkable that one short life out of eternity could do the job, and therefore we arrive at the thought that we must have come back again and again to this plane. One thing that does appear from spiritual research into the laws of repeated earth lives, is that we reincarnate in groups. Our friends, our colleagues, the members of our family, are almost certainly souls with whom we were together in earlier lives. We have all been through the earlier epochs, in Chaldea, in Egypt, Greece and Rome and in the Middle Ages, to experience the progressive evolution of the earth consciousness and with it human consciousness. Our soul is thus a repository of history. Could we but develop the faculty of memory we might begin to get recollections of rowing as a slave in a galley, or marching on a crusade. We apparently experience each great age with the group of souls who are on our wave-length, sometimes as mother and daughter, sometimes as brothers, sometimes as friends and companions. This is a powerful thought to strengthen us in the inevitable difficulties in personal relations, particularly in this age leading up to the great spiritual turning point in human history at the close of this century. Any who are working for spiritual enlightenment must therefore treat with the greatest possible respect the friends, the colleagues, the family with whom they are now incarnated, for there is almost certainly purpose in our being together.

This picture surely restores for many the lost sense of meaning to life, bringing to us a supreme hope. The world is not just a desperate place full of death and hate, murder and disaster, as we would gather by listening to any news; we are watching the turmoil of the coming to birth of a New Age and a new quality of soul in man. We recognise that death is the great illusion, and we need have no fear of it. Since life is eternal, all that can happen is the discarding of worn-out sheaths. A beautiful analogy is that of a daffodil. It sags and it drops and we throw it on the compost heap as a dead thing. There it breaks down and becomes humus, which is the matrix of all life. It holds within it this little point of formlessness, chaoticised matter, the seed. When this is put back into the living soil and water, sun and air play on it, out comes the resurrected daffodil. Where is the death? There's nothing but the breaking down of the outward form. It looks as if the earth forces are the ones which do the breaking down of form, not into death but into the life-filled structure of mother earth, and that from the Cosmos streams in creative power which can bring forth and make new flowers, new animals, new men.

If this is all true, if we are really denizens of a higher plane, opting to live for periods of experience and work upon earth, then this planet is of immense importance. It is not a speck of dust in a dead Cosmos; it is **a** living seed in a living Cosmos, carrying this immeasurably important burden of self-consciousness with the potentiality of God-consciousness. Any who doubt the importance of this planet should consider that it was seen fit for the Lord of the Solar Logos to incarnate on it, which is no little compliment for the Heavens to pay to a tiny planet. As Alice Meynell says in one of her poems, this planet 'holds as chief treasure one forsaken grave'. We are approaching the possibility of true understanding of resurrection and what the resurrection body really means.

Now all this is not just an academic theory. The notable thing about this spiritual awakening in our time is the sense of urgency, the sense that something is happening now, and that the end of this century is one of the great turning points in the spiritual history of man. It is the end of an epoch, and the possibility of the new consciousness is really with us. Man has reached the point when he can take the leap of uniting his thinking with the Creative Spirit, lifting his soul to the Higher Soul level, stepping beyond the limitations of the physical. He appears, therefore, as what has been called the tenth hierarchy 'a little lower than the angels' for he is the spiritual being who has been given the God-like faculty of freewill. This is something the angels have not got, since they are simply one with the will of God and their whole delight is to serve His will. We have all gone through separation and the Prodigal Son's experience, and therefore only with freewill turn back to our Father.

Remember, of course, that only a very small proportion of the human race is in incarnation at any one moment; a huge proportion of them are on the next plane or planes beyond that. Those friends of ours who have left the body, and have not yet incarnated in another body, are all there on higher levels of consciousness, and we are very close to them because telepathically we can blend in thought with beings on higher planes. When we meditate, pray and lift our thinking to a friend who has moved on to that plane, that soul picks up our thought. This is amply proved to any whose minds are not closed to the forms of evidence before us. The way that your friend can speak to you is not by appearing like a ghost outside you, but within your own thinking. It is wonderful to realize that within the heart and within the thought answers to our questions can come, and new ideas can come alight from the worlds of being and the beings in those worlds.

Therefore now comes the increasing possibility that human consciousness can blend with the beings of the higher realms. It would appear that the higher worlds are deeply concerned with this planet, and that the veils are becoming very thin between the levels. If this planet is a living organism then the whole solar system must also be seen as a great spiritual organism, and each of the planets is comparable to the endocrine glands in our own body. As these tiny organs influence the entire structure of the whole body, so the tiny planet influences the entire structure of the solar system.

We come back in a quite rational way to the medieval concept of the reality of the crystal spheres, as they were called. Mars is not really that point shining in the heavens, but occultly Mars is that great field of force and influence which is enclosed within the whole great circuit that it makes, the huge sphere; Jupiter is another vaster sphere, and the Moon a smaller sphere. We come back to this realization that we are all in these great spheres of spiritual influence. Now and in this room we are in Mars, in Jupiter, and in Saturn, and can draw from their forces. The beings on the higher planes are deeply concerned that man does not blow this planet off its course, because it would damage the whole solar system, much as harming the pineal gland would the human organism. Hence the concern of the higher worlds to work with man and to awaken him to the possibility of co-operation.

We are called on now to open our thinking to contact these higher worlds because the forces of light, which can be called the forces of Michael, 'the countenance of Christ, Wielder of the Sword of Light', cannot just invade our darkened planet. Since they must respect the divine principle of freewill, we have got to invoke them and invite them. If we can learn to co-operate with the higher worlds there is nothing that could not be done for the de-polluting and redemption of this planet. Change could come rapidly because if human consciousness blended with the higher consciousness, light and power could sweep through human lives and bring about a veritable new society, a New Age. Many are convinced that this is coming, and that great changes are already afoot, but man is doing such damage to the whole structure of the planet that the very living being of Earth may react against him. We may be faced with considerable disasters one way or another, but disaster is not the last word, since there is no dying without re-birth. Therefore, we are seeing the dying of an old set of laws and the coming to birth of the glory of a new set of laws, the veritable New Age in which human consciousness can blend with the consciousness of higher beings, for the redemption of man, nature and the earth. We have got to do our part in invoking and calling down the forces of light, but we may feel the assurance that the Cosmic Christ, He whom Tudor Pole called 'The Revealer of the Word', is already overlighting mankind and working in human hearts and thinking.

I will end by quoting again the splendid passage from Christopher Fry's *A Sleep of Prisoners*. Soldiers locked in an empty church bicker and quarrel through the night, breaking at times into inspired speaking from higher consciousness. The sergeant says:

> The human heart can go to the lengths of God.
> Dark and cold we may be, but this
> Is no winter now. The frozen misery
> Of centuries breaks, cracks, begins to move;
> The thunder is the thunder of the floes,
> The thaw, the flood, the upstart Spring.
> Thank God our time is now when wrong
> Comes up to face us everywhere,
> Never to leave us till we take
> The longest stride of soul men ever took.
> Affairs are now soul size.
> The enterprise
> Is exploration into God.
> Where are you making for? It takes
> So many thousand years to wake,
> But will you wake for pity's sake?

3

THE EXPANSION OF CONSCIOUSNESS

THIS GREAT gathering is itself a sign that a new vision is drawing people together with a heightened sense of the meaning of purpose of life. The greatest tragedy is to lose this sense of meaning, After the war a great Austrian psychologist named Frankl found that the breakdowns in many of his patients were brought about through a sense of complete purposelessness of life. An enquiry revealed that over 80% of students in American Universities at that time saw no real meaning in life. Frankl developed what he called 'logotherapy' which simply meant healing through restoring a sense of meaning. It is interesting that a recent enquiry by the News of the World revealed that among seven hundred young people in this country sixty-seven percent declared a belief in God, though making it clear that they meant universal ever-present consciousness and Being. They had recovered a sense of meaning and the majority confessed that the discovery was for them quite recent. Something seems to be happening in human consciousness and. it is full of hope.

The great scientist Sir James Jeans wrote a generation ago:

What does life amount to? We have tumbled, as though through error, into a universe which by all the evidence was not intended for us. We cling to a fragment of a grain of sand until such time as the chill of death shall return us to primal matter. We strut for a tiny moment upon a tiny stage, well knowing that all our aspirations are doomed to ultimate failure and that everything we have achieved will perish with our race, leaving the Universe as though we had never existed ... The Universe is indifferent and even hostile to every kind of Life.

Can we not see that man's aspiration must ultimately come to a stop if that is the truth? Sooner or later despair must set in, with the sense that life is without meaning. It is indeed miraculous that we go on so bravely hoping, believing and worshipping in face of the heavy load of doubt. Later in his life Jeans modified his attitude, sensing that the universe was ultimately of the nature of thought:

> The tendency of modern physics is to resolve the whole natural universe into waves and, nothing but waves ... If annihilation of matter occurs the process is merely of unbottling of imprisoned wave energy and letting it free to travel through space. These concepts reduce the whole universe to a world of light, potential and existent, so that the whole story of creation can be told with perfect accuracy and completeness in the six words 'God said, Let there by Light'.

But Light we know is Life, is Spirit, is God. So close are we to the bridging of advanced physics and mysticism. It is this conviction of the divinity of all life that is now flooding our thinking. We see that the universe is in fact spiritual in essence, that matter is derivative from creative spirit, that the planet earth is not to be seen as a dead speck of dust but as a living seed bearing on it that most precious cargo – human consciousness. Furthermore, the earth has been seen worthy to receive the incarnation of the Lord of Spiritual Light, the 'Christos'. That is no small compliment to be paid to our tiny wandering planet.

It is a strange paradox that the view that man is wholly unimportant has led to his arrogance in our ages. If matter is merely dead and we are an accident of evolution in a nature wholly indifferent to us, then why should we not exploit it to our own gain? The alternative world-view accepts the truth of the words:

> In the beginning was the Word and the Word was God ...
> By Him were all things made ...

16

First came the primal oneness of Being and Spirit and from this our world of diversity is derived.

We wake up with something of awe to realise that man is the purpose of evolution, integrally part of nature, and that we are the stewards of our planet with the task of serving it. What are we doing with our stewardship? A new humility awakens once we recognise that man is indeed important to the universe and his evolving consciousness is part of a great plan.

Human thinking is now hovering between those two world-views and expanding of consciousness is leading many to see the limitations of our materialistic outlook.

Materialism essentially is not wrong, but it is a partial truth and dangerous when taken as the only value. It is part of the spiritual evolution of man that his thinking plunge into the mastering of matter even to the point of disintegrating it into the energy of which it is constituted. The great challenge is now to step beyond materialism and widen our vision to include the spiritual planes of creative being. Man is at a turning point in which materialistic thinking could drag him blindly down into a new bestiality, unless he can awaken to a deeper truth and rediscover the lost sense of meaning and spiritual purpose. To this end he is called on to expand his consciousness.

Here we may profitably consider the picture of evolution given by the great French scientist and seer Teilhard de Chardin which could well bring about a marriage between scientific thinking and religious inspiration. Teilhard's argument is that every cell and molecule is alive and has a 'within'. Its core is energy and energy we must see as 'frozen spirit'. Thus there is no dead matter. The outstanding feature in evolution is that these living cells and atoms have an inbuilt faculty for clustering together to create ever more complex structures and organisms. Even the smallest plankton has an incredibly complex structure. How much more so in animals where consciousness has developed.

Throughout evolution there is manifested this purposeful turning-in of atoms upon themselves, first to create minerals, then plants, fishes, animals and finally man. Each stage results in

17

a release of tremendous creative energy. Each step in 'complex-ification', to use the word coined by Teilhard, results in greater consciousness . In man an organism is made so complex that it becomes self-conscious. Here evolution becomes conscious of itself and can reflect. Man is the first organism to be conscious that it is conscious. All Heaven must have rejoiced when that tremendous stage was reached.

If matter is dead then it couldn't manifest purpose and drive towards a consummation. That matter is alive is shown by this inbuilt drive towards a consummation. 'I came that ye could have life and have it more abundantly.'

Dryden wrote:

> No atoms casually together hurled,
> could e'er produce so beautiful a world.

It is all too common to judge the values in our universe on the basis of mere size and distance. We are appalled by the small-ness of our planet in the vast expanses of space and therefore conclude that man is unimportant. Not so, says Teilhard. The true measure is complexity.

These great red giants among the stars have an extremely simple molecular arrangement – one nucleus and one electron moving around it. Compare this with millions upon millions of cells in a human brain, making self consciousness possible. Only a temperate planet could have achieved this.

Man is thus seen as the crown and purpose of evolution and of supreme importance to the universe. We can, in imagination, view the sweep of life from the simplest organisms up to man and realise that in some sense the life within the atom, being eternal, has passed up through mineral, plant and animal into man. We become more aware of our profound relationship to the whole of living nature and its kingdoms, for we are part of a single sweep of ever mounting consciousness. Furthermore we realise that the inner core of man is spiritual in origin and that it has descended from eternal worlds to which it must return when freed from the drastic limitation of a physical body. Thus we must grasp the idea of a spiritual evolution in the being of man which unites with the upward-striving urge of physical evolution.

We too often tacitly assume that man as the crown of evolution is a more or less finished product and we therefore look for advance to be in the way of social improvement. Teilhard submits something much more exciting. The drive within evolution will not stop. It logically follows that the human molecules will turn in upon each other to create an ultra-human clustering. The power manifested in each cell to cluster with others on the same wave-length must ultimately be recognised as of the nature of love. Each human molecule is becoming conscious of this rise of love and is beginning to unite in human clusters, or new groupings. Those can only have one purpose, to raise consciousness to a higher level. Self-consciousness was achieved in man. Now, in greater complexification, he advances towards cosmic consciousness and God-consciousness. He moves towards the real consummation, the re-uniting with God.

Thus Teilhard. welcomes the crowding of our planet as a symptom of the end of a great evolutionary epoch. We are rushing inexorably into a world society merging into one world, one family. We may expect a new form of collective life. We need not be discouraged by the fact that the first attempts by Hitler and Stalin were sinister in that personality was sacrificed to the worship of the state. This involved a most unspiritual view of man. As man takes the next stop in consciousness he will form groups bound creatively in love, in which the individuality of each member will enrich the group and itself be enriched by united activity.

Teilhard has made us familiar with the concept of the 'noosphere', the thought layer surrounding the plant, created by human thinking and yet to be seen as an objective reality. It is a great unity, a mind which actually extends the consciousness of the planet. As love awakens in the heart, uniting kindred souls, we may expect the real spirit of Earth to develop the new Man Heart. Consciousness has risen from low life through the animal sensitivity to self-consciousness. Next it will open up towards

God consciousness. The love in each of us is connected with the Cosmic Personality, the Christos, the Lord of all Light, the Son of God, who said 'I am Alpha and Omega, the First and the Last'. As the human soul breaks out from the mould of matter it discovers its goal. Teilhard has called this 'homing upon the Omega point'; like a homing pigeon it yearns for the bliss of cosmic consciousness. As we awake to the glory of the prospect ahead and realise the drastic limitation of consciousness involved in living in the body with its five senses, we recognise as a brother every other soul which has taken the same step. Out of these will come the new groups, aware of the meaning of life, the purpose of man and the power of unpossessive love which literally makes the world go round.

Indeed this is the forming of the Body of Christ, the New Society, the New Jerusalem. Might it also be seen as the building of the Ark? What is going to be the New Ark if the deluge comes? Surely it will be made of those souls which have orientated on to their Divine source. The society that is formed out of this vision is bringing in the New Age. A new flow of love and sympathy is apparent between souls on the same path. It brings a joy, excitement and zest which will override any dissenters in this life. For we shall have disasters and are having them as the inevitable symptom of the breaking down of the old society, but if we have set our foot upon the upward path we shall be guided through all the disasters and brought together with kindred spirits.

A veritable new society is forming in our midst and a new age is emerging with the strength and inevitability of the coming of spring. We are filled with the stupendous hope that something new is coming to birth and that there is indeed a higher world closely watching and deeply concerned with the welfare and redemption of mankind.

Man's path now is upwards into ever widening fields of consciousness. Even while in the body we can learn through meditation to free ourselves from its limitations and contact the sphere of absolute being, the Primal Oneness which is every- where and permeates every living form and yet is beyond all the manifestations of diversity. We learn to see our lives on earth as an allegorical journey in which, through the overcoming of obstacles and trials, we may unite with our higher self and make ourselves worthy to enter the realms of expanded awareness. As we grasp the majestic picture everything recovers the meaning which we thought was lost, seeing the endless vistas ahead for soul development and exploration in our earth span, and in every human contact. It implies that to adult education in the truest sense there is no limit. We are preparing now for the entry into what might be compared with a university of the spirit when we have left the restrictive body. Alas that so many are moving on with absolutely no knowledge of what it implies or of the possibilities of ever-widening consciousness which will be ours.

An aspect of the expansion of consciousness is that in thought we can be united with those in the greater life on higher levels of being. Whether they be our friends who have gone on ahead of us or angelic beings of exalted spiritual nature, a communion is possible within the thinking and through the intuition of the heart. Communication through trance mediumship is being superseded by fully conscious clairaudience in thought, and also by this form of communion which is truly a blending with spiritual powers. Through this we may expect an immense enhancement of human faculties and capacity for knowledge and wisdom.

Already we are seeing examples of individuals who have demonstrated that expansion of consciousness is possible. Rudolf Steiner was one of these. As mystic and scientist he showed that it is possible so to lift human thinking that it becomes one with the processes of the universe. Then the supposed limits to knowledge were overcome and it became possible to tap the source of knowledge directly and immediately, within his own thinking. His life was devoted to demonstrating the truth of this claim. The fact that it could be done by one proves that there are latent faculties of perception in us all if we can learn how to develop them. It is the great challenge to a scientific age. The excitement of our time is that the frontiers of reality are being crossed. This offers a different form of space exploration. We shoot our own moon rockets and though this represents a stupendous group achievement, we are still exploring on the physical vibration. The new attack on reality, uniting religion and science, will be across the frequency bands till planes of spirit are reached, entering through developed faculties of thought into realms where consciousness can blend with beings on higher planes. In co-operation of this sort there is nothing which the human race could not do. The hope is therefore that we are on the edge of a new renaissance not only technological, but artistic and religious, as human thinking learns to unite in communion with the flow of spiritual power and higher knowledge.

It is Teilhard's conviction that such expansion of conscious-ness is an evolutionary drive which nothing can stop. Man is moving, in the direction of an experience of the unity and divinity of all life, and once he has tasted the possibility he will strive with ever more zeal to move along this upward path.

Consider these quotations from Teilhard's 'Future of Man'.

> The sense of the earth opening and exploding upwards into God; and the sense of God taking root and finding nourishment down-wards into Earth. A personal, transcendent God and an evolving Universe no longer forming two hostile centres of attraction, but entering into hierarchic conjunction to raise the human mass on a single tide. Such is the sublime transformation which we may with justice foresee, and which in fact is beginning to have its effect upon a growing number of minds, free-thinkers as well as believers: the idea of a spiritual evolution of the Universe. The very transformation we have been seeking!
>
> From this standpoint it is at once apparent that, to unify the living forces of humanity, at present so painfully at odds, the direct and effective method is simply to sound the call-to-arms and form a solid block of all those, whether of the right or the left, who believe that the principal business of present-day Mankind is to achieve a breakthrough straight ahead by forcing its way over the threshold of some higher level of consciousness. Whether Christian or Non-Christian, the people inspired by this particular conviction constitute a homogenous category.

What more do they need that they may know and love one another? The 'union sacrée', the Common Front of all those who believe that the World is still advancing: what is this but the active minority, the solid core around which the unanimity of tomorrow must harden?

Despite the wave of scepticism which seems to have swept away the hopes (too ingenuous, no doubt, and too materialistic) on which the nineteenth century lived, faith in the future is not dead in our hearts. Indeed, it is this faith, deepened and purified which must save us. Not only does the idea of a possible raising of our consciousness to a state of super-conscious show itself daily in the light of scientific experience to be better founded and psychologically more necessary for preserving in Man his will to act; but furthermore this idea, carried to its logical extreme, appears to be the only one capable of paving the way for the great event we look for – the manifestation of a unified impulse to worship in which will be joined and mutually exalted both a passionate desire to conquer the World and a passionate longing to be united with God: the vital act, specifically now, corresponding to a new age in the history of Earth.

Here indeed is an inspiring prospect for the future. A gathering such as ours holds a great responsibility. It is to be seen as an active deed in offering our lifted thought towards the reality of the worlds of light. We recognise, without dogma, that the worlds of higher consciousness are present everywhere, binding all together in the great unity of life. Groups coming together in this way will evoke a response from higher powers waiting to help mankind.

Man reaches the step in his evolution when he begins to break free from the restricting mould of matter and discovers that his thinking and his consciousness are not limited. We are not our bodies. The physical body is the sheath essential to the eternal being of man if this is to be conscious and act upon the earth planet. The coloured aura radiates out in all directions. The magnetic field of a man, according to Dr. Glazowski, reaches out as far as our understanding can go. Our consciousness can be anywhere in this field where we chose to direct thought. It is an illusion that we are enclosed, in the central point of the body.

The doors are open to us to explore behind the veils which normally hide the higher planes from us. We truly are where we direct our thought beam. First we must free ourselves from the illusion that we are bound in consciousness by the body. Man is called on to take a glorious step in reality that there is essentially nothing to stop him from expanding his consciousness to the limit of his 'field'. Thus he can explore space in a new way, reaching through ever subtler levels to achieve transcendental consciousness. The thought is well put in a remarkable sonnet, *Bodily Extension*, by Charles Earle.

> The body is not bounded by its skin;
> > Its effluence, like a gentle cloud of scent,
> Is wide into the air diffused and, blent
> > With elements unseen, its way doth win
> To other frontiers, where take origin
> > Far subtler systems, nobler regions meant
> > To be the area and the instrument.
> Of operations ever to begin
> Anew and never end. Thus every man
> > Wears as his robe the garment of the sky
> So close his union with cosmic plan,
> > So perfectly he pierces low and high –
> Reaching as far in space as creature can,
> > And co-extending with immensity.

To quote Einstein: 'Religion without science is blind, and science without religion is lame … The most beautiful emotion we can experience is the mystical. He to whom this emotion is a stranger, and who can no longer wonder and stand in awe, is as good as dead.'

'If man today does not find a new way of thinking, humanity may well be doomed to extinction.'

4

THE COSMIC CHRIST
IN THE NEW AGE

THE COMING OF the New Age is heralded by a spiritual awakening which is to be distinguished from what has commonly been understood by the phrase 'a religious revival'. It has not grown out of the churches or conventional religions, though it can bring fresh ardour into every church. Yet this broad movement is truly religious in its nature in that it is a recognition of the stupendous Oneness of all life in its infinite diversity. All life is of God and everything is of Divine origin. Furthermore, there is the wide-spread conviction not only that higher worlds of spirit are a reality, but that a 'pressure' from those worlds is breaking into our lives and lifting human consciousness in this very generation. Many great seers have foretold some great spiritual 'crisis' or evolutionary turning point for mankind by the end of the 20th century. This in some way must involve an expansion of consciousness to take in other dimensions of reality, for it becomes very clear that our earth-bound consciousness is by no means the only level that the human mind can experience. We are, it appears in essence, spiritual beings, droplets of the Divine Source, sojourning for a while, in the drastic limitations of a physical sense-bound body. The spiritual kernel, the 'I' in each of us, when released from that body, remains very much alive and is capable of progressing into ever wider and more light-filled spheres in its long journey back to the Divine Source to which it truly belongs.

The recognition that life is a Divine Oneness and that mankind is indeed one great family becomes an essential part of our world view. We can at least accept it intellectually and then with the imagination strive to understand the implications. We can recognise that 'Spaceship Earth' is truly a living sentient being or creature of which we men are a part. Man is that point where evolution becomes conscious of itself. In us the planet can think towards God, who can experience Himself reflected in Man. We come to see that not only is the planet alive but that the whole Cosmos is in very truth shot through with creative intelligence and spirit from which all physical substance is derived. To quote R.M. Bucke from *Cosmic Consciousness* speaking of the experience of mental illumination:

> Like a flash there is presented to his consciousness a clear conception (a vision) in outline of the meaning and drift of the universe. He does not come to believe merely; but he sees and knows that the Cosmos, which to the self conscious mind seems made up of dead matter, is in fact far otherwise – is in truth a living presence … He sees that the life which is in man is eternal, as all life is eternal; that the soul of man is as immortal as God is. He obtains such a conception of The Whole or at least of an immense Whole as dwarfs all conception, imagination or speculation springing from and belonging to ordinary self consciousness, such a conception as makes the old attempts mentally to grasp the universe and its meaning petty and ridiculous.

Commenting on the awakening of our age, the late Tudor Pole, one of the great adepts of our period, wrote in his last book *Writing on the Ground*:

> It is my belief that the 'Revealer of the Word' (the 'Christos') for the historic times in which we now live, has already descended into the invisible spheres that surround our planet and that those with eyes to see and ears to hear, can begin to discern the Message he is bringing, even if the Messenger may not be clothed in form or outwardly discernible. He will bring with him the inspiration and the spiritual impetus we need in order to lift human consciousness out of its present darkness into the Light of new Day. One thing is certain. If we are to equip ourselves to receive

and understand the Revealer, the coming Messenger from God, we must arouse ourselves from sleep and prepare ourselves for this arrival.

Who and what is the Christos? Clearly an exalted Being of Light must overlight *all* mankind. He must illumine every race, creed and nation. There can be nothing sectarian about Him. Truth and Love must play down on to every man, whether atheist or believer. The great world religions need not merge and indeed should not merge, for each of them carries a tremendous facet of the Truth. But over all a real and all-embracing world religion could begin to appear in recognition of the Lord of Light, overlighting all mankind.

The name the 'Christos' is the Greek for this Exalted Being of the Spiritual Sun. The worship of the Spirit of Light and Truth is common to all the great religions, which acknowledged His approach to the Earth for the redemption of mankind, though there was disagreement and uncertainty concerning the time and nature of this deed of entry. To Christians He is the Christ, but clearly the present vision would lift us far above the sectarian conflicts which have through history caused such bloodshed in the name of the Christian religion. We are dealing with concepts which would renew and widen Christianity so that veritably the coming of the New Age would be seen to include and express the Christ Impulse for all mankind.

Let us look at it from the teachings of Rudolf Steiner. Though very many great teachers have spoken on this theme, Steiner's clarity of perception truly heralded the present awakening. Rudolf Steiner, born in 1861 and dying in 1925, was a great scientist who also from youth possessed complete clairvoyance, so that the reality of the spiritual worlds was obvious to him. However, as a scientist, he saw that this faculty must be transmuted into a thinking which was consonant with scientific method. If Divine Intelligence was the creative power behind all nature and life, then the human mind must be able so to lift its thinking that it could blend in consciousness with the world process. Then true investigation of higher knowledge by immediate experience would be possible. Truth would then be apprehended directly within the risen thinking. This would be worthy of the evolved intellect of our age. It would be something quite different from an atavistic clairvoyance. It would mean the opening of dormant faculties of perception present in every man. By meditation and the training of his thinking he achieved this step. He has described his 'Anthroposophy' as 'A path of knowledge leading the spiritual in man to the spiritual in the Universe'.

Having developed this power of exploring higher worlds and putting his findings into thoughts, he set out on his investigations into the 'akashic record'. The earth, it appears, is surrounded on a subtle level by an immense field of a spiritual substance known as 'akasha' in which is impressed, like a celestial tape recording, every impulse of human thought, will and emotion. It constitutes therefore a complete record of human and planetary history, and those adepts who have lifted their consciousness until they can 'read the akashic record' are able to investigate history at source without the need of written documents. This Steiner claimed to be able to do, and was able furthermore to reach right back in his thinking to experience the earlier incarnations of the planet itself. This immense span is covered in his book *Occult Science*.

As a researcher, without preconception, prejudice or dogma, he surveyed back to the dim past of human and planetary evolution, using his developed faculties of cognition. To his astonishment he came up against the fact of the descent of the Christ as the absolutely central event of evolution, the turning point which gave meaning to history. Be it said that in the 1890s, working in the intellectual and scientific circles in Berlin, he had publicly attacked Christianity. It seems that he must have undergone something comparable with Paul's experience of meeting the Living Christ on the road to Damascus. As Paul must be seen as the first discoverer of the Cosmic Christ, so Steiner re-discovered Him and became His apostle for our century. Of this period in his life he writes in his autobiography:

> I stood before the Mystery of Golgotha in a most profound inward festival of knowledge.

From about 1910 on his entire teaching is Christo-centric. Naturally it does not always conform to church dogma, for this was spiritual research which was able to arrive at Truth afresh without need to draw on written documents. With a certainty which he claimed to be in line with scientific method he researched into the unseen worlds, crystallized his findings into thoughts and gave them out in lectures, books and teaching.

He frequently made it clear that he was never demanding belief or 'faith' in the usually accepted sense. He merely declared what as an adept he had seen, contending that every other person who had developed his faculties of perception to enter the unseen worlds would find the same. He invites us, if we feel drawn to the ideas, to *think* them. Live with them as thoughts, and if they are truth they will, through the years draw a deep certainty to themselves. If not true, or if we are not ready for them, they will fall from our thinking.

What then did he find about the Christ?

His cosmology is always built on his certainty that behind *all* manifestation in the diversity of the relative world is the great Oneness of Creative Intelligence and Spirit, the Divine Source. 'In the beginning was the Word and the Word was with God and the Word was God. By Him were all things made and without Him was not anything made that was made'.

Thus the celestial bodies are not mere gaseous balls but are the spheres of action of exalted spiritual beings. The solar system seen with spiritual knowledge is a huge living organism shot through and through with living thought. Each of the planets represents a vast sphere of forces. Indeed the movement of the visible planet marks the periphery of this sphere of influence and spiritual quality. We come back again to a recognition of the basic truth of the old concept of the 'crystal spheres' of the planets which was still an active tenet in Shakespeare's day.

The field of action of the highest hierarchy, the Elohim, is the Sun. Since all manifestation in the world of matter is a reflection of spiritual reality on an eternal plane beyond time and space, we must grasp the concept of the *spiritual sun*. The visible sun is the vortex or channel through which the most exalted beings of light can work. The Lord of these sublime beings is He who was known as the Christos, the Son of God.

We remember Blake's outburst:

> Do you think that when the sun rises I see something like a golden guinea? No, no, no, I see the Cherubim and the Seraphim crying 'Holy, Holy, Holy, Lord God Almighty'.

The earth in this view is not a dead speck of dust in a vast indifferent mechanism of a cosmos, which some modern astronomers believe it to be. Rather it is to be seen as a living seed, a planet given the charge of a priceless inheritance – the development of consciousness and the home of a spiritual being who can develop to free will and to God-consciousness. Man, in the spiritual world-view, is not a chance accident of evolution in a cosmos wholly indifferent to him. He is part of the primal archetypal vision of the Creator. Though last to appear in physical form, he is, as spiritual archetype, first to be created. Man, in this sense, was there from the very beginning, and the whole of evolution has been concerned with developing a new hierarchy, a spiritual being who can accept the divine gift of free will and in time expand self-consciousness into cosmic-consciousness and finally God-consciousness. Thus man can become veritably a companion to God, that point where in thought God can experience his own reflection.

> When I consider the heavens, the moon and the stars which Thou hast ordained, what is man that Thou art mindful of him or the son of man that Thou visitest him for Thou hast made him a little lower than the angels and has crowned him with glory and honour.

None can know how many other planets in the Universe carry conscious sentient beings, but Planet Earth in our solar system bears a supremely important burden. It was a high compliment that the Sublime Lord of all Light and of the Elohim saw fit to descend and blend His power and life with the stream of earth evolution.

Alice Meynell in her poem *Christ in the universe* writes that our '… wayside planet … Bears, as chief treasure, one forsaken grave'.

Steiner's picture of the evolution of the solar system and the way in which the celestial bodies became related to each other as they are now is too large a theme to deal with here. His findings do not essentially conflict with the findings of astronomy. Very briefly be it said that Steiner contends that in early phases the celestial bodies of the solar system were merged into an enormous whole, shot through with spirit and being. As this condensed, the refined Beings of Light found the increasing density intolerable and drew out to a certain distance to play upon the developing earth from outside. Thus appeared what in time became our sun, behind which stood the Spiritual Sun. The result of this withdrawal was that the speed of condensing and hardening greatly increased. Since earth was the field for evolving man, the danger arose that the contracting processes would so harden him that evolution would become impossible. Thus the forces and beings concerned with his condensing also withdrew from the great body to a distance in which their influence could be controlled. Thus appears our moon.

If it be true that all the celestial bodies are spheres of activity of spiritual beings then we must see that evolution has both a physical and a spiritual aspect. Aeons of time have gone to develop a physical organism capable of carrying a self-conscious 'ego', yet what has been the evolution of that ego itself? If we can take the thought that Man as archetypal idea was created in the beginning, then there must have been a time when this droplet of the Divine Source first began its descent into matter. This is perhaps indicated in Genesis in the verse:

> And the Lord God formed man of the dust of the ground, and breathed into his nostrils the breath of life and man became a living soul.

The immortal entity begins to embody itself, though first in a form far different from our present body. This according to Steiner takes place far back in the Lemurian epoch, long before Atlantis. By alternating between embodiment and life on the higher planes the human being gradually gets deeper into the material world and himself is actively involved in working upon the physical vehicle. Thus we see a spiritual evolution of the entity of man working with the physical evolution.

There comes a time, however, when those beings who were responsible for drawing man down ever deeper into matter had so advanced the hardening and condensing processes on earth that it became likely that human life would become impossible. Had this trend gone on unchecked, then the human being would have become so encased in matter that he would have lost all touch with his spiritual worlds of origin.

Thus some redemptive deed became necessary.

The Exalted Lord of the Spiritual Sun now took the decision to enter the stream of earth evolution. This great fact is recognised in all the world religions, for it is the supreme turning point in the whole of earth history. The Hindus knew this Being as Vishva Karman. The ancient Persians worshipped Him as Ahura Mazdao, Lord of Light, who opposed Ahriman, the lord of darkness.

The Egyptians knew him as Osiris, and the legend of his dismemberment and rescue by Isis tells of his descent to Earth. The Hebrews awaited His descent as the Messiah. The Mystery Temples of antiquity foresaw the redemptive descent of the God of Light who would reverse the trend of hardening into matter. Precisely how and when the Christos would enter earth they could not know, but the initiates knew that when the event happened they would be aware of it since the whole aura of the earth would change and be shot through with light. The descent of the Christ Being is a unique event in history in which God for the first and only time experiences human death. There had of course been many cases of divine beings temporarily taking over the individuality of a man. This is often described in Greek legend, but is quite different from the actual identification with man so as to suffer and experience death.

Steiner describes the event which can be seen by all initiates in whom the inner faculties of vision are developed. To enter earth evolution the Christos needed a perfected human instrument. This was Jesus. The Holy Spirit had prepared this vehicle through long periods. That a human body could carry in himself

32

the Cosmic Being who had declared himself as 'I AM THE I AM', implies the highest possible preparation. In Jesus there flow together two streams, the one bringing all the Wisdom of the Ages, the other pure love and compassion. The Gospel of Matthew indicates the royal lineage from Solomon and David to whom the three Wise Men are drawn. The Gospel of Luke describes the soul of Innocence who draws to himself the simple shepherds and the creatures of nature. Now these two merge in an occult mystery, which Steiner investigated. It explains the remarkable discrepancies between the two Gospel stories. Suffice it to say that we are being told of the preparation of the sublime vehicle, who could receive the Cosmic Christ.

The moment of entry is seen to be the Baptism by John in the Jordan. Then the individuality of Jesus gave place to the Christ Being, the Cosmic 'I AM'. At the moment when 'the Holy Ghost descended in the form of a dove', this Exalted Being took over the human body. For the next three years it is the Christ who is speaking in Jesus. The previous thirty years had been a preparation of the vehicle.

This view of the event, drawn from esoteric vision, of course differs from the tacit assumption that the Christ was born in Jesus as a babe. We are invited to re-think. There is usually such close association of Jesus with the Christ that the concept of the descent of the God of Light is lost. Esoteric Christianity sees Jesus as the human vehicle for the Cosmic Being of the Christ. This was clearly accepted in the first two centuries by the followers of Christ. They celebrated the 'Christ-Mass', the true birth of Christ, on January 6th, Epiphany, the day of the Baptism. It was only in the 4th century AD that Christmas was moved forward to the date of the birth of the babe on December 25th. This suggests that the occult knowledge of the descent of the God of Light was too difficult to be generally understood when all Roman citizens were baptized into the Christian faith. Therefore the knowledge was lost and indeed was driven underground as heresy.

It is, however, most significant that the gospels of Mark and John both begin with the Baptism in Jordan and only deal with the three last years. Matthew and Luke tell the story of the birth of Jesus in both cases in what is really a surprisingly short introduction, and then quickly move on to the Baptism. The early followers of Christ were chiefly interested in celebrating the Baptism and the Resurrection rather than the birth and the Crucifixion, for they still knew of this sublime event of the descent of the Christ.

The events during the three years of His life in Jesus are to be seen as the continuous process of incarnation of the Cosmic 'I AM'. Thus the Temptation marks the takeover of the astral body of Jesus, the Transfiguration the complete mastery of the etheric body. When on the Cross He called out the words 'It is finished', it amounted to a triumphant declaration that matter had been fully mastered, the complete incarnation was achieved and death conquered.

This Deed of Christ is to be seen as the absolute turning point in history and evolution. It may be said to have reversed the Fall of Man. It indeed starts the Ascent of Man, opening the possibility of his recovering his lost knowledge of the Spiritual Worlds.

Steiner spoke always of the 'Mystery of Golgotha', thus implying that Christ achieved thereby a transformation of the ancient mysteries which in the temples of antiquity initiated pupils into esoteric knowledge of the higher worlds. So profound is the Mystery of Golgotha that we only begin to understand its implications for the future of mankind. At that moment the Christ Impulse entered into earthly evolution and continues to work as a leaven to redeem the human soul and body.

A God experienced human death. At the moment when the blood ran into the earth from the body on the Cross, the whole aura of the earth was changed. Steiner, in a lecture called 'The Etherization of the Blood', describes how the Divine blood was transmuted on to an etheric level so that it was able to extend into the whole 'ether body' of the earth. It was 'potentized' in the sense that the word is used in homeopathy. While the body of Jesus lay dead, the Christ being became the helper and redeemer of the souls of the dead who had lost their divine nature. The Greek conviction was that the dead were as shades. Achilles, when Odysseus visited him in Hades, said that it was 'better to be a beggar on earth than a king in the realm of the shades'. The entry of the Christ into what we now call the Borderland brought a flooding of light and hope. Much the same situation holds good today. So many souls who 'go over' with no understanding or belief in the immortality of the soul find themselves as 'shades' in a surrounding of gloom and obscurity and may even not know that they are dead. The Living Christ in this age comes again to redeem lost souls.

Christ's resurrection overcame death. A spiritual being has to 'embody' itself in whatever sheath is necessary for it to enter another plane of being. Thus a physical body with a hard skeleton is essential if it wishes to incarnate on earth. If it enters a gaseous or a liquid planet then a gaseous, fiery or viscous body will be needed. When its task is finished the particles of the sheath should be dispersed and should return to source.

Thus the survival of the corpse is seen as something essentially unnatural. 'By man came death'. As the etheric forces return after death to the great etheric pool, so it was meant that the physical particles should dissolve without leaving the corpse. The Christ had such power that He could control even the physical body, so that the corpse disappeared. Instead of the etheric body dispersing, he was then able to hold it together in a human form which appeared identical with the physical. By so doing he demonstrated that man will in time be able to overcome death and dematerialise the physical sheath when it has done its task.

The descent of the Christ meant the entry of an Impulse into the dying body of the earth. It checked the tendency to over-hardening and condensing which was present in evolution through the working of the adversary forces. Hence from that Easter Sunday the possibility of rising again was given to man.

Redemption from the ultimate hardening into matter is thereby achieved. Had the Christ not descended, human life upon earth would in time have become impossible and souls upon earth would have become so deeply embedded in matter that all knowledge of the spiritual worlds would have been lost.

For over a month the Risen Christ moved among the disciples in the Resurrection Body, able to come and go and be in more than one place at a time. Thus John in his last sentence in his Gospel writes that if all the deeds of Christ after the Resurrection were to be written down 'I suppose that even the world itself could not contain the books that should be written'.

Then came the Ascension, when the disciples appeared to lose Him as He was taken 'up to heaven'. Here Steiner gives an illuminating interpretation. The Christ has taken over the direction of the life of the earth. Thus he moves into this 'higher' realm of the etheric which, being the life structure which permeates all form and holds together the particle of substance, is absolutely ubiquitous. He disappears to physical view, but from now on is everywhere and within the etheric body of every plant, tree, animal or man. 'I am with you always, even to the end of the earth cycle'. Certain medieval maps of the globe show the Christ standing behind the earth and holding it, so that head, hands and feet just appear. The following poem by Joseph Plunkett attempts to express the stupendous truth:

> I see his blood upon the rose
> And in the stars the glory of his eyes,
> His body gleams amid eternal snows,
> His tears fall from the skies.
>
> I see his face in every flower;
> The thunder and the singing of the birds
> Are but his voice – and carven by his power
> Rocks are his written words.
>
> All pathways by his feet are worn,
> His strong heart stirs the ever-beating sea,
> His crown of thorns is twined with every thorn,
> His cross is every tree.

The Ascension is to be seen as a deed for all men. As the physical sun shines on all, so every human being is redeemed by the Deed of Christ and by His sacrifice in taking over the Regency of the etheric earth. The event of Pentecost at Whitsuntide offered the possibility that the individual soul who from within itself made the approach, could be flooded with Christ Power. Here the Comforter, the Holy Spirit, came in the form of the Gifts of the Spirit on the first Pentecost. Thus Whitsun is a festival for the redemption of the individual ego in its attempt to overcome the desires of the lower self and surrender to the Higher Self. Each man has his Higher Self or spiritual principle, and this is Christ-filled.

The two festivals, Ascension and Pentecost, come alive for our time in a wonderful way. The Christ Impulse floods all life, rejuvenating the soul. No longer need man harden into matter and lose touch with the higher worlds. The Ascent of Man has begun as a result of the Christ deed. The redemption of the race has been begun.

To quote the last words of Christopher Smart's *Song to David*:

> And now the matchless deed's achieved,
> Determined, dared and done.

It needs, however, the inner initiative of the individual soul to lift and open itself to the entry of the Christ. This is the task of our age. To quote Steiner: 'The supreme mystery of the age in which we are living is the Second Coming of Christ – that is its true nature'.

Now we see the true nature of the Second Coming. The Christ is now overlighting all mankind. He is present everywhere in the etheric. If men can lift their consciousness into this super-sensible, invisible realm they will find Him. In this sense the Second Coming has already happened. It is for us to bring it to individual consciousness and realisation.

Our epoch is the Cosmic Whitsuntide when the individual ego can, through its own conscious initiative, unite with the 'I AM'. This is Teilhard's 'homing upon the Omega point'. This fulfils the age and leads us through into the new epoch.

We see that the 'body of Christ' is being formed everywhere by the individual souls who unite themselves with Him. Each is like a blood corpuscle in this Body, and it is essentially the New Age society, bound by the Love for the Divine in all things and in each other.

There is clearly no need for the Christ to incarnate again and live through a physical body and so pass through death. That was done once and need not be repeated. He can appear in a thousand places at the same time anywhere in the world. In the resurrection body he can appear and then mysteriously withdraw, and there are more and more cases of this happening since the middle of our century. Nor need He always appear in the traditional white robe. As Lord and Creator of all Life, he can overlight any human form. He has, with the eye of vision, been seen as the great scholar in academic robes, for surely He is the master scientist, the Lord of all Wisdom. He could appear in the Olympic Games to show what sublime beauty and achievement is possible with the human body. He could overlight a politician or public figure, speaking through him in the Risen Language of the spirit. As a new society is formed out of the chaos of our age, this Redeeming Power of the Second Coming may be expected in infinitely varied fields.

Steiner himself must have experienced something of Paul's vision at the Gates of Damascus. He tells us that more and more people from now onwards and through into the coming centuries will have the same experience and know with absolute certainty that the Living Christ exists.

Thus the wonder of our age is that through all the darkness and negation the Christ Impulse is flooding. There is a resurgence of light and a new consciousness which can redeem the pollution of the planet through the instrument of the individual souls who receive the Power of the Spirit and allow it to pour through them for the healing of mankind. Christ is the Great Healer, who can restore the imbalanced body to its true relation to the Whole. To quote from the Creed of the Christian Community, the Church founded by Steiner: 'He will in time unite for the advancement of the world with those whom through their bearing He can wrest from the death of matter'. By its nature esoteric Christianity contains concepts so advanced that they could not possibly have been accepted by the general public in the early Church or even in our time. Truth, however, is so many-faceted that there need be no essential conflict. If we are drawn to accept that the Christ is a Cosmic Being who entered into the human vehicle of Jesus, this does not in any way reduce the stature of Jesus. Rather does it raise and expand the whole picture of Christianity as the impulse which can lead to a new world religion. Christ is not merely a great teacher. Christianity, in Steiner's phrase, is a mystical fact, a great Event in history. The entry of the Cosmic Christ for all men relates Christianity to the other great religions. The recognition of Jesus as the vehicle of the Christ places Him in His true relation to the other prophets. The Buddha prepared the way six hundred years before the Event of Golgotha, by showing the path to enlightenment. Six hundred years after it Mohammed made his revelations of the One God. Modern research, particularly into the works of the Islamic sage, Ibn al'Arabi, reveal that the esoteric core of Islam is truly teaching knowledge of the Cosmic Christ. As we recognise the reality of the spiritual worlds, we shall learn that the Buddha is now working in close association with Christ for the redemption of mankind through illumination of understanding. The Master Jesus is ever present with us as leader of the group of the great spiritual Masters. Thus this concept of the Cosmic Christ helps us to lift clear of the apparent contradictions between the religions and points the way to a vision which unites all men who have found their way to the health-giving power of the Christ Impulse. What name we give does not matter. We are united in recognition and worship of the Lord of Light.

5

THE SIGNIFICANCE OF
THE GROUP IN THE NEW AGE

W HAT DO WE mean by thinking into the New Age? Basically it means recovering the vision of wholeness. First we must by an effort of imagination grasp that the planet on which we tread is a living being, a great 'creature' of which the human kingdom is an integral part.

Nature is a great living oneness. But more than this. The vision of the Whole must include the different planes of being which interpenetrate each other. Higher worlds of spirit are indeed a reality but not in the sense of being spatially infinitely distant. Modern science familiarises us with the idea of vibrations and higher frequencies passing right through matter, which is revealed as merely a very slow frequency to which our five senses are tuned in. Subtler senses will reveal higher worlds, and the higher frequencies are not merely to be seen as realms of shorter wave-length but as planes where extended consciousness and Being can be found. Ultimately the whole universe is seen as being composed of Thought, the product of Divine Imagination. All these realms can interpenetrate each other and the spiritual and super-sensible realms will therefore be found within our sense world and experienced by our intuitive thinking.

All the great religions are now expecting a new Advent. In some sense it would appear that the higher realms are pressing in upon our material world. The veils are becoming thin and to many comes the experience of an extension of consciousness and understanding of the higher reality. It seems that a spiritual event is taking place in which the supra-mental realms impinge upon the physical world: the breaking upon us of a New Age is imminent and taking place before our eyes. The channelling of the inflow of new forces, ideas and impulses must be through human groups, consciously formed and dedicated. Man must be the creative channel, both invoking and working with the higher forces and beings who can transform our world and our society.

It is so easy to be a prophet of doom, fixing attention on the sinister symptoms of our time. These must never be belittled. Indeed it is certain that the vast majority of people have no notion as to how grave is the human situation and what calamities we may bring upon the world through conflict, mis-applied science, materialistic greed. It is well within the bounds of possibility that man will turn this into an uninhabitable planet.

The more important is it therefore to throw all our attention and thought into the birth of the new age which is coming into manifestation as the green shoots of spring appear in the desolation of winter. The first shoots are individually weak and can easily be crushed out, but they are signs, for those with eyes to see, of a power so invincible that winter cannot stand against it. It is with a spiritual Spring that we are now working and it bids fair in time to redeem the world we know.

New age groups will come together consciously as channels for the entry of new thought. Living ideas which carry a trans-forming force may be expected to flow into all the different aspects of our society.

Society, quite obviously, has always been composed of a pattern of groups related in infinite complexity. It is important to grasp that in a deeper sense a group is an Entity. Behind the band of individuals we must see, on a higher plane, a Being. This concept, if acceptable, greatly helps us in understanding how the new age ideas can enter our thinking. Behind a nation we can see the Folk-Soul who inspires a national culture.

That which makes us expressly Englishmen is a great angelic being whose impulse can fire us in time of crisis. This concept gives a picture of a family of Folk-Souls, themselves forming a great Group, each nation having its special contribution to world culture. It helps us to see the possibility of a true world unity when conflict is superseded, not by the oneness of a dictatorship or a uniformity, but the organic wholeness of complementary cultural traditions, recognising the need for co-operation in world economy and political contacts.

Every grouping of men must be seen as being backed by a Spiritual entity who may either have brought the group together or even have been formed by the thought of the group. The life of these entities will vary infinitely, that of the national or tribal folk-soul being very long-lived and that of a college or even such a group as an orchestra being much more ephemeral. In our smaller groups consciously brought together for meditation we may sense a 'guardian angel' as guide and protector.

The tribal groups have played a tremendous part in earlier centuries in developing human society. They have mostly been bound by a blood tie. We must recognise that in the old age, love and hate were carried in the blood. This survived even in the Scottish clans. A Macdonald hated a Campbell and his blood rose as his rival entered the room. Love flowed in the blood-bond to all fellow clansmen. It appears that so strong was the tribal tie in biblical days that even memory could pass through several generations. The essential impulse which the Christ brought into the world as a spiritual fact was the possibility of love flowing from individual to individual without any reference to blood. This gives the key to the new brotherhood of man. The Christ Spirit lives in the higher self of every man and women and each is therefore in the true sense brother to his fellow. Love can transcend all barriers of colour and blood.

This is the deeper aspect of what has so notably developed in our modern age – the consciousness of individuality. This indeed is a key to history. It is as if the age of man has, as the centuries progressed, stepped down ever deeper into his physical vehicle until in the last century he came to identify himself entirely with his body and his five senses. Before the Renaissance he could still, like Dante, see with a higher faculty into the realms of the nine hierarchies, and recognise himself, in his inner core, as a spiritual being descended for a spell of time into the allegorical journey through the world of the material. When this vision faded in our own age he lost all contact with that divine world, forgot its very existence and proudly declared himself a materialist. There was as such nothing wrong with this. This evolution was necessary not only that he might master the world of matter, but that he should have the psychological experience of being alone and cut off from his divine source. He 'came of age' as a child of God and experienced freedom. Each of us must go through this experience, which is described in a thousand ways in allegory and myth. Each must in freedom rediscover his divine origin and out of his own inner initiative take the step which, like the prodigal son, sets him on the path back to his Father. It is thus a free moral act to take this Way, and no outer or inner compulsion drives him to it.

Thus the New Age group is something quite different from earlier groups which have been formed out of the impulses of the collective unconscious or for the many and varied reasons of human aspiration or interest. It must be a group of individuals brought together in an Inner bond of understanding, love and dedication to a task involving a creativity which recognises the reality of the divine forces. Such a group, a conscious creative channel, will have a strength far greater than the sum of its individuals, because it will be an integrated unit. It will recognise that the summit of individuality is to work in a greater community. Individuality will not be lost but heightened by coming together with the bond of love and service in a new identity with others. Old age groups in our time have all too often shown the possibility of the individual being swept away by group passions of hatred or fear or sheer excitement. The New Age group formed from the conscious individual in co-operation with beings and impulses from higher planes of thought will show a new character.

We can look at different aspects of social life and sense the kind of way these groups may be expected to form. In psychology a new vision and new techniques will come to birth through recognising the reality of the higher self of man as a creative cause in his personality. No truly 'scientific' psychology can any longer ignore the higher or spiritual self of man as being too vague a concept. The new science must include it, also recognising that all cultures but our own have known of its truth and importance. In science we may expect the 'vision of wholeness' to lead to groups for investigation of the interpenetration of spheres of being. Already it looks as if the research of the physicists is coming very close to the findings of spiritual science. The new age will know that the divine is in all matter and that true science and research must include the spiritual. Teilhard de Chardin, as both scientist and seer, gives us the lead towards research into the 'divinisation' of our planet. Medicine and healing will call for groups which become channels for the inflow of divine energy bringing a re-establishment of harmony and thereby health in the organism. Educational groups will be formed to research into new ways. The new age will be recognised as a mental age in which powers of creative thought, as yet hardly envisaged, may be expected to develop. Spiritual science shows that the universe is of the nature of Thought and that when human thinking is lifted to intuition it is one with the whole world process. Where individuals have achieved this step in consciousness they have demonstrated that human thinking can be used as an instrument of direct knowledge and even of creativity vastly ahead of anything we have yet seen. Instead of the laborious process of storing facts in the memory for passing examinations, education will increasingly be directed towards the development of mental powers of perception. The creative arts will show the impact of new-age thinking in wonderful ways. When an artist is able to take the step in awareness and vision so that he can become a channel for the spiritual formative forces, we may expect new art forms to be created. The inspiration will show itself in a new architecture reflecting the great light-filled forms of the etheric planes invisible to the physical eye. Painting and sculpture will again show the nature of matter and man imbued with spiritual reality. The new vision

45

will fire poetry and drama, since the great truths enshrined in mythology and older drama are rediscovered as the eternal verities in the story of the human soul and its evolution. Drama is likely again to take its real place as a formative force in the inner nature of man.

In industry and sociology and politics, new age groups will form. Industry will increasingly be recognised as a great organic structure of human relations. Individual firms will enter into new human relationships of true profit-sharing. The true three-fold balance of society into economic interests, political rights and obligations, and the freedom of cultural and spiritual interests, will be realised. The recognition of the great spiritual entities behind the social and national groups will call for new groups to become conscious channels for new understanding. It will in time no longer be seen as the sign of a 'practical man' that he ignores the spiritual ideas. The vision of wholeness reveals that we must have our feet firmly planted on the ground while vision is raised towards the stars. The agriculture of wholeness will call for new age groups arising from the realisation of what man is doing to the fertility of the planet through his faith in chemicals and his failure to understand that our earth is indeed a living creature whom he must serve rather than exploit for gain.

Esoteric groups of various sorts will be essential to new-age thinking. Study and research into spiritual reality will bring people together. Meditation groups will become the feature of centres through which the Light can enter the dark realms of the earth and the borderland. These are essential as a network of channels for the descent of the Christ energies. Religious groups for direct contact with the divine powers are essentially part of the emerging pattern. So also are groups concerned with telepathy and kindred subjects, since the new age must learn to use mental powers in a new way. All the varied groups will be recognised as part of the new understanding which brings a religious character into every aspect of life, because it knows that the spiritual realms are to be found within the material world and at every point in space and time.

The chief force bringing new age groups together will always be love. Therefore they will have less need for regulation and rules as in old age groups. Indeed they are likely in time to have what might be called an 'astrological' character, in that their members may be found to have been brought together to represent different polarities of human talent. On a deeper level it will be found that the members have probably been related to each other as friends or family in earlier lives. Thus a new quality of Love will develop wholly unpossessive in its nature, based on respect for the uniqueness of the other souls and the joy that will come by experiencing united work in service of the higher guides and entities. Man in his groups will be seen as a creator as never before because in freedom and love he has dedicated himself to the divine forces which are bringing to birth a new world.

The New Age groups can at the present time be seen as 'bridgeheads' which are offered as channels for the invading forces of light to enter. They will be used and guided, and are each part of a great network.

May I end with a mention of Michaelmas. This weekend is held at the Feast of Michael, a festival as yet hardly recognised in our society. It stands as a polar opposite to Easter, as New Year stands over against midsummer. It has not yet been born as a festival because it concerns the future. Michael is that exalted being who is the Lord of the Cosmic Intelligence and the Standard Bearer of the Christ. We are entering the age in which he has taken over rulership of human affairs from the spiritual realms. The essence of the Plan is that human freedom must be maintained. The Christ impulse never coerces belief: it must be accepted in freedom and love and will only enter when man invokes and invites. Our groups, composed of free individuals bound in love, must therefore dedicate their thinking and their creative will to the higher forces. It is a spiritual co-operation between man and the higher beings. Michaelmas can be seen as a festival of social co-operation in creative intelligence. Its forms and rituals will be developed as we recognise that the New Age calls for new forms and that all aspects of social and personal life will be given a deeper meaning and significance as they are shot through with the new enthusiasm of the spirit and the Living Word. This course is offered to Michael as part of the birth of a true Festival of Michael as human thinking is dedicated to the coming of the New Age.

6

THE ADVENTURES OF DYING

MANY ARE FACING the evening of life with anxiety despite the comfort offered in the teaching, life, death and resurrection of Our Lord which demonstrated once and for all the unreality of death. In our time we are offered a fresh understanding of the meaning of his life and deed. The teachings of modern spiritual science, and the communication of modern clairvoyance and conscious mediumship offer evidence of survival so abundant and overwhelming that any mind open to the truths of the spirit must find it acceptable. The critical intellect may always raise doubts but the understanding of the heart brings certainty.

We see that the life in each of us is eternal as all life is eternal. We must each clear from our hearts any vestige of fear of extinction, realising that the gateway of death opens through to a realm of ever widening consciousness. The higher worlds are indeed real and the messages now coming back to us through sensitives describing the life of those who have left the body are extremely convincing and interesting. Once we accept the idea that the core of each individual is an eternal spiritual being and that we come down from a higher plane to take to ourselves a body for our temporary sojourn upon earth, then it surely follows that so-called death is a release back to the realm to which we truly and permanently belong. This conviction opens the heart to a flood of hope and joy. Death, however, is so often looked upon with dread. We tacitly equate spirit and body and do not see how we can be conscious of self without the brain and organs of sense. It is essential to recognise that 'we' are not our bodies But that, as eternal beings, we live through our time-ridden bodies. These in the end are shed like a worn-out overcoat.

Elementary logic shows us that if spirit is primary, and God created man first on a spiritual plane, thought must exist before and beyond the brain. The brain, miraculous organ that it is, is the product of thought. It exists that we may become conscious of ourselves in the separated condition of earth life. The five senses and the brain-bound thinking are the necessary instruments of earth life. Modern spiritual research is based on the discovery of the possibility of 'brain-free' thinking, when in meditation and sleep we are lifted free of the normal limitations and our auras can extend to touch the worlds of light and higher vibrations.

Not all can research in this way, but what we can all do is to study and understand the findings of the seers and the 'knowers'. If we can build for ourselves the spiritual picture of man and grasp the reality of higher worlds, and of our continuing life therein, then our whole attitude to our later years must change from anxiety to keen anticipation and hope.

With all the advancements in medical knowledge and improvement in living conditions, our society today has given everybody the gift of a dozen free years, more or less, at the close of their lives after the working career is finished or the family brought up and launched upon the world. It is the first time in history that this has been achieved. Perhaps it is highly significant that it should be to this generation that the 'gift' is offered, since the new understanding now bursting upon us enables us to use these last years as a period of preparation for what comes after. They are not to be seen merely as a time to put by with ever-failing powers. A new possibility develops of a society of senior citizens consciously dedicated to the great task of preparing the soul for the great transition into expanding consciousness. The very limiting of physical powers, rightly seen, means a flowering on a subtler inner plane. New faculties may develop which bring understanding of the deeper meanings of life and death, and as we actually approach near to that mysterious gateway; our joy and anticipation should increase.

Death from the viewpoint of soul and spirit must be seen as a beautiful and solemn birth into light. Yet our modern thinking is so conditioned by the negative image of death. The renaissance pictures portraying the horror of the 'dance of death', the fear of extinction and eternal darkness, the sense of hopeless loss, has worked into the marrow of the bones of our thinking. Even the constantly repeated concept of 'rest in the grave' is a profound misunderstanding. The last thing that the young soul, passing over, wants is rest! There may be a period of transitional rest but the Joy of the 'new' view is that we enter into endless realms of possibility of creative action on the planes of light. Death is release into light but there is no word in our language to express this majestic concept. Furthermore, we must take as absolute certainty that on the further shore we shall find our friends and those we loved. Where there is love there can be no separation. This is the great truth often so sadly lost. Those who have 'lost' a beloved friend are in fact among the privileged of our age, because the passing of one on to the ethereal plane opens a possibility of inner communication such as is impossible in the limitation, of two bodies. Every pair of kindred spirits 'separated' in this way are given the choice to demonstrate by their understanding the new and deeper unity of experience, making thereby an important bridge between the two planes of being. Freed from the body, the soul enters a world much shaped by thought since the 'substance' of the next plane is much more malleable than here on earth. Thus it is true that people tend at first to find what they expect. If they resolutely believe in extinction of consciousness, they may find themselves alive but in a fog. They will be lost until, with the help of guides and friends, something wakes them up to the fact that they are dead and yet alive. Then the soul can proceed.

More and more books are appearing which give us 'post mortem' experience and a picture of what life means on the higher planes. Suffice it here to say that, with the common attitude of fear or refusal to think about death, with the frequent exaggeration of grief at loss, or the tendency to forget those who have passed on, a kind of fog develops which cuts us off from contact with the planes of Light. When we do move on, it is often entirely without preparation or understanding. We carry with us, to the next plane, that which we have spiritualised in our thinking. If we have given no consideration to the higher worlds we shall be ill-equipped to enter what might be called the University of the Spirit. The prospect is enthralling and the field for exploration infinite. 'Is not the whole of eternity mine?' to quote the philosopher Lessing. Once we have considered the great truth, an inner serenity and joy can flood the soul. Then we can accept the limitations, loneliness and pain of an ageing body, awaiting the certainty of release into Light and freedom and using the last years to prepare in understanding for this supreme adventure.

7

DEATH – THE GREAT ADVENTURE

O F ALL SUBJECTS calling for a rethinking in our time, Death takes a foremost place. We seem to be a death-ridden culture. Death in one form or another seems to be the chief 'news'. Yet at the same time it is a theme we avoid. It is not quite nice to talk about it. It must be hushed up. All possible medical means must be taken to keep a person alive even at immense cost of money, suffering and difficulty.

The dread of death looms large in many minds. In others there is basic unconcern. As we can know so little about what, if anything, happens hereafter, it is best to ignore the whole unpleasant subject – such is often the attitude.

In the materialism of our time we tend to identify ourselves with our bodies. How can consciousness continue without the brain? This is perhaps the strongest argument of those who do not believe in survival. Even among believers and religiously minded people the stress is constantly on rest hereafter: 'Thou in the grave shall rest …'

> Mony a lad and lass
> Are lying 'neath the grass
> The green, green grass
> Of Traquair churchyard.

R.I.P. and the inscriptions on a thousand tombstones, some of which are deliberately witty, for example one in a church porch for a pauper:

> The further in the more you pay
> So here lie I as warm as they.

53

Or in the ballad *Clerk Launders*:

> My bed it is full lowly now,
> Among the hungry worms I sleep …
> Cauld mould is my covering now
> But and my winding-sheet,
> The dew it falls nae sooner down
> Than my resting place is weet.

Quite obviously such concepts imply the tacit assumption that we are our bodies and that the soul is tied to the body when it dies. But to those who believe in extinction of consciousness after death and demand proof of survival, perhaps the right answer would be to counter attack and say: 'on the contrary, you produce me one shred of real evidence that you are extinguished. I challenge you that your belief is sheer supposition. An immense body of circumstantial evidence is now available for any mind that is prepared to look at it openly, and without prejudice, to show that the soul continues very much alive. No evidence has been produced for its extinction'.

It is indeed remarkable that there is no word in our language to imply that most majestic and solemn of processes, the release of the soul into light, for this is what the passage through the gate of death truly is. 'Death' has in the last centuries become so much associated with the hideous corpse and rotting cadaver. Dürer's 'Dance of Death' portrays the sinister form coming to tap us on the shoulder with the fearful summons. It is time we broke clear away from this outdated attitude and recognised that the spiritual entity of man is imperishable. We should therefore drop out of our vocabulary those words identifying the soul of man with the mechanical process by which the physical sheath is discarded and decays. We must wake up to the great conception that on all levels there can be no 'death' without rebirth, a 'becoming' through release on to a subtler and more light-filled plane of life. We may thus have the certainty that the liberated soul is free to range in wide realms of life and that the possibility of exploration, joyous adventure and creative activity open up to us in the hereafter.

Let us approach the subject from a wide viewpoint. In our time a spiritual world-view is emerging, rising like a tide in the consciousness of very many and restoring a sense of meaning to life lost in the materialistic thinking of our time. We are rediscovering what the Orient and the older civilizations have always known – that behind the relative world of appearance is a realm of Being beyond time and space yet interpenetrating everywhere; that the material world is derivative from the planes of Creative Intelligence and Spirit; that the Universe is basically a great Presence, shot through with thought and life. We give to this Primal Source the name of God. Each human being is seen to be in essence a droplet of this divine source. The inner core of each of us is therefore a spiritual being who always was and always will be, eternal and therefore imperishable. This eternal droplet belonging to the realms of Light has through the divine plan, as symbolized by the myth of the Fall, entered deeply into the material plane here to undergo soul trials and ordeals in order that it may, with heightened consciousness, rise ever farther towards the source from which it descended. 'Earth' is thus seen as the great training ground, a 'vale of soul-making' in Keats' s phrase. Blake wrote, 'we are set on earth a little space that we may learn to bear the beams of love'. To sojourn on this plane of dense matter and slow vibration the vibrant living spirit needs to take to itself sheaths or bodies. A being capable of moving through time and space at the speed of Ariel needs to be slowed down. Entrance into a body involves drastic limitation.

Man must be seen again as a threefold being of spirit, soul, and body. The imperishable droplet of spirit needs to take to itself a soul sheath and an etheric body of vital forces, which then draws together the particles of matter to make the physical body. This is a vehicle for the eternal soul/spirit being. A very good analogy is the diving suit. We stump about with leaden boots to hold us down to the ocean floor and gaze at the wonders of that world but forget the two tubes which connect us with the upper world. If we rise to the surface and again breathe fresh sunlit air, we know we do not really belong to the ocean depth, and when we descend again our attitude is changed. So it is when in meditation or soul travel we experience higher spiritual planes and learn that we are only sojourning temporarily in the lower density of matter.

When the diving suit is no longer needed it can be discarded. The body, for all its wonder, is to be seen as no more than an overcoat which when worn out can be thrown away. To assume that 'we' cease with the discarding of our overcoat is, to say the least, illogical

How can we know these things? What assurance have we that this spiritual world view is true? We must recognise that since the turn of the century a breakthrough in consciousness has been taking place. It has become possible for certain advanced minds in fullest consciousness and with a clarity of thought comparable with scientific method to lift thinking and investigate the higher worlds. These 'seers' or adepts, developing a new clairvoyance and clairaudience, have shown that there slumber in every human being organs of perception which when awakened give knowledge of the reality of higher worlds.

The great seers of our age never demand belief. They say in effect, 'This is what we find when we develop our faculties of perception. All who achieve this will find essentially the same. You are not asked to believe anything. Rather if you are drawn to these ideas you are invited to think them. Live with them as thoughts and if they are true they will draw a certainty into your consciousness and the meaning of life will for you be enhanced'. Here is really the beginning of a new form of spiritual investigation. The mind has the capacity for grasping at an idea for its very beauty. We can then hold this idea as a living thought and watch whether supporting indications and evidence are drawn to our consciousness. Truth never constrains. The new understanding is offered to us with no demand for belief.

It does appear, however, that what modern sensitives are finding is essentially the same knowledge of higher worlds taught in the Mystery temples of the ancients and passed on through the esoteric teachings of such bodies as the Rosicrucians, the Knights Templars, the Masons. It is the ageless wisdom re-emerging in our time in a form that our intellectual and scientific minds can take, and it supports what has been known through the ages in the East.

The core of man is seen as an imperishable spiritual entity, a droplet of the Divine source. As such it cannot be extinguished. It is eternal as all life is eternal. The outer sheaths can be discarded, there can be metamorphosis, but death in the sense of extinction of the 'ego' or droplet is impossible. Live with this idea and see where it takes us. 'Survival' becomes axiomatic. Of course you survive. How can you do other since your 'I' is a spiritual entity? A much more important implication is that you were there before you were born. Pre-existence as a concept needs to be recovered. The desire for survival may have personal connotations. The recognition of pre-existence is a sobering thought bringing a deeper sense of responsibility. As an already developed soul entity we descend to earth to take on a body and – when that body is discarded – we are released from limitation once more to expand in the wide fields of consciousness on higher planes.

It is basic to our thinking to see that human brain-bound Consciousness is but the lowest level, in the darkness and density of matter. Above it, tier upon tier, are planes of higher consciousness, all filled with spiritual being, reaching right back to God, the Creative Source. The eternal soul of man is moving up and down these levels of consciousness on its long journey down into earth and back to the worlds of light. To use Blake's phraseology, it moves from innocence (Eden Garden) through Experience (bodily and sensual life on earth) to Imagination (the Holy City, New Jerusalem). This is the passage of every individual life and of the race of men.

Now it must be clear that the phrase 'higher worlds' does not imply spatially far distant, but rather a higher frequency and vibration. Our five senses are tuned in to the slow vibration of earth substance. If we could develop the subtler senses we would become aware of invisible worlds interpenetrating the physical everywhere as wireless waves pass through solid matter. Thus the widening of Consciousness would give entry to other kingdoms of being. As a great teacher has said, 'Every cubic centimetre is shot through with all that is'.

Wordsworth expressed the belief in pre-existence in his great *Ode on the Intimations of Immortality in Early Childhood*:

> Our birth is but a sleep and a forgetting.
> The soul that rises with us, our life's star,
> Hath had elsewhere its setting
> And cometh from afar,
> Not in entire forgetfulness
> And not in utter nakedness
> But trailing Clouds of glory do we come
> From God, who is our home.

Everywhere in living nature the process of death takes place in order that old forms may give way to new by a process of metamorphosis. Every death is accompanied by a resurrection, a new 'becoming'. Goethe wrote, 'Nature invented death that there might be new life'. The eternal being is released to take to itself a new form. The daffodil 'dies' and is thrown on to the compost heap where it breaks down into humus, the matrix of life. Meantime, the seed holds the core of new living form. In the soul life of man, psychological 'death' is often necessary that an inner step be taken. William Blake in jocular mood, wrote his own epitaph: 'William Blake, who delighted in good company, born 1759 and died many times since'. Goethe gives us the great truth:

> For if you have not got this, this DEATH AND BECOMING,
> You are but a dull guest in the dark world.

Let us now think into our subject of death on the hypothesis that the spiritual individuality of man (or what is loosely called the 'soul') is imperishable. Released from the body it is still itself, but moving now in greater freedom in a subtler world. This is born out by all communications received from the 'Beyond'. To the newly dead it is often a surprise to find oneself very much alive and very like oneself, essentially the same person but in a lighter body, free from illness, aches and pains. It appears that our friends are there to meet us in a surrounding, at first much like the world we are used to, though more beautiful. The explanation is simple enough. The 'next world' is made up from thought and imagining. It is subtler plane of finer vibrations and therefore 'substance' is immediately responsive to thought. Thus there are houses, trees and rivers, which are experienced as solid since they are on the same vibratory rate as our new bodies. We know that solid matter on earth feels hard to us but is in reality composed of widely spaced particles of energy. So on subtler and higher planes a world created by imagining indeed exists. In the area known as the 'Summerland' and described by many communicants it can be exceedingly beautiful. This is a soul plane where the heart's desires can be fulfilled. Therefore once reached many feel it simply to be heaven and are content to sojourn there a very long time.

Of course it is true that this is a plane of illusion. This does not make the experience of it any less real or important. It is no more illusion than our own earth plane. The 'maya' of the material world is real and necessary enough for us while we are here. The important thing to realise is that the true realms of spirit are on far higher planes, attained after long soul development and catharsis.

Before reaching the Summerland the departing soul passes through the Borderland. After an initial period of sleep or unconsciousness, we wake to find ourselves in a surrounding formed really by our own preconceptions. The soul before death sends out 'the call', and those it loves will gather to receive it into the next world. This can clearly be a very joyful moment and those who have prepared their understanding may find they move quickly through to the planes of light.

What, however, of the many souls in our materialistic age who go over with no certainty of the reality of life after death? Many now are agnostic and even atheistic and are complete disbelievers in survival. They will awake to find themselves alive. The result is that many refuse at first to believe they have died. If they are totally unprepared, they may find themselves in a fog or maze, or lost in some gloomy setting which is really the symbolical counterpart of their belief or unbelief.

The important fact, born out in so many reports, is that their friends from the realms of light have difficulty in getting through to a soul held in the condition of blindness to the spirit.

Until the soul is ready to respond it cannot be reached from above. Thus in the present age of unbelief the Borderland is apparently a very dark place. Thousands of souls go over without the understanding enabling them to make contact and break through. Thus there are 'rescue centres' with the object of redeeming and awakening these lost wanderers between death and new life.

We on earth have here an important part to play. The soul after death will turn back for contact with those it has loved. It can take knowledge from those still alive on earth. Truly the initial soul nourishment is drawn from the spiritual thoughts of those with whom it has affinity on earth, particularly while we are asleep. But since so many now go into sleep at night without having developed any spiritual thinking, the crying need of the lost souls hungry for nourishment remains quite unmet. Furthermore, where the one bereft on earth is filled with unreasoning grief, a kind of smokescreen is created which prevents the soul in the beyond even finding its friend. Hence the immeasurable importance of rethinking death. For the soul moving on, it is essentially a release which can be filled with joy. The gist of so many communications is that 'I am all right and very much alive and it is wonderful over here'.

Thus our sorrow, let us face it, is largely for ourselves. This is not to belittle the pain of parting and the sense of loss for us here. But we must accept the basic fact of telepathic contact. The higher world is a thought world. Those living in it are free to move with speed and souls can blend with each other, sharing consciousness. This implies that our thought, prayer and love to a departed friend are instantly received. Even though most of us cannot register this. We can take it as a concept and can act on it. Talk to your friend or relative. Bring him or her into your life and plans. Mentally discuss things. Support them with love and joy and courage as they explore ahead. Emphatically this does not bind them to earth in the wrong way. It is our unreasoning

and persisting grief which binds and hurts, and many communications strive to convey the message that the blind grief is really
hindering the soul's onward progress. Furthermore, they really
are with us frequently. They can speak within our thinking. and
in the impulse of joy in the heart. They will not appear to us like
sad ghosts outside of us, but will respond to our advance in this
delicate and subtle way as if we have answered our question
within our own minds. It is through such conscious communion
and blending thought in full awareness that modern sensitives are
able to give us the picture of the life beyond. This ability to tune
in to discarnate souls is the developing of faculties which lift us
beyond the communication through trance mediumship. It opens
beautiful possibilities, for it is the beginning of the possibility of
infinitely rich and joyful relationships, in truth closer than before.
Our beloved friends can indeed be 'closer than breathing, nearer
than hands and feet'.

Of course we have lost them as physical companions and this
loss may be grievous. Only a limited number of people can yet
really experience subtler telepathic blending in consciousness. To
describe the possibility is not to belittle the genuine suffering of
bereavement. The new outlook can, however, lift us courageously
beyond the despair often felt at the sense of the finality of loss.
We are really called on to open our hearts in love, transmuting
the sense of tragic loss into the comfort and joy of certainty that
in God's good time we shall be united again.

What then is the actual event of dying? Man consists of a
physical body, the substance of which is held together by a vital
body of formative forces known as the etheric. Then there is the
'astral body' or soul, and the 'ego', the eternal spiritual entity
which needs to take to itself those sheaths in order to live in the
density of earth. In sleep the astral body and ego withdraw and
are then in the spiritual worlds, though of course most of us have
not developed organs of perception to experience what happens.
We are then with our friends who have passed on, and those who
have awakened their deeper faculties of perception can report
their experiences during sleep. This is one of the important
sources of spiritual research. The physical and etheric bodies lie

on the bed unconscious but are linked by the so called 'silver cord', by means of which the wandering soul may be instantly recalled. Then waking occurs. In death this silver cord is broken and no return is possible. During sleep the etheric forces restore and energize the body. After death the etheric body flows out and returns to the vast pool of etheric forces from which it was drawn. As it departs, the physical body begins to disintegrate. This is seen in the changes taking place in the two days after death.

Death has been called the 'Great Anaesthetist', for it seems that the one who is passing feels no pain. To us who watch, it may seem that the body is distorted in a last spasm or death struggle, but at this moment the soul is rarely conscious.

It seems that at the moment of passing the soul has a glimpse as of a passage-way opening up into a great light. Goethe's last words were 'Light – more light', and that exuberant life-giving Victorian artist, William Petty, called out loudly at the last moment, 'Glorious, glorious, this Death!'

The ritual of the lying in state for two-and-a-half or three days has deep meaning, for the soul during this time often hovers round to get used to the fact that it has left the body. There are many descriptions as to how the 'dead' person finds himself floating above his body. Here we see the importance of flowers around the coffin, candles and, on occasions, vigil. The astral body and etheric body are drawn by the flowers and the light, and the process of transition becomes more beautiful. The stillness and dignity of the situation helps the soul to free itself. Hence the importance of avoiding fuss or busy activity about the chamber. After a time the soul will probably fall into a period of sleep and will awaken to find itself perhaps in a beautiful 'hospital' room with friends or family to greet it. As soon as we accept the fact that we have discarded the body, that we are still very much alive, that all illness and pain has passed, we are free to move on into a new and beautiful world.

It is at this stage that we who are left on earth can most support our departed friends by loving thoughts, sending them forth courageously on their new adventure.

It must be re-stressed that man is in core an eternal being of spirit, housed for a time in a soul and body. This truth of his threefold nature has largely been lost and is being recovered now in our thinking. Furthermore, as a spiritual being he belongs to the spiritual realms. In descending to earth life he takes on drastic limitation and his five senses are really filters that allow only a little of the glory of light and sound of the cosmos to enter his consciousness. To think that this free spiritual being is identified with the discarded and rotting corpse or that he sleeps there in the grave or is extinguished in the fire of the crematorium is sheer ignorance arising from a limited view. Let us grasp in thought and imagination that the free-ranging being can indeed explore into the realms of light.

'In My Father's house are many mansions,' said Christ. Many assume that the Summerland is Heaven. It is called the Plane of Fulfilled Desires and also the Plane of Illusion. It is but the lowest heaven realm, though infinite rich and enjoyable experience is found there. The soul, however, must in time 'die' again to be reborn on higher planes until ultimately it is free for soul-travel in the divine realms of pure spirit.

It cannot move on until it is fit through cleansing and catharsis. Each step is a deeper initiation. Frances Banks, in her post-mortem communications through Helen Greaves, set down in her *Testimony of Light*, describes how she decided she would enter the Halls of Learning, and confidently strode up the steps of this temple university of the spirit, only to be thrown back by blinding light. We cannot move on to the more refined vibrations till we are prepared for it, and in this long soul journey towards the Source there are clearly many difficulties to overcome. All these planes interpenetrate. The finer frequency can pass through the coarser as wireless waves pass through 'solid' matter. It is a question of learning how to tune in and so move through. The prospect of free soul travel is open to us all. We do it in sleep but without conscious awareness. Richelieu's remarkable book *A Soul's Journey* gives a description of the lifting of this experience into consciousness.

John Donne opens his great sonnet with the lines:

Death be not proud, though some have called thee
Mighty and dreadful, for, thou art not so,
For those whom thou thinks't thou dust overthrow
Die not, poor Death, nor yet canst thou kill me
From rest and sleep, which but thy pictures be
Much pleasure, then from thee much more must flow
And soonest our best men with thee do go
Rest of their bones, and souls' delivery.

Clearly the imperishable soul has infinite aeons for this long development and exploration. The fact that this earth level exists as a field for experience of self-consciousness within the limitations of a gravity-bound body, means that the evolving being will use this training ground many times. As the whole consciousness of the earth and of mankind evolves so the individual monad will need to return for further experience. It is a long education, but, as the philosopher Lessing phrased it: 'Is not the whole of eternity mine?'

Though we speak of the Summerland and of 'release into light', this does not imply that the higher worlds are without suffering. The whole immense process is soul development and education. Therefore, released from the body and the five senses, the soul will have to face its own limitations, inadequacies and ill doing in the form of remorse and pain. Just before the moment of death we experience in one great flash an instantaneous panorama of our past life. This is often born out by those rescued from drowning. It is accounted for by the release of the etheric body which is the storehouse of memory. Later the soul lives through a long retrospect of its life which apparently takes something like a third of the time of the life span. Here we re-experience our deeds but in reverse, in that we experience in our own soul the pain or pleasure we caused. Thus if we had been cruel to another we are starkly faced with what our action meant by experiencing what he felt. This means we are filled with a pain that brings understanding and remorse. We know that our own soul development is held up until we make compensation. This can often be done by repentance and forgiveness on the higher plane, but if the wrong was too grave we incarnate again and find the soul we have harmed, in order to do some deed of sacrifice which will rectify the karmic damage and free us for further progress. Thus a purgatorial experience is a very real one through which the soul must pass. It is not however, a question of a harsh God issuing judgment. Clearly the soul is its own and only judge, by being set in situations where within its own feeling it faces the real truth of the results of its actions. Then is implanted in it the urge to make amends and restoration to others, and forgiveness can release it to advance upon its journey. We are responsible for creating our own Hell. If the soul is tied to corporeal desires and appetites it will suffer because after death it has lost the physical organs for their satisfaction. Here is the truth behind the myth of Tantalus, for ever striving to reach the grapes which are always just out of his reach.

Some souls will hurry back to Earth as soon as possible since they cannot tolerate a body-free existence filled with unsatisfied lusts and longings for the flesh. Some will gladly put themselves through the refining fires of 'purgatory' to purge the Soul of its faults and obtain release on to the next heavenly stage.

We are still bedevilled in our subconscious by the medieval pictures of Hell and Judgment. The notion of eternal damnation in hell is quite at variance with the picture which now emerges of the self-judgment of the soul by compassionate experience of the suffering it caused to others. It is a very primitive view that the good or ill done in one life settles the fate to eternity. The very word 'eternity' is here misunderstood. We move on to an 'eternal' plane in the sense that it is beyond our time-space continuum of earth life. When it is fitting we can choose to return from the higher planes into the temporal sphere for further experience and service.

The fear of death which arises from ignorance or uncertainty of conscious survival is lifted by even a partial understanding of the spiritual world-view. Modern communications are bringing to light a wonderful picture of the fields of experience after death. These bring an assurance that we really do find again those whom we loved and 'lost'. We might say that the 'gravity force' in the beyond is sympathy and antipathy. We are naturally and inevitably drawn again to these with whom we have affinity. In this body-free realm, souls can blend and merge so that consciousness becomes one while identity is kept. Thus the experience of the ecstasy of love will be heightened, though in a subtler form than in the body. Let us remember that, as Goethe said, 'Everything on the temporal plane is but a parable, an image'. Every earthly thing is a reflection of creative ideas and archetypes in the spiritual spheres. Thus physical loving must be but a reflection of the glory of experience when light and love-filled souls blend on the higher planes. There need be no fear that by dying we have passed beyond the possibility of ecstasy.

The blending of souls also gives us the clue to the important concept of the group souls. We shall be drawn into a concourse of kindred spirits to whom we karmically belong. The group will probably be overlighted by some great master spirit. With friends in these groups we shall incarnate again. It appears probable that those whom we find in life as friends, colleagues or relatives are souls with whom we have a karmic connection and with whom we were in incarnation in earlier lives. This thought, of course, adds to our respect for our friends and colleagues and heightens the interest in our contacts with them and our work together since this will bear fruit into the future.

Though this wide picture of endless living lifts the crude and ignorant fear of death, it does not mean that all life in the beyond is a rosy heavenly experience. Over the aeons life on whatever plane is a continuous educational experience. Many of us will, to a greater or less degree, have failed to fulfil the life task and purpose for which we incarnated. We may even fail to find what that task is. When in the 'beyond' we recognise our failures there may be agonies of remorse. Though it is said that 'Destiny is always kind', the law of cause and effect holds good and compensation for failure and wrong-doing is inevitable. Therefore among advanced souls who have seen these tremendous truths there may well be a certain dread of death lest we have failed to take the steps in inner development and outer service for which we came to Earth. This concept shows how vitally important it is to think through the true picture of the Great

Transition lest we miss the opportunities and have to repeat the experiences all over again.

However, the Lord of Karma is Christ himself. Knowledge of the reality of the Glory of Light and the imperishable nature of the soul, realization of the power of Love and Forgiveness, fills us with a joy which overlays and transforms all doubt. We realize that we are a great process of moving towards the great Oneness while at the same time going through a long training so as individuality possessing free will, we can learn to become a companion of God.

For man is indeed a creature

> God begotten, God companioned,
> God-ward striving.

By Pope he was called: 'The Glory, jest and riddle of the world'.

8

RELEASE INTO LIGHT

W E HAVE RECENTLY at our adult college in Shropshire run a week-end course called 'Positive Attitudes to the Third Phase of Life – commonly called Retirement'. A new phenomenon has arisen in our society. We are being offered a third phase in life. Till now there have been two stages, nurture followed by work until we are worn out. Now for the first time in history everyone is offered a gift of perhaps a dozen free years to harvest the experiences of life. Many go on to the last years with anxiety, perturbed at the sudden break from the self discipline and routine perhaps of office life. Many feel that their faculties are waning and that there is little point in starting fresh creative activities at this stage. Yet these last years should be seen as a God-given opportunity for freedom and creativity. Let me quote from Yeats' poem *Sailing to Byzantium*:

> An aged man is but a paltry thing,
> A tattered coat upon a stick, unless
> Soul claps its hands and sing, and louder sing
> For every tatter in its mortal dress,
> Nor is there singing school but studying
> Monuments of its own magnificence;
> And therefore I have sailed the seas and come
> To the holy city of Byzantium.

This verse gives the true key to adult education in later years. 'Byzantium' to Yeats had of course a double meaning. It could be read as the city of miraculous works of art and beauty but it also stood as a symbol for the attaining of a higher degree of consciousness.

> 'Old men ought to be explorers' wrote T.S. Eliot,
> 'Here and there does not matter
> We must be still and still moving
> Into another intensity
> For a further union, a deeper communion ...'

The timid attitude towards retirement arises from the too common belief that death means the end. We identify ourselves with our bodies and feel that as these fail a limitation and restriction is setting in. The truth is that consciousness can be increasingly released and extended as the physical faculties fade – 'In my end is my beginning', to quote Eliot again. As we 'shuffle off this mortal coil' and discard the body like a worn out overcoat, we move out into a wider consciousness, maintaining our identity. As that stupendous truth penetrates human consciousness, as the bogey of death is 'debunked' and overthrown, a whole new attitude towards the third phase of life will come about. We shall then realise the task we have in the remaining years we have been given. It is a splendid challenge.

It is strange that in human history medical knowledge has freed man from early death and given him this extra time of greater leisure and free creativity, precisely at the time when there is emerging into our consciousness the truth that so called 'death' is a step into extended awareness. So many people in our age have not bothered at all about what they carry with them into this further life. It is as if we are moving into a new university, with the possibility of immense width of understanding and research in a new and light-filled land, but we realise with consternation that we have done nothing whatever to prepare ourselves to qualify for this change. The soul carries with it on to the new plane that which it has been able to spiritualise in its thinking. All that is concerned solely with the material plane, above all what has to do with merely getting money and things for ourselves, is left behind. That which we have given in creative thought or feeling or will towards beauty, goodness and the spirit, and spiritual understanding, will be brought forward on to the further plane.

Thus we should consciously use these free years to prepare ourselves for the next exciting stage. Retirement is the lifting out of the scramble for getting on, for getting one's living. We may find ourselves in straightened circumstances but we are free to choose our own activities. We may hope to see the emergence in our society of a true culture of the senior citizens, those who have 'retired'.

Now let us picture the realms the soul will enter when it is released from the body. It will enter a society in which the scramble to 'get on' is wholly removed. There will no longer be the need to get money in order to eat. It will be left to its own enthusiasm and creativity in thinking to explore the light-filled world and carry its consciousness on to ever further planes. In other words the vision of a new culture for the retired, the third phase of life as it could be on this earth plane, is but a faint image of the society we shall enter and live with on the higher plane. Once we have woken up to the fact that there is no such thing as 'death' in the sense of extinction, a new excitement will awaken, a new ardour and earnestness about what we do with our last years in conscious preparation for the great release into light. Truly we shall enter another civilization, but one based on the affinities of love, enthusiasm and creativity. This civilization is not far distant, but is interpenetrating our material plane and in it we shall find those we have known on earth. We ourselves are even now part of this great society, though we are temporarily 'seconded' to the darker earth plane with all its illusion of separation.

A new phase of understanding of these worlds beyond 'death' is coming in our time, and the rush of new uniting, recording of experiences and of communion with those who are on the higher plane suggests a great thinning of the veils between the different levels of consciousness.

It is a very strange thing that there is no word in our English language to express this most majestic of all conceptions, the release of the soul into light. There is only the word 'DEATH' with all its suggestions of rotting cadavers and corpses and skeletons. It has been endowed with a note of morbidity and even horror, and is often taboo as a subject for discussion. It almost seems as if there is a conspiracy to hush up the fact of death. We need to create a word to express this concept of 'release into light'. Teilhard de Chardin has shown us how we can coin new words to express our new vision of the organic oneness of the planet and of life. Why should not the spiritual movement in this country find and adopt a scholarly word which would bring this light-filled concept into our modern and living language? Any suggestions?

We grasp now that the universe is of the nature of thought, that the so-called higher planes are not vastly distant but are ever present within our sense world, on a higher frequency which our physical senses cannot detect. We need to be able to tune in to a much higher wavelength if we are to have communion with those who have left the body. We discover that the human organism is truly the most marvellous radio set or computer. Where there is real love and affinity between souls there can never be any separation. There is telepathic connection between the planes but while we are limited within a body, this 'muddy vesture of decay', we have difficulty in learning how to tune in. The important point to grasp is that discarnate entities or beings can speak to us within our own thinking. Too many people still hope to see their 'lost' friends in some outward vision. The one who has left the body has psychic powers beyond ours and can pick up all our loving thoughts. We can ask them questions and the answers will usually be given at the moment of waking, as if it were in our own thinking. This is why communion is so often missed. People fail to see that the message must appear to have been thought by themselves. When we are asleep and the soul and 'ego' are freed from the body, we are then together with those with whom we have affinity on higher planes, but are naturally not conscious of it in our ordinary experience, so when we wake we know nothing of it. We must watch our dreams, however, for in these important days of the thinning of the veil the 'clear dream' may be a way in which our friends or spirit guides may wish to communicate with us.

This true communion within thinking is wonderfully subtle and obviously by its nature does not in any way conflict with our free will. It would be so easy to follow and obey the Archangel Michael if he appeared before us with his flaming sword! But the nature of the grand experiment of God is that man has to experience being cut off from the divine to which he belongs. In our materialistic age he has come to the point of allowing the faculty for seeing into the higher realities to atrophy. Therefore he proudly declares they do not exist and concerns himself solely with his outward-looking concerns in the material world.

Once having experienced separation the moment can come when he is called on, like the prodigal son, to 'come to himself' and turn again and say 'I will go back to my Father'. The impulse comes from within the heart of man himself to overcome the aloneness and set himself once more on the path of return but this impulse has to come in freedom from within each of us. There can be no constraint from higher worlds.

A new and wonderful picture emerges from modern spiritual science of world within world, interpenetrating fields of light vibration of which our physical world is but the lowest frequency. To enter those worlds we have to learn to look within recovering that faculty which is so much dulled in our intellectual training today. William Blake, artist and seer, writes:

> I cease not from my great task, to open the eternal worlds, to open the immortal eyes of man inward, into the realms of thought, into Eternity, ever expanding in the Bosom of God, the human Imagination.

Looking inwards is not mere introspection at our personal psychological state. We discover that in Blake's sense to look within is to look through and that imaginative thinking is able to enter the realms of Divine Imagining. In Imagination we have a key to those worlds which we enter when released from the body at death. Our generation is called on to begin to explore space in this new sense, not resting content solely with outward looking and action, but re-awakening and developing the organs of perception which enable each of us to look deep within and through.

The picture emerging from the vision of spiritual science is of interpenetrating planes of vibration and light. These are the 'eternal worlds' in the sense that they are lifted beyond time as we experience it on the material plane. However the 'higher' worlds are not to be thought of as vastly distant. That mistake comes from thinking spatially. They are ever present wholly interpenetrating the sense world but on a higher frequency which our ordinary sense cannot detect. Our inner thought, however, if lifted towards intuition, can learn to explore them.

The inner core of man's being is seen as belonging to these timeless realms, descending to go through an allegorical journey through dark forests and stormy ocean, undergoing soul trials and ordeals until he can unite with his higher self, the symbolical princess of all fairy tales, returning again to the world from which he descended. It is strange that confirmation of spiritual science is found in all mythology, all legends and fairy stories, and much great drama and poetry. The symbols when interpreted in this way are found to enshrine this great truth so important for the modern mind.

We live in an age when doctrines like Marxism contend that the whole of the fabric of religion and art is but a super-structure built upon the one reality – matter. Never was there an age when it was more important to revive and reinterpret the old legends, because they speak direct to the heart and the imagination within the soul of the eternal truths which the logical intellect can so easily miss. Look beneath the outward form of Shakespeare's plays and the Odyssey you find the same great truth which can convince the soul that it is in fact going through an entirely meaningful journey on the earth plane.

Always the allegory reveals that the timeless being of man, the eternal entity, enters the temporal sphere of earth for this journey of initiation. This gives us the clue of greatest import-ance – *we were there as eternal entities before our conception and birth*. Much concern has been given to survival after death. The much more penetrating concept is that of *pre-existence*. Spiritual science, supported by mythology and the intuition of the poets, estab-lishes this important truth. We do not need to try to convince the sceptical intellect by finding 'proofs of survival'. The intellect can always debunk and disprove anything! We need to think ourselves into the understanding that these are timeless realms of spirit, interpenetrating the slow vibrational plane of earth and that the entity of man is eternally at home in these higher planes, re-entering them in sleep, in deep meditation and after 'death'. This is the finding of all the 'seers', ancient or contemporary. They tell us what they experience of the higher worlds. They never ask us simply to believe or to accept on faith. We recognise that the higher worlds are realms of Thought and that our imaginative thinking can apprehend them. Do we not all know the experience of our thinking leaping to grasp an idea which is so beautiful that we know it must be true? Recognise that this faculty is the beginning of spiritual knowledge. We all have latent organs of perception and the first step in developing them is the use of this power of thinking. Hold the pictures in thought, and if they are true they will be supported as time goes on by inner conviction.

In our day conscious communion with the beings of the higher planes is becoming possible as never before, carrying with it a conviction of truth which no scepticism can shake. Individuals and groups are able directly to listen within their own thinking. But this is not only for our personal comfort – far from it. We are called on to co-operate with the higher worlds in the entry of spiritual forces on to the earth plane. We are to be the channels through which the angelic world can descend. We are needed by them.

The world is in a very critical state and the dangers are appalling. Communications bear out that there is immense concern on higher planes about what man is doing to the planet. In his reckless greed and Ignorance he is exploiting the forces of life to his own advantage in ways that imperil the very survival of life upon the planet. It is even feared that he may do things which will tip earth off its axis, with damaging effects through-out the whole solar system.

Now it would clearly defeat the whole Divine plan of devel-oping man as a free moral being if there were direct intervention to change our thinking. This change must come from within our own hearts and minds. There can, however, be intervention through calamity. Our failure to see that the earth is a great living being is so disturbing the great elemental forces throughout the whole body of the earth that it may pay us back in disturbances such as earthquakes and atmospheric change. Worst of all our nuclear bombs, breaking through the etheric envelope of the earth, allow the instreaming not only of harmful rays but also of dark beings. Many communications are now being given which suggest that catastrophes and cataclysm may manifest on the earth if we do not change our thinking. Time is short and the only way of saving this planet is for enough of mankind to become channels for the inflow of light and the flow of spirit.

Calamity will also be cleansing. This picture is one of supreme hope, since the entry of the spirit means the flow of the light of the Christ impulse. Teilhard de Chardin speaks, with intense excitement, of the 'Christification' of the planet, a process and phenomenon both scientific and spiritual in which every particle of matter and every soul-atom is being filled with inner light. The forces of light will enter, when men as groups and individuals take the initiative and invoke them, offering themselves as channels. We who meet in this way are in the position of a fifth column, holding a kind of bridgehead at a time when the warning of impending invasion has been sent out. We are not to be discouraged by our own littleness. Many vital positions in the war were held by tiny groups. It is a terrific picture to be taken absolutely seriously. All our little meditation groups are centres which should lift themselves in dedication towards the light so that spiritual power can pour through on to the earth plane.

All the great religions are expecting a new Advent, many believe it may be in the next year or two, though in what form, whether within the soul or in outward manifestation, it is dangerous to speculate. A great change might shoot through human beings. No one has yet written a science-fiction novel about this possible event. Suppose that at midnight the Christ love and the mighty forces of light struck all human hearts. What would happen throughout our society? To those concerned with selfish or evil ends it would look like the angel of death. There would be uttermost confusion and those who were turned in to the Light would be filled with the great joy in recognising the Second Coming. It may well be that this great adventure is really upon us. Teilhard writes 'How many of us are genuinely moved in the depth of our hearts by the wild hope that our earth will be recast ... The flame of expectation must be revived at all costs. At all costs we must renew in ourselves the desire and the hope for the great Coming.'

James Elroy Flecker wrote:

> Awake, awake, the world is young
> For all its weary years of thought
> The starkest fights must still be fought
> The most surprising songs be sung.

Truly we need 'to be prepared for the most surprising events', but facing them with a joyous courage, since we know that we have guidance and protection if we can turn to the light and lift our thinking towards the Christ power throughout our daily activities.

Then we are ready for anything. We can be filled with the splendid hope of the emergence of a new world out of any turmoil which arises in the submergence of darkness in the Coming Light. Then the bogey of 'death' will be wholly expelled from our minds and we shall know that the planes of consciousness interpenetrate so completely that it matters little whether we find ourselves on this or that side of the thinning veil. The river of death turns out to be the merest brook and we may step over it into a country of wider light-filled consciousness.

Let us close with the great passage from Christopher Fry's *A Sleep of Prisoners*:

> The human heart can go the lengths of God
> Dark and cold we may be
> But this is no winter now
> The human misery of centuries begins to crack and break
> The thunder is the thunder of the floes

The thaw, the flood, the upstart spring.
Thank God our time is now, when wrong
Comes up to meet us everywhere
Never to leave us till we take
The longest stride of soul men ever took
Affairs are now soul-size.

    The enterprise is exploration into God.
Where are you making for?
It takes so many thousand years to wake,
But will you wake, for pity's sake.

9

THOUGHTS ON CHILDBIRTH IN THE LIGHT OF THE HOLISTIC WORLD PICTURE

THIS ESSAY is written for a lass who has a baby on the way and who is troubled by the doubt as to whether it was justifiable to bring a child into so awful a world as surrounds us now. Let us look at this in the light of the 'holistic' world picture. It is always good and valid to lift our view-point and look at every problem from this greater light. Be it repeated that none of this is dogma to be believed. If you respond to these ideas, learn to live with them as thoughts, learn to act as if you believed them, and yet reserve judgment. You are not asked to believe but to think. Watch life in the light of them. This is a way of exploring into further reaches of imponderable truths. They will, if true to you, draw an inner certainty to themselves as the weeks go by. Something in us quickens in response to an idea. We are experiencing the opening of buds of perception, of new vision.

So, think that all life is One. All is Consciousness, a divine field of creative thought interpenetrating everything everywhere. We are each a point of self-consciousness in this sea of consciousness. Thus there can be no problem it does not touch. All aspects of our lives can be illuminated.

So to our problem of childbirth.

The soul is immortal and imperishable. It always was and always will be, for it is a droplet of the Divine Source. For it

79

there can be no death, though the body sheath can age, break down and be destroyed. The conception of a child is thus the initiating of a process whereby a free ranging spiritual being begins the long process of anchoring itself into the material world and descending into the field of gravity.

Since the true spiritual 'I' of man is eternal, it follows axiomatically that it was there before it was born, as an already developed entity. Hold to this tremendous thought. The child quickening within you is not a soul starting 'from scratch' at conception. It is already matured by experience through long ages. This point is best illustrated from a verse by our metaphysical poet Thomas Traherne (d.1650) who possessed the faculty of remembering back into the womb – and beyond. All his poems and writings try to convey this experience to us. It is significant that his works were lost until discovered in an attic about 1900 for they could not have been understood earlier. Now they speak to us a profound and vital truth. Listen to them. He is palpably describing the embryo.

> Before I skill'd to prize
> Those living Stars, mine Eyes;
> Before I knew these Hands were mine
> Or that my sinews did my Members join ...
> I was within
> A House I knew not, newly cloath'd with skin.
>
> Then was my Soul my only All to me,
> A living endless Eye
> Scarce bounded with the Sky
> Whose Power and Act and Essence was to see;
> I was an inward sphere of Light
> Or an interminable Orb of Sight
> Exceeding that which makes the days,
> A vital Sun, that shed abroad its rays,
> All Life, all Sense,
> A naked, simple, pure intelligence.

The same intuition is developed by Wordsworth in his great *Ode on the Intimations of Immortality in Early Childhood.*

Our birth is but a sleep and a forgetting;
The soul that rises with us, our life's Star,
    Hath had elsewhere its setting
    And cometh from afar:
    Nor in entire forgetfulness
    And not in utter nakedness,
But trailing clouds of glory do we come
    From God, who is our home
Heaven lies about us in our infancy
Shades of the prison-house begin to close
    Upon the growing boy.
But he beholds the light, and whence it flows,
    He sees it in his joy;
The Youth, who daily farther from the East
    Must travel, still is Nature's Priest,
    And by the vision splendid
    Is on his way attended;
At length the Man perceives it die away
And fade into the light of common day.

We now, in the quickening of spiritual knowledge, are indeed recovering that 'vision splendid'. It is not dead. Only the organs of inner perception have gone dormant as we grow to self-consciousness and they call to be re-awakened.

What a thought this is for parents, doctors or teachers! When we see a wee puling infant let us not say 'Look at this tiny little soul'. The soul is ageless. You may be watching the beginning of a lengthy process of incarnation of a mature and highly developed soul, limiting itself into the drastic restriction of embodiment. The body is the wonderful tool for action and creation in the heavy density of the material plane, but the entry into a body is, nevertheless, for a free-ranging spirit something like an imprisonment. It is a sort of tomb. Gravity is the grave. Birth is in this sense a kind of death, death truly a birth, it is perhaps a blessed provision that we wholly forget the world of light we came from. This coming child of yours – where, then, did it gather its experience? We see that in addition to the phys-ical evolution of the body we must come to terms with the idea of a spiritual evolution of the 'I', that spark separated from the

Divine Fire. Can we take it that entry into the field of gravity and form, obviously involving the experience of separation from the spiritual source, could be a kind of training, a method of getting experience? The whole drive of evolution is towards what Teilhard de Chardin calls the process of 'complexifying', the coming together of cells into ever greater complexity, each stage involving a heightening of consciousness. Indeed he comes to the conclusion that there is an inbuilt drive within the cell to complexify, and he concludes that, if this be so, it reveals higher purpose in all evolution. As Pope put it:

> Mere atoms casually together hurled
> Could ne'er produce so beautiful a world.

(Live with that wonderful idea. Don't believe it, but live as if you believed it. Don't let critical mind say 'Yes, but …')

So it looks as if our beautiful earth is the great training-ground for souls. Here within the limitation of body and senses we learn self-consciousness and responsibility. Keats called Earth a 'vale of soul-making'. From the concept of pre-existence we arrive at the likelihood of many visits to earth – re-birth or re-incarnation. Again this is no doctrine to be believed, but enormous strength comes from living as if you believed it. For it implies that we choose our environment for soul training. Spiritual research bears this out, and the seers from Plato onward have known it. It appears that no soul incarnates until it agrees to do so and that then it is shown its destiny and given a preview of its coming life experience.

This concept is presented by Robert Frost in a remarkable poem called *Trial by Existence*. The scene is laid in Heaven and he describes:

> The gathering of the souls for birth,
> The trial by existence named,
> The obscuration upon earth,
> And none are taken but who will,
> Having first heard the life read out
> That opens earthward, good or ill
> Beyond the shadow of a doubt.

But always God speaks at the end.
One thought in agony of strife
The bravest will have by for friend
The memory that he chose the life:
But the pure fate to which you go
Admits no memory of choice
Or the woe were not earthly woe
To which you give assenting voice.

How infinitely strengthening it would be if we could act as if we believed this. Modern psychology has implied that our personalities are made from heredity and environment. This justifies us in transferring blame for our shortcomings on to someone else or something outside ourselves. The noble picture of re-birth puts the responsibility squarely on our own shoulders. Seen on a higher level we chose our environment and are therefore in a real sense total cause of our circumstances and our difficulties and limitations. If we can accept this (or act as if it were true) we become a much more tolerant, tolerable and positive human being, for we shall no longer grumble about anything. We gain a great deal and lose nothing whatever by this way of thinking and we still remain free from any dogmatic belief in a difficult field.

Now that child on the way – the implication is that it actually chose its parents in order to get a suitable body for its round of earth experience. Be flattered! You have a great task. You didn't make that child – you are giving it a body.

One of the most important aspects of the concept of reincarnation is that we return in groups of kindred souls. Grasp the idea of the Group Soul, formed out of the coming together of many souls held by affinity and the attractive force of love. When you descend to earth you do not go down with your whole being. What might be called your 'permanent soul' puts out a sort of feeler into the gravity plane to act as a feed-back for earth experience into the Group Soul. Your present personality is no more than the limited self-consciousness built up during this sojourn on earth. Your immortal eternal 'I' is something beyond personality and we shall learn to see that the purpose of earth life is to achieve this trans-personal consciousness. This is no less than achieving the Life Eternal not after death but now, while we are in the body. When we have done that we are sure to go forward after death into the Eternal realms of Light and not be stuck in the gloomy Borderland.

We incarnate in kindred groups. Therefore the friend or colleague you find in middle life was probably a relative last time, and perhaps will be a brother, sister, mother, son next time. Again there's no need to believe this. But how enriching a possibility! Surely this adds a profound respect for both our relatives and our friends or colleagues and helps us to face up to personality difficulties. It is wonderful to think what experiences we must have had together. It seems that after the release of so called death we are allowed to look back down the corridors of time and see what our real soul's history has been. For you and I truly are history. But alas we may too likely find that we have by no means fulfilled the task we undertook when we chose to descend!

Now to consider that grave question – am I justified for my pleasure in bringing another child into our over-crowded and in many ways awful world?

Firstly, it is not only the concern of you and your husband. That being has chosen you and with its eyes open saw the world it was entering. Born in 1979 it will come of age in the year 2000. The turn of the century is likely to be a time of tremendous spiritual transformation of man. In all the turmoil of our present time we are perhaps experiencing the prelude to the greatest events in human history. Apocalyptic change is upon us, to be followed after the time of tribulation such as never was by the 'coming of the Son of Man with power and great glory'. This is perhaps the most exciting and important generation in human history and you young people are involved and on your shoulders will be the great responsibility. Is it not likely that many souls are crowding into incarnation to share the experience of earth change and the Second Coming? So far from doing something wrong by having a child, you are giving a soul the opportunity of sharing this great experience. You are being joined by one of the group, maybe an advanced soul who can really help to lift mankind through the coming changes. You see the sort of scale of thinking that must come if we brood upon the holistic world picture. How great a responsibility and joy to give the chance of a new birth. Look into the eyes of the young child and know that in that smile a great and exalted soul may be looking out at you.

We recognise that a result of the rationalist reductionist thinking has resulted in the development of a medical science which treats the body essentially as a machine, even now to the supply of spare parts to keep it going efficiently. From this thinking it has seemed valid, for hospital efficiency's sake, to separate the new born babe immediately from the mother, hold it upside down and slap its bottom to make it take its first breath and cry its first cry, wash it and label it – all very clinical. Now from the lead of Dr. Laboyer and others concerned with 'natural childbirth' it is realised that the infant may be left quietly with the parents of which, soul and body, it is truly part, that the first breath will be taken naturally at the right moment, that what is all-important is the unbroken flow of love and life from the mother to the new born child. This may be seen just as a wise improvement in ante-natal technique allowing for the tenderness which we know to be so vital a psychological factor. But if we try to relate this to the holistic world-picture, we shall see that this change of method, now rapidly spreading to the joy and delight of so many mothers, may be a real sign of the inflooding of the energies of synthesis, harmony, wholeness and love. These powers of the spirit, it is contended, are now being released into human consciousness to bring about the *metanoia*, or change in thinking which will bring mankind into an era of greater harmony, based on a knowledge of the Oneness of life. This must inevitably reveal itself at the key point in the life process, when the spiritual entity first passes from the Timeless realms through the narrow gate of birth into the world of form. Just conceive in this light the terrible shock of bewilderment when this being of its own free choice begins its adventure of plunging down into the fascinating and dangerous adventure of earth life to be received with a callous indifference of being taken from the mother, slapped and washed and catalogued. Thus the movement for natural childbirth may be truly seen as a step towards a holistic medicine which will come to recognise man as being of spirit, soul and body, and birth as a wonderful step into incarnation.

In light of this knowledge, the study of embryology is quite fascinating. Here is found one of the greatest sources of spiritual research into the history of the evolution of the planet earth. As Steiner and his fellow researchers have shown, the embryo recapitulates in miniature not only the story of bodily evolution but of the various incarnations of the planet. These are described in Steiner's great volume *Occult Science*.

The young child naturally holds a dim recollection of the land of light from which as a spiritual being it has descended. This we have found so well expressed in Traherne's poems. Thus so often it will ask the puzzled question 'Mummy where did I come from?' Too often the modern mother, assuming tacitly that life begins at conception, will reply by telling the child prematurely about the so-called 'facts of life'. But it is not desire for instruction about sex that lies behind the question, for the child, as Wordsworth knew, still 'beholds the light and whence it flows'. There are indeed 'intimations of immortality in early childhood'. With Taliesin he can rightly say: 'I come from the region of the summer stars'.

It is so easy for the rationalist-minded mother to assume that the tiny child has only very limited consciousness and awareness. Yet consider the implications of a single authentic case. A woman was put into a hypnotic state to help her to be freed from some traumatic mental blockage. She was carried right back to the moment of birth, when she suddenly said in a loud Yorkshire accent, 'Eh but the master will be mad when he sees this fun.' These were the words of the midwife immediately after the birth and the subconscious of the child heard and understood it and knew she was an unwanted child – and never forgot it!

Traherne has another extraordinary poem called *Dumbness* in which he describes how, before he had learned to talk, all natural objects spoke to him and told him of their Divinity, but, when he began to speak they relapsed into silence. We may try, with wonder, to conceive what is really going on in the inner world of the child.

One of the most wonderful moments with the tiny child is when first it really smiles – as distinct from the grimace associated with wind. If we know that we are watching the majestic process of incarnation of an already mature soul, then with deeper vision we can look through that smile into the light-filled beauty of the descending spirit. In Traherne's words again:

> How like an angel he came down
> How bright are all things here.

A friend of mine heard a small boy of four declare to his mother, 'These people are all giants. But they don't know it because they can only see the part that's down here.' He was delighted and amused at his discovery. That child had clairvoyant vision of the oversoul. So it is with many children, who are able to 'see' into the supersensible, elemental world, the realm of 'faery'. They know the truth, but how shattering it can be for this sensitivity when a prosaic parent declares that the child must stop imagining things and be sensible. So let us close with Wordsworth, again from the great Ode.

> Thou, whose exterior semblance doth belie
>   Thy soul's immensity:
> Thou best Philosopher, who yet dost keep
> Thy heritage, thou Eye among the blind
> That, deaf and silent, read'st the eternal deep,
> Flaunted for ever by the eternal mind –
>   Mighty prophet! Seer blest!
>   On whom those truths do rest
> Which we are toiling all our lives to find
> In darkness lost, the darkness of the grave;
> Thou, over whom thy Immortality
>   Broods like the day . .
> Thou little Child, yet glorious in the might
> Of heaven-born freedom on thy being's height ...

Full soon thy Soul shall have her earthly freight
And custom lie upon thee with a weight
Heavy as frost, and deep almost as life.

10

OUTER WORLD, INNER WORLD

THE SUPERFICIAL experience is that we are each a separate entity, more or less cut off from our fellows. Our understanding now gives us a different picture. We recognise that really we are particles of a stupendous whole and that no life, human or natural, exists of itself. The world is a great organism and the whole life structure consists of organism within organism in incredible complexity. We begin to see that when we discard the body at so-called 'death', we find ourselves in a soul condition in which we can merge consciousness with other souls. As spiritual beings we shall be able to touch auras and enter lovingly into the thought and feelings of our fellows. We have, as Teilhard puts it, 'glimpsed the marvels of a common soul', and the experience of this can begin on the earth plane, as the selfless and unpossessive love characteristic of the new age begins to bind individuals into the new groups.

The mental grasp of the idea of Oneness is the first essential. To experience it consciously is the aim. An imaginative turning-about is here necessary in our thinking. We accept that soul trials and ordeals are the nature and purpose of life on earth. Earth, says Keats, is not so much a vale of tears as a vale of soul-making. A major clue is given in Shakespeare's tragedies. The hero is shown with a flaw in his character. This draws to him conditions of temptation. If he fails, he is thrown into mental confusion which makes possible a second attack. If he again fails to rise and to react from his higher self, he passes the point of no return and the situation deteriorates into calamity. For

Macbeth, the flaw of ambition is touched by the Witches and by Lady Macbeth. For Othello, Iago is the counterpart of the flaw of jealousy. In each case an outer person or situation is the exact counterpart of the inner weakness which needs to be overcome. In a true sense the flaw actually creates the counterpart and draws the personality again and again into similar situations of ordeal and testing.

Do we not all know this in ourselves? Each of us, in our little way, is living out a Shakespearean soul-drama, and this is why the plays, in their deeper symbolism hold their eternal appeal.

Yet we must not fall into the trap of self-centred thinking. If Othello draws Iago to himself to bring about the trial, so does Iago draw Othello. Lady Macbeth has her flaw in character which is challenged by Macbeth. The dance is very intricate. The souls we meet are also meeting us. A complex pattern of trials is taking place, always like a changing kaleidoscope. We may see all our relationships during the day as meaningful. We must conceive of a planning and direction of events perpetually in action from a higher and wider sphere of consciousness, bringing people into relationships which give experience to both parties. Then we can feel a new sympathy for the other souls as we recognise that they have their own destinies into which we have ourselves been mysteriously drawn.

The heightening of consciousness is of course a process of pain. We become aware of the flaw in character and recollection of past events is seared with remorse as we see the folly of the way we reacted to certain opportunities or situations.

T.S. Eliot, in *Little Gidding*, speaks of 'the gifts reserved for age':

> ... the rending pain of re-enactment
> Of all that you have done, and been; the shame
> Of motives late revealed, and the awareness
> Of things ill done and done to others' harm
> Which once you took for exercise of virtue.
>
> From wrong to wrong the exasperated spirit
> Proceeds, unless restored by that refining fire
> Where you must move in measure, like a dancer.

The agony of past failure ceases to be intolerable if we can lift our thinking and see ourselves playing out a soul drama with a real purpose. This purpose is, of course, development of self consciousness, evolving of ego awareness and then opening this to our own Higher Self, ultimately the Christ-filled Ego, the I AM. Every soul-step involves suffering, though it will be made in joy. The turning-about in attitude comes when we accept that we are not here by chance but have entered life by choice and taken on a body and personality in order to develop soul and spirit quality. We return again and again to the plane of earth in order to undergo soul trials until a step into inner freedom can be made.

Robert Frost, in his great poem *Trial by Existence*, says:

> 'Tis of the essence of life here,
>   Though we choose greatly, still to lack
> The lasting memory at all clear,
>   That life has for us on the wrack
> Nothing but what we somehow chose:
>
> But the pure fate to which you go
>   Admits no memory of choice,
> Or the woe were not earthly woe
>   To which you give the assenting voice.

The flaw in our character actually draws us to events or people who provide the temptation and trial. If we fail to 'overcome', the inexorable fate will find us again or, more correctly, we shall ourselves seek out and stage for ourselves another set of circumstances to repeat the trial. By the nature of human psychology it can never be avoided. The subconscious, closely linked with the superconscious part of our nature, will lead us gently into temptation which our conscious personality must then face.

Now the soul experience is an inner thing. Inside our hearts we know fear or jealousy, hate or resentment, yet the provoker of each dark emotion is a being or person 'outside' ourselves. Almost all 'events' when analysed turn out to be people or beings impingeing upon us. The real battle ground is in ourselves. We discover we are fighting resentment or fear inside ourselves stimulated by an outer remark or action. The whole field is an 'inner' affair, or rather the distinctions of inner and outer begin to get inextricably merged. The 'event', this is the other soul, becomes really part of our 'inner' field.

The soul battle is solely against ourselves. The supposed insult thrown at us can be seen as a challenge to control our own reactions. We are duelling not with an outer enemy but with the low-self reaction in ourselves. Truly the fencing symbol is powerful here. Normally we parry the attack and riposte direct at the other person in anger or resentment. This is just what the devil wants – to create a flare-up and leave a wreck of jangled emotions. If, however, we can parry, not his attack, but our instant and habitual reaction to his attack inside ourselves, then we remain free to act objectively and calmly. The temptation representing the flaw has been met and overcome. We owe a debt to the tempter for presenting us with the obstacle.

Seen this way all the events which meet us in the day are part of our inner world. All are features in a battle between light and darkness going on inside ourselves. Our negative emotions are the only enemy. All resentment against others is lifted if once we see that, on a higher level, we ourselves have planned and drawn ourselves into the trials. 'To him that overcometh shall be given ...' (It is interesting in Chapters 2 and 3 of the Book of Revelation to read consecutively the series of rewards 'to him that overcometh'.)

All this about the temptations and pitfalls of the lower self may seem somewhat negative. Clearly it is the counterpart of something much grander – low-self may draw a man into situations which tempt him to fall; high-self stages situations which challenge him to rise. As we progress, the emphasis changes towards this latter. Once conceive and grasp the reality of a higher self, a spiritual self, leading us upward towards the overself in the eternal world, and we see that man's purpose here is to rise into this contact. First he learns to overcome low-self temptations. Then desire is transmuted into aspiration and the soul yearns towards its spiritual origin and goal. Then we must admit that we are innerly drawn into situations which present the opportunity and challenge to take a step in character. Always this must be into the new. We are having to learn to act into conditions we have never experienced, to behave as if we were something bigger than our habitual self. Thus we are presented with opportunities. Often these are very painful, as is every step in awakening consciousness. Do we not all know these moments when we are suddenly faced with crisis and have no notion which course to choose? There seems to be no guide and for a moment the soul reels in indecision. Too often then the rational mind persuades us to react along habitual paths and we take the tamer course, afterwards upbraiding ourselves for lack of courage. At such moments, we should bravely act into the highest we can imagine of ourselves. We are giving the chance for the higher self to enter as a power into our lives. As we learn to recognise these moments, it is born in on us that they repeat themselves with regularity as if they are really being arranged from a higher level. It is agony of pain when we realise we have failed again and again, but the time will come when we can respond with certainty. This is the real training of the human soul, made possible through the recognition of the reality of the realm of the higher selves to which we aspire. We ourselves truly bring about these situations of opportunity as well as the moments of temptation. It is said that the Chinese have no word for crisis, and that the nearest translation would be 'important opportunity'.

Recognise that the outer world of events which comes to meet us is closely and mysteriously related to our inner world of soul experience. Know that all that happens has plan and meaning and that we are all moving in an intricate dance and drama. Plunge with joy into the 'refining fire' of that dance. It is our own choice whether the direction is towards light and unity or darkness and despair. Of this we are certain, that in the dance we are not alone, but are guided and directed from realms of higher being. We pass through events as in a fairy story and each has inner purpose.

Through each soul-trial overcome we come nearer to the true union with the realm of our higher self. We can choose to give ourselves freely to the dance, lifting ourselves in an act of faith to recognition that it has meaning. In these extraordinary days, when so many believe that an enhancing of consciousness through a change in 'vibratory rate' is upon us, we can add little more than consciously accept the invitation to the dance in the refining fire. Moment to moment we can learn to accept what comes to us in inner tranquillity.

Goethe wrote 'all that is transitory is but a parable'. Did you ever achieve the real experience of the Viennese Waltz? If so, you will remember that a stage comes in the dance when all the surrounding room with its twisting throng becomes a moving whirl of colour and music, in which oneself and one's partner are the only 'still point in the turning world'. We feel no giddiness since we are completely surrendered to the dervish spinning which can continue unbroken for half an hour. There comes the experience of complete tranquillity and absolute control. When this inner stilling is achieved through meditation, then we can be guided by the world of spirit. Perhaps this is the most important contribution we can each make in preparation for a time when we may be called on to move into events and changes, inner and outer, for which there is no precedent. The primary task is to prepare ourselves as best we can to be channels for the Coming Light, by creating an inner centre of stillness, carrying this over into the events and contacts of daily life.

11

SHAKESPEARE AND
THE VISION OF WHOLENESS

THE VISION of wholeness colours the whole of Shakespeare's writing. It is the key to the hidden allegory which runs through all his plays and new light is thrown upon their interpretation once we begin to look upon them in this way. The concept was still current in the world-view of Shakespeare's day. It was assumed that in the beginning was the vast unity of divine imagination. This then began to divide itself into great polarities, balanced opposites in a harmony of antagonistic action. Among the primary polarities were the *voluntas* and *noluntas*, the opposition of male and female running through all life. Gravity and its opposite known as 'levity' till the seventeenth century, is another example. The incredible diversification in nature is the picture of this ever increasing partition into subtler polarities. It is the process which Teilhard de Chardin called 'complexification', and it created that complex environment which makes it now possible for the human organism to survive.

This division means that all parts are an image of the whole and the whole is contained in every part. Man is thus the microcosm and the image of the macrocosm. Modern radionics rediscovers this truth. The bloodspot is found to radiate on the same wave-length as the whole body and thus diagnosis and healing, can be achieved at a distance through restoring the imbalance in radiation pattern.

The opposing view sees the world as the aggregate of separate parts integrated in growth. The distinction is fundamental.

Our scientific age is largely founded on the second view. It is clearly accepted in the Marxist doctrine that all the achievements of art and religion are but a superstructure of human thinking built upon the one reality – matter. The current views of evolution make the tacit assumption that species have grown 'by chance' through natural selection. Man is thus essentially an accident in a realm of nature indifferent to him and his presence. The planet on which we tread is seen as a tiny speck of dust in a vast dead mechanism of the cosmos and life a puff of light to be extinguished in the vast and slow death of a solar system. No wonder that man, finding himself an unimportant accident in a world of death, feels himself at liberty to exploit and 'mine' the planet 'ad lib' for his personal gain and pleasure.

Into this thinking now impinge disturbing thoughts. Perhaps this is not the true picture. Perhaps our assumption of unimportance has led to a vast arrogance. At least we awaken to the fact that it is not the only picture. Perhaps after all we must take more literally the phrases that we say so lightly.

> In the beginning was the Word
> and the Word was with God and the Word was
> God. By him were all things made.

As Pope had it:

> 'All are but parts of one stupendous whole
> Whose body nature is and God the soul'.

We must recognise that until recently the 'vision of whole-ness' was the basic tenet of the thinking mind. It still coloured all thought in Shakespeare's day. Indeed we must admit that ours is the only culture since the world began which has not in some way held that life began in a great unity and that life on our earth plane is held by a great and living organism of spiritual being. Our arrogant age has abandoned this world-view, writing off the earlier thinkers as victims of superstition. Now it begins to reawaken. Stammeringly and with a new humility we begin to recognise that the older thinkers may have been right. Man may after all prove to be the centre of a living organism of being; the

SHAKESPEARE AND THE VISION OF WHOLENESS

planet instead of a speck of dead dust, may prove to be a living seed, holding in the crown of its evolution a spiritual future of enormous importance. Certainly man as a free and conscious kingdom seems to have been the concern of God or the Gods.

> What is man, that Thou art mindful of him –
> For thou hast made him a little lower than the angels.

In the new understanding we can see the human kingdom is that field in which nature becomes conscious of herself. The living organism of the planet looks out through human consciousness into a cosmos shot through with living thought and being. Man is indeed responsible to God for life on the planet. The divine world has handed over to him the task of tending and developing life upon the planet. We are the channels for the inflow of the spirit and of light but in our greed, with its offspring fear, we turn it all to confusion and darkness. In a new humility we must take up our task of stewards of God and of ambassadors for the divine.

All mythology, all fairy stories, tell in terms of symbolism and allegory of that truth which it is so essential for modern man to rediscover if he is to keep his sanity. The inner core of man is eternal spiritual being belonging to a timeless world of light. This descends into the world of matter to undertake an allegorical journey, through dark forest or dangerous seas, until it can find and unite with its own higher or spiritual self. When this mystical marriage has been achieved, return to the eternal realms becomes possible. A thousand variants on this timeless theme are found by all who know how to read in legend and drama. The hero in all mythology is one who journeys into the timeless realms to bring back the elixir of life, be it Golden Fleece, Holy Grail, talisman or jewel, with life-enhancing power.

Shakespeare's plays constitute, in this sense, a great body of mythology. Once we have seen the 'vision of wholeness' and the truth of the eternal being of man we can re-read the plays on a different level. They strengthen the soul in the truths they reveal.

The theme of unity runs through them all. First comes the primal unity diversified into polarities thrown into confusion by human error, the task of the hero being to restore the harmony through uniting with his higher self as symbolised by the heroine. A cosmic process is portrayed on the level of human relations.

The Comedy of Errors is one of the clearest examples of this. Here a condition of Elysian unity is first described, then division into pairs, paired yet again, like cells dividing. The uttermost confusion comes about through human error and frailty, until finally the right pairs find each other and the original harmony is restored. A comedy indeed, some would say a brilliant youthful farce. Yet at the same time in this early play Shakespeare gives us his whole thesis and follows it through in all the other comedies. The greatest error is to think that this play is simply a comedy. It is a great allegory, but as with all Shakespeare, no moral is forced upon us. We have no need to bother about the hidden allegory. We may take the plays at their face value. The very title, *As You Like It*, shows this. *As You Like It* turns out to be the most complete morality play, with not one character or even name that has not its significance in the pattern. Space does not allow analysis here and only the hint can be given to urge the reader to explore further. 'Feed yourselves by questioning,' is Hymen's final injunction. Orlando, representing the awaking powers of affection, revolts against the dominant Will (Oliver, his brother), to find his higher self (Rosalind), is separated from her to go through soul trials until he can truly come back to her again, worthy of the mystical marriage. Exiled to the forest, an eternal symbol of the journey through time, he finds her in disguise and is trained by her in love. When Will and heart and thinking are in harmony through the integration of the personality a composite marriage is celebrated.

> Now is there joy in heaven
> when earthly things made even
> Atone together.

In allegorical interpretation all characters must be seen as aspects of the personality. This is well known in the psychology of dreams. The unbelievable genius of Shakespeare is that he is able to keep this psychological unity while giving us outward stories of adventure and conflict which even have political patterns as well.

The Merchant of Venice compares remarkably with *As You Like It*. In both plays we have the clear indication of the need to attain to a higher level of consciousness (city, forest and court; Venice, the rich city, and Belmont the fair mountain where lives the rich princess). The hero Bassanio wins his higher self, Portia, through a wonderful fairy-story lottery, but in that instant has to be separated from her to return to Venice to watch what is virtually the ritual murder of his friend by the Jew.

The task of man on this plane is to find and unite with his spiritual self. The higher worlds waste no time. Once the two, hero and heroine, have recognised and loved each other they are allowed no time for enjoyment. They are separated by an apparently cruel fate and made to endure more ordeals and trials until they prove themselves worthy of final union. How often does this pattern show itself in our actual lives, suggesting that we are all engaged in an allegorical journey working out a web of destiny with a goal set in a higher plane of consciousness. Portia, the higher love and wisdom, comes to the rescue in disguise, the only one who knows the overall picture and can see how the citizens of the worldly Venice have lost their way in their search for earthly gain. 'Tarry a moment there is something else,' she calls as Shylock's knife comes up to take the pound of flesh from the merchant. This line sounds like a clarion call to our materialistic culture, an eleventh hour warning that there is a whole set of values and vision of the world which we have missed. The story ends again with the uniting in composite marriages in the Elysian world of Belmont, the true unity of personality and spirit now established.

So also with that great mystery play *The Tempest*. Again the hero Ferdinand sees and loves Miranda, 'They have changed eyes.' Once the inner unity is secure the initiating priest, Prospero, separates them with apparent cruelty until after fitting trials – 'thou hast strangely stood the test' – Ferdinand is allowed to marry his higher soul of love and is shown in pageant form the great vision of the spiritual meaning of the world. The whole play is the picture of an initiation. On the magic island two more parties undergo ordeals fitting for their nature. The court party is drawn to repentance and the characters representing sensual man (Stephano and Trinculo) meet the tempter Caliban and re-experience the Fall.

An important clue in the imagery of *The Tempest* is that all characters are shown as moving up and down through the symbolical elements from the mists of confusion into clear air, from air up to celestial light or down into the literal mires and bogs of sensuality.

So we can tackle play after play and they will break down into allegory. The strangest and most improbable situations, such as no modern dramatist would dare to present, take their place with an inevitable rightness when looked at in this way. For instance, the almost absurd 'happy ending' in *The Merchant of Venice*, when Portia gives back his lost ships to Antonio, is seen as the only possible finish for the picture of the integrated soul. 'That which thy child's mistake fancied as lost I have kept for thee in Heaven. Rise, take my hand and come.' (*Hound of Heaven*).

It seems that Shakespeare uses the Comedies to present his picture of the transmutation of the soul by lifting it to other levels of consciousness. All these plays have profound cosmic meaning, but this never intrudes itself. There is no constraint or obligation to bother about it, and never is there a sense that Shakespeare is imposing teaching upon us. This is understandable in that in his age the esoteric knowledge could not be outwardly spoken. To write mystery or morality plays was unacceptable to reformation thought. The inner significance of the plays is in line with the stream of hidden wisdom which has been passed down from the mystery temples of the ancients. 'Shakespeare', whoever he was, is certainly an example of cosmic consciousness. To quote from Arnold's sonnet:

> Others abide our question. Thou art free.
> We ask and ask: Thou smilest and art still
> Out-topping knowledge ...

The wholeness of life, the interpenetration of matter and spirit, was all included in his tremendous vision and if we could know the whole cycle of plays we should have revealed to us the whole mystery of life.

Each generation is called upon to re-interpret Shakespeare in its own way. Perhaps the allegorical and imaginative interpretation is fitting for our times. Those who are not drawn to the world-view of spiritual wholeness will assuredly challenge this as a forcing of the plays into a pattern which suits the interpreter. Be this as it may. It will seem so if the basic view is not held. But there are many in our time for whom the 'vision of wholeness' throws a new flood of light on the whole meaning of life, restoring lost values and giving to man a new significance.

12

MUSIC AS A COSMIC
AND SPIRITUAL POWER

THE MATERIAL WORLD is essentially a picture of the formative realm of Spirit. 'Alles vergangliches ist nur ein Gleichniss,' wrote Goethe. Our earth plane is but the lowest, slowest and densest frequency and is interpenetrated by planes of higher frequency up to the spheres of spiritual light. Music in its archetypal form is part of the workings of the Logos, the creative Divine Imagining. Every thing on our earth plane is formed out of spirit. First it existed in Divine Idea; then in celestial rhythm, colour and sound until, passing down through the ethers, it can be materialised on the earth plane. In this sense everything is music. The human organism itself is made up of musical relationship and harmonies, as was well known by Renaissance architects. Music is the soul-stuff of the Universe and on higher planes is inseparable from colour.

The great composers are to be seen as channels for this free formative music to enter the earth plane. They did not so much invent their symphonies as record them. They 'found out beautiful tunes'. Here I quote Ernest Newman on the 'Eroica' from *The Unconscious Beethoven*:

> Here, more than anywhere else, do we get that curious feeling that in his greatest works Beethoven was 'possessed' – the mere human instrument through which a vast musical design realized itself in all its marvellous logic ... We have the conviction that his mind did not proceed from the particular to the whole, but began, in some curious way, with the whole and then worked back to the

particular ... The long and painful search for the themes was simply an effort, not to find workable atoms out of which he could construct a musical edifice according to the conventions of symphonic form, but to reduce an already existing nebula, in which that edifice was implicit, to the atom, and then, by the orderly arrangement of these atoms, to make the implicit explicit.

Mozart records that he would hear a whole symphony as a single form in an instant of time. Cyril Scott, in his little book *Music, Its Secret Influence Through The Ages*, contends that the composers are to be seen as channels for soul-formative power. They all seem to appear two generations before the corresponding psychological developments in society. They are not so much reflectors of society as inaugurators of new soul quality. They actually make the psychology of the coming age. They are handling the soul stuff of the world. Steiner as mystic describes the plane of the archetypes. It is a realm of creative being, where beings of sound and colour and light are perpetually weaving and forming and experimenting in new patterns, any of which can be selected to be materialised into the forms in the material plane. Thus behind every form of plant, animal or crystal we can see the weaving forces of creative spirit and, conversely, realise that a sphere of Divine Music interpenetrates the cosmos on an exalted frequency. Music pre-exists, and the composer is one so constituted in his earth incarnation that he can reflect it and shape it creatively. We know well that music and architecture are closely linked. On the heavenly plane souls released from bodily limitations find themselves in temple structures of light which are also formed out of living music. It is these which are apprehended and in some sense experienced by our architects and reflected in shadow form into man's earthly temples. We are in these realms in meditation and in sleep and they will therefore colour our creation on this plane.

Here I wish to speak about the phenomenon of Sir Donald Tovey. It was said truthfully when he left Oxford after reading Classics that he could write down from memory every note that Bach and Beethoven had ever written. In later life he seemed to have read all Western music from the earliest plainsong to the music of his own life time, and once read it was remembered. His pupils could never find a work he did not know, and in such detail that he could tell them they should have A sharp in bar 172. If you told him you knew a work, his answer was 'Can you write it down?' He could. Here we are simply up against a phenomenon. It is easy to say Tovey had a photographic brain. This materialistic explanation is not good enough. He had not time in his life to turn the pages of every work of music written since 1300, let alone study them. Surely we must feel that in him is a faculty which supervenes our normal powers of study. He could somehow apprehend all music direct. Somehow, as a Being, he was all music.

I suggest that Donald Tovey stands before us as a phenomenon inexplicable in any normal mechanistic way. In some way beyond our comprehension he is the incarnation of an exalted being who is one with the whole sphere of music. He is the music. Imagine an archangelical being, close to the Logos, identified with the sources of music, who chooses to enter an earth body. He would never have to learn a work. He would simply direct his attention to that part of his own great being and consciousness which was the symphony and it would pour through him afresh in conscious knowledge. Every time he would tap the symphony afresh at its source, not digging it up out of his memory.

Tovey must be such a being. Many of the wonderful stories about him suggest how ill adjusted he was to ordinary life. It is as if he hardly belonged to our sphere.

We know that every human thought, feeling or will impulse is impressed indelibly on the akashic record, that celestial 'tape recorder' of spiritual substance surrounding the earth plane. Thus each symphony once realised and recorded is available for re-experience by every one who knows how to tune in to it. The great composers are the channels for recording eternal musical form in the earth vibration. Tovey may be an example of the yet more exalted being who is the total sphere of music. His incarnation at the turn of the century is significant.

Steiner came then to show a new way of lifting human thinking into the wholeness of knowledge. Thinking is also inexplicable on a mechanistic level. He showed in his series of lectures on so many different subjects, that the human faculties of clear thinking, lifted beyond the limitation of the senses, could become so one with the Thought Processes of the World that there were no limits to knowledge. In like manner Tovey showed that the framework of music could be available to pour afresh through one human consciousness.

Now consider the significance of all this for the New Age which is breaking upon us. The urgent need is that man should awaken to the fact that matter is interpenetrated by Spirit, that the higher worlds exist. Man in the 19th and 20th centuries has gone through the stage of being so closely identified with the material world and the five senses that he loses all knowledge of higher worlds and even denies the existence of the Divine. This is of course a critical stage in the evolution of consciousness since, through this separation from his Divine source, he attains freedom. Then in full consciousness he may now 'return to this Father'.

Here the concept of Teilhard de Chardin is magnificent. The 'noosphere', having enveloped the earth and discovered its unity, now, particle by particle, soul by soul, begins the triumphant surge towards unity with the Divine source, 'homing' at last on the Omega point, which is, of course, the Christ Being. It is in precisely these years that this process is being consummated. A great acceleration is taking place. Consciousness is being raised. A realm of higher frequency is impinging upon our human awareness. The spiritual world is 'raising the pressure', turning on the heat. Evidence pours in from all parts of the world and from all religions suggesting that some sort of advent is imminent. Many believe that a heightening of consciousness is likely to manifest in the near future. Such an event would be immensely disturbing and disruptive

Those who have no recognition of spiritual reality would feel they were going mad and be bewildered. Those who knew could recognise in it the coming of the Christ. The world situation is so critical and man has, through his ignorance, brought the planet so near to disaster, that the realms of spirit are watching and preparing to intervene, in ways which, however, will not interfere with freedom. Great soul-changes may be expected. In the plane beyond bodily limitation, beyond so called 'death', is truly a society, a civilization, a culture based on creativity, love and affinity, not on acquisitiveness. Communications show that groups of soul-entities are striving to work with and through man. We know, for example, of the so called 'Myers Group', scientists who are working for a break-through so that their higher knowledge may be received into the thinking of scientists on our plane.

Once this was achieved the importance for the salvation of man would be enormous. Doctors who have passed over are also grouping to help in healing. So also with music. There must be groups on the higher plane working to release the formative power of music into our consciousness. As the soul-stuff of the Universe, a flood of music rightly used would break up and disperse false thought-forms and lift the spirit of man. In the New Age and in the apocalyptic changes which are upon us the power of music is absolutely primary. It will be a creative bridge towards understanding of spiritual reality and of lifting human consciousness. Thus we must expect that the great souls who were the composers would be working together as another of these soul-groups, seeking to make their break-through as part of cosmic plan for the redemption of mankind.

13

THE SEEING EYE
IN ARCHITECTURE

NOW WE ARE to look at Architecture. To look at architecture and think what it is really about. Alas many of us have got on to the wrong line. We believe that when we have dated a building and named the architect we are free to stop there, particularly if we have 'got a picture'. The obvious truth is that we have not yet begun. Art History is of enormous importance and huge strides have been taken in it since the war. It is essential that we learn all we can about the facts and periods. But let us be clear that this intellectual approach is not the architectural experience. In our intellectual age it is possible that too much admiration of art history is bedevilling our real looking and a balance needs to be restored. Doubtless in Renaissance days the whole city was moved by architecture. We have descriptions of throngs turning out to see the unveiling of a statue or admire a new facade. Theirs was a society in which everything was geared to creativity. Every boy learned several crafts from an early age. In succeeding centuries the intellect became highly developed, but at the price perhaps of loss of the faculty of vital looking.

> For this, for everything we are out of tune
> It moves us not.

So wrote Wordsworth about Nature. Despite the amount of art we can now see, through travel and reproduction, we have mostly lost the power of being deeply moved. If this were not so, some people on their swift holidays would be overwhelmed. In the various arts we need consciously to discover and recover the art of looking. In this essay let us try to see what we need to do in order to release the magic from a building. What I wish to say can be easily demonstrated to a group. It will be more difficult for the reader to make the effort of imagination in reading a few pages, but the approach is important and it is worth the attempt.

The approach first came to me as something of a discovery in Venice. We were drinking coffee on the Piazza of St. Mark. My eye was idly running up and down the huge Campanile. To ordinary looking the two slightly tapering sides of this noble tower are quite straight. Suddenly I found that, if I ran my eye down with strength and determination at a certain speed, I discovered a bulge. It was there and then gone again, about 'chest level' and quite invisible if one did not look in active movement. Perhaps it was no more than an inch in the whole 250ft. but it was enough and the eye could detect it. I found my companions could also get the experience, so we began to explore. The bulge was only there and alive during the split second of active eye-movement.

This revealed the important truth – *seeing is an active deed* and not merely a passive reception of images. Recognise that you can put out an eyebeam and touch a pillar. The fingers of your looking can delicately stroke down the grooving of a column. Some day scientists will doubtless explain how this is so, and what radiation of light emanates from the eye. For the time being all that matters to us is the conscious experience of using the eyebeam to explore a form, recognising that the tip of the eye-beam is sensitive. Our consciousness is at the point where our two eye-beams cross and this touching of a form is, I repeat, to be seen as an active deed.

In this manner let us take that basic architectural form – a Doric column. We all know about *entasis*, that subtle curving which makes a Greek column so vibrantly alive. The mind recognises it easily enough. But do more. Stroke that column strongly up and down with your eye. Soon you will feel the bulge

110

as an actual movement. Next you will begin to feel the strength of the column in your own body, the entasis reflecting the bulging of muscle. The whole dynamic of the pillar will be revealed to you as a sensation within your own body structure and you can experience how, in steady silence, it holds the weight of lintel and entablature.

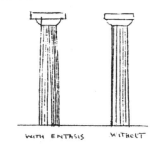

WITH ENTASIS   WITHOUT

A new meaning is now given to the Caryatids on the Acropolis. Truly a pillar in a certain sense represents the Divine structure of the human body and the goddess figures can rightly take their stand in that portico.

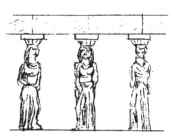

Do we begin to get a clue as to what the use of pillars is really about? Why the three orders, Doric, Ionic and Corinthian, used one about the other on a classical or Renaissance facade? To discover the answer we must consciously indulge in a kind of looking which is obvious when pointed out but seems to be practised by few. Allow your eye to rest on the building. Watch what it wants to do and which way it wants to go. Unless you actively inhibit its movement your eye will begin to flow along continuous lines, vertical or horizontal, and to leap from one image to another of kindred character. Allow it to do so. Take the obvious detail, say a column. In every building the process is quite unique. You should approach the building with no pre-conceptions. You need absolutely no knowledge of art history.

You merely need the readiness to *stand behind your eye and what it does*. I stress again that your interest is not so much in the building as in watching what your eye does when it impinges upon that building. This is a totally different thing. Perhaps it explains what Blake meant in saying 'I look not with my eye but through it'.

The trick is first of all to take kindred forms. Take that Doric pillar at the bottom, stroke the eye up and down it until the

entasis moves and you feel its dynamism. Then jump your eye up to the ionic column or the next storey. Do this two or three times back and forth. The upper column being lighter, you will discover that one image 'clicks' into the other, registering an apparent movement, as if the thicker column became suddenly more delicate. The differences between the two images is discovered by this apparent movement. We are doing a very simple thing. We are taking the after-image of the first column and placing it over the second.

As the after-image merges into the new image, the differences register as movement. We are concerned with what is really a quite scientific observation of a phenomenon rarely considered. We are observing not the building but our own eye beam with its leap from one image into the next.

Now move up to the second floor with its Corinthian column. This is revealed as being still more delicate and by moving now through the series of three images we clearly experience this lightening. We recognise that a metamorphosis of form is going on which will include all subordinate features in the design. Be it stressed again at this point that this process has a naivety at which the intellect may scoff. Of course we all know that the orders reduce in scale. Anyone can see that. We are concerned not with this intellectual fact, but the dynamic experience of forms changing. The great string courses and architraves dividing the building seem to say to us that the image stops here and starts again above in its metamorphosed form. You might almost say it re-incarnates. Now bravely go over the whole thing from the bottom 1, 2, 3 and 4. We suddenly see that the statue against the sky is indeed another metamorphosis. Man, the measure of all things, is released from the imprisonment in the column into a new freedom. Like Michelangelo's slaves, he is struggling to free himself from the rock. Suddenly the very orders themselves begin to speak. The united human organism is threefold, a head system, a chest and heart system, a metabolic or limb system. We see that the Doric on the ground floor represents the limb system, seat of the will. Rightly it is the column of the Greek athlete. The Ionic symbolises the heart system and the Corinthian the head or thinking system. It is truly the Philosopher's column. The three make up Man and it is inevitable that they stand thus on the great facade, transformed, released and united in sculpture against the sky.

But that was a flight into imaginative interpretation. Let us keep to the active looking. Let the eye be drawn in each building to the significant units. These may be flat surfaces. Here a quite different thing happens. We fill the whole shape with what might be called the liquid of our looking. Eliot writes, 'The pool was filled with water out of sunlight'. So we can fill a surface, an alcove, a spandrel, a roundel with liquid of our looking which will spread like oil and take in quite a complex area at a glance.

Thus on a facade a kind of key pattern is discovered around the windows; when the lower key is placed upon that of the next storey one image leaps into the next and the sense of movement discovers to us the difference. The eye will come to rest in the perfection of a circle. If there should be a circular dish, here you will stop, until with an effort of will you launch out again into forms and surfaces that keep you moving and changing. So piece by piece we can 'account for' all that is happening on a facade.

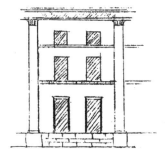

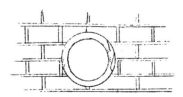

In this brief essay we can only hint at a few forms, difficult to get from reading alone and a few bad drawings. Faced with a building we find that all architectural forms can in time be coaxed to speak and reveal their secrets. The eye will be found to make very different movements. Along a colonnade of pillars it will make a series of major jumps.

Along the dentils in a cornice it will trip lightly. Along an iron railing it will rattle like a boy's stick. In interior plaster work and cornices, a thousand different eye rhythms will be discovered.

We discover that in each case we can only describe our experience in some rhythmical phrase, however simple – 'dum diddle dum diddle dum, dum, dum.' Yet this naivety begins to give us the clue that we are releasing the hidden musical relationship in the building. 'Architecture is frozen music' it has been said. In this active looking we begin to see what this means. All the parts are beginning to move in relationship to each other. Every form begins to harmonise with the rest, some more strongly pressing the subordinate features to conform.

Thus consider the so called venetian window of Palladio. Look at its pillars, relate the two outside lights to each other, experience

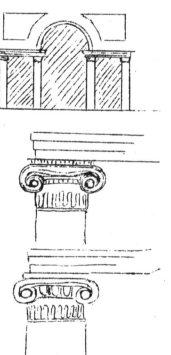

that the cornice has been broken in the middle to allow for the 'pressure' of the central light. It is a dynamic form and it has forced up the half circle and has pressed the slighter spandrels into conformity.

Or look at the Ionic capital. What does the eye do? Obviously it grasps the central bulge of the volute and runs first one way and then the other into the twisting horn-shaped extremities. It needs quite an effort of will to escape, because the swinging movement is so complete.

Compare this with the second example, looking actively from one drawing to the other. Here we feel the capital is still asleep. The greater example is breathing and is very

114

much alive. Remember also that we sensed that the ionic was related to the breathing system.

Every building will offer a completely different set of experiences to the looker. Be it stressed again that no knowledge whatever of facts and dates and names is necessary. We are discovering something quite different. We are really exploring the harmonic relationships within the structure of our own bodies. Man is the measure of all things. He is the microcosm that holds within him the macrocosm. 'Man know thyself and thou shalt know the universe.' This was carved at the gateway of the Greek mystery temples. The purpose of architecture is being discovered. It offers us a set of forms on such a scale that the eye can thereby experience movement and relationships which make conscious to it the harmonious relationships in the body. We are exploring our own life process in this strange procedure which seems to make the building alive. Be it stressed again that we start with a very definite and almost scientific observation of our own eye images and their changes, not with any personal feelings about buildings. Yet when individuals try to describe what they have discovered, they are compelled to use either musical terms or epithets such as 'thrilling', 'terrifying', 'exciting', to convey a sudden movement of light or breaking of forms into each other.

We have been discussing one way of securing a sense of movement – by placing two images upon each other and watching how one clicks into the next. This compares to the movement of images in a film achieved through a series of still screens. There is another notable form of movement. If I walk gently past a building it will appear to swing. Parts will change relationship – to my thought image it makes no difference whatsoever if I walk past a stationary object or if I stand still and it moves past me. Thus by the simplest act of imagination I can get the building on the move. I can swing St Paul's, a trinket on my wrist, and literally, as far as my image is concerned, it is on the move. All that is necessary is to be prepared to play with the imagination and not be discouraged by the rational and, debunking intellect. 'Except ye become as little children ...'

Combining these two kinds of movement the entire structure comes alive and into relation with you. Indeed it may be declared that *'Architecture' does not begin until we have released the forms by active looking*. Everything is previously bewitched into a set of stone forms. Then suddenly by your deed of dynamic looking and your own initiative you bring it alive. It begins to move and to sound and sing in your limbs and heart and thinking. The pillars stand like great dignified Beings, archangel sentinels gazing across at each other. You discover the points where pressure of space is bursting out into shape and remoulding other forms. For a few seconds perhaps the whole is ARCHITECTURE and you are part of it. Then you lose it and it falls back into its bewitched state and is no more than so many stone pillars and windows designed by so and so, at such and such a date. If, however, you can discover how to release the hidden music and animate the forms, you will never be the same again. You have been one with the building and thereby have experienced its power within your own organism. It may be that we are touching a great mystery and that the building itself will never be quite the same again. Perhaps there is some great Being held into matter by the skill of a Michelangelo or Palladio or Scamozzi, and our looking has done something to release it. In his living looking at nature or at art, man possibly has a great task in redeeming the spirit which has been bewitched and frozen into material forms. Be that as it may, the experience of an hour spent in active looking at a building is not describable in words. A flowing change has taken place in our whole living organism and the sense of 'in-touch-ness' has a redemptive quality.

We soon discover that enclosed space can be made dynamic. It has power and is thrusting to escape. You come to feel the whole enclosed space, for the active eye can of course look through a wall or through a column. It does not need to stop at the surface. Thus consider the obsession of the great Renaissance architects with the centralised church as the noblest expressions of worship. Look at the plan first and see how from the central circle imprisoned in a square, the energy of space bursts out into the four apses.

Now see the elevation, and feel the apses blown out and then see that dynamic space has thrust an upward form out of the cube. First came the drum and then the dome. You can imagine the whole deflating again and reverting to the cube as the basic sleeping form.

A dome is a great experience. Take St Paul's, in reality or photograph. Let your looking touch the top of the dome and, then spread and stroke it down. Do this several times until you can, so to speak, stretch your act of looking in all directions at the same time. Where and how do you experience this? Is

it not in a sense of tension in the dome of the head? Suddenly we are given the understanding as to what these centralised temples represent. They are the human archetype. The dome is the head, the great drum with its pillars is symbolic of the chest system and the centralised alter is the heart. The lantern above is like a fontanelle, open in the child and symbolic of the 'chakra' or spiritual centre through which the cosmic light can pour into human understanding. Wren's dome on St Paul's is then seen as the symbolic Temple of the Ancients, standing on its platform of the conventional Christian church. As a great Renaissance figure he needed to express the same oceanic transcendental experience of Christ Pantocrator, the risen Cosmic Christ.

Experiment with the columns of St Paul's drum. On the storey above they collect themselves into greatly reduced pilasters and then are metamorphosed into the ribs of the dome. You might say that the dome is made of transformed columns all bent in together until they meet in the centre and their capitals transmute into lantern and golden cross. This concept creates an experience of terrific power in that dome. In St Paul's, of course, the centralised altar is on the ethereal plane, invisible in the space inside the Whispering Gallery. Only the eye of imagination knows it is there.

117

Once we have tuned-in into a building, we can move gently through its rooms and experience the changing of space as if one room-form metamorphoses into the next. Every detail, every pilaster, every design in ceiling plasterwork helps to heighten the experience of organic life and movement. It is interesting that this form of 'active looking' can far best be done with Renaissance buildings, and Palladio's buildings most of all. Perhaps this is why his work so fascinated English travellers. In the Renaissance, Man was still known to be the measure of all things. The Golden Section was seen as fundamental to the structure of the living body. Now we have abandoned this concept. Modern architectural form is not related in this way to man and for this reason it is rare that we can get this experience of movement in a contemporary building.

A profound experience can be had in a Palladian church. Five of us spent the morning in the Redentore in Venice the day after we had discovered this way of looking. We got the church swinging and as we moved through the interior towards the crossing, we found how the curves of the great dome broke into each other, in swinging parabolas, all drawing towards the moment when they would transmute into a series of concentric circles as we came dead centre under the lantern. Then Perfection would be achieved. On the floor, inlay gave guide lines for our steps, leading to a central circle. As we reached it we were filled with a holy awe. Were we worthy to step into the magic circle? It seemed to be a radiation point of power, and only with a prayer dared we step over into its ultimate confines. Then the spell broke, the living watching Beings reverted to pilasters, the magic went and tourists walked unthinking over the holy central point. But we had experienced the real truth that Palladio was offering. After one and a half hours we stopped for coffee, not because we were suffering from 'tourist's feet', but because so much life had flowed through our looking into our limbs, that we were compelled to pause to quieten our excitement and enhanced vitality. It should be said that four out of the five of us were almost completely innocent of architectural knowledge.

I submit this as an approach which can vitalise architecture for anyone. Then the study of art history can profitably follow. The buildings begin to speak and the forms begin to tell their meaning. Note that the initial method of approach is in no way sentimental or imaginative. It is a perfectly factual and 'scientific' observation not of the building but of the way your own eye wants to register changes of form on that building. In this way you can account for everything that happens on a façade, and since the movement is experienced with the whole sense organism and not just the mind, you do not forget it. Next day the image of movement can be recalled and it will have grown in strength. Thus a new style of drawing buildings will result. You can endeavour to put down on paper not the forms of the building, but the movement of images which you experienced. If you keep honestly to this and recall the linked series of experiences, you will find you have memorised an entire building in a way impossible for the static observation by intellect alone. The claim for this method of looking must be kept in proportion since many architects and great architectural historians doubtless look in this way. The approach is offered rather as a teaching technique to enable the layman to explore architecture. I believe that this method is fitting for our time. Almost everyone to whom I have spoken has responded with enthusiasm, as if it makes conscious something within themselves for which they were already asking, and which they are now ripe to receive. We are at a turning point in man's development. It seems as if he is passing beyond the age of highly developed intellect, into understanding of the great oneness of life. Intellect separates and analyses. Imagination apprehends the living whole. Teilhard de Chardin and many other seers urge us to grasp the unity of all life. Active looking at architecture gives us the experience of our own organism as part of a far greater structure. This approach may therefore be ripe and fitting as we pass into the Aquarian age, the age when all forms flow into the great unity. The purpose of architecture is perhaps to teach the whole of man what he is in relation to the cosmos. Architecture does not begin until our looking becomes active. The architectural experience is a flow between the looker and the forms and when the dynamic looking stops the 'living' building reverts to mere stone or brick or plaster. While within the architectural experience we are for a few seconds in a magical world, which cannot be entered or held without our own initiative in the deed of active looking.

A second essay is needed concerning Gothic architecture in which the mysteries of movement are subtly different.

This may be enough to start some people in looking in this dynamic way and discovering that the architect, whether consciously or unconsciously, is really externalising the mysteries and harmonies of the Divine pattern of his own organism into the temples that he builds.

14

THE DEEPER SYMBOLISM
IN HERALDRY

IN SOME now forgotten book I remember reading a sentence
to the effect that a heraldic coat of arms gives a precise
picture of the man who bears them. The remark seems
outwardly absurd. In what possible sense could arms awarded to
a crusader in 1200 picture the descendant working in the Stock
Exchange in 1970? Yet the thought went on irritating me. There
must be some key to this. I even committed myself to lecture to
the Birmingham Society of Genealogy and Heraldry on the
theme of 'Symbolism in Heraldry' while still having no notion of
what the lecture had to say. Fortunately light came a few days
before the date! I discussed it with the College of Arms who gave
the official view that Heraldry was not essentially a symbolic art
but that its purpose was practical and utilitarian. With all its
colour and splendour, its primary purpose was to distinguish
knights in tourney and battle when their faces were covered by a
visor. There was obviously symbolism in certain charges and
Guillam in the first half of the 17th Century had tried to develop
it, but for the medieval College of Heralds, the object was
essentially practical. Such seemed to be the official view.

Yet does it ring wholly true? Picture the young aspirant for
knighthood in vigil all night before the altar, his sword and
armour, his helm and shield set before him, in prayer to Christ
the King in preparation for the day when his earthly king should,
in the accolade, touch him on the shoulder with the Sword of
Michael and say, 'Rise, Sir Roger'. Then he is to go forth into the

world to carry light and justice into the confusion and cruelty of daily life. There he is to do doughty deeds and rescue fair ladies from the clutches of dragons or wicked men.

It becomes clear that there must be a double aspect of heraldry – the outward practical side of it will hide an inner meaning for those who can find it. Here is a wonderful and colourful art which gave the opportunity for the courts of Chivalry to splash the jousting ring with gorgeous effects of gold and red and blue. The very names 'Chivalry' and 'Heraldry' ring with the joy of idealism and aspiration.

How closely allied it seems to be with the medieval vision of the Arthurian legends. Indeed we must recognise that all legends, all mythology, even all fairy stories, have behind their outward tales, an 'esoteric' or hidden meaning. They tell, in allegory, truths about the human soul and its passage through the darkness of life on the earth plane. The basic picture is always the same though couched in a thousand different forms. The symbols tell that the core of man's spirit belongs to an eternal realm of Light outside time. It descends into the earth plane, taking to itself a body. There it goes on an allegorical journey through dark forest or stormy ocean, undergoing soul trials and ordeals until it can find the princess with her golden locks, bewitched and waiting for her rescuer.

Then is consummated the mystical marriage and the return to the realms of light is achieved. The princess represents the higher spiritual self which we must find and awaken in ourselves. This is the integration of the personality. In our age, when so many assume that matter is the only reality, it is vitally important to give assurance to the questing mind that the eternal realms do exist, that the higher self IS a reality, that the soul trials we all undergo have got meaningful significance and that the soul released at last from its worn out sheath, does in fact return in heightened awareness to the planes of light.

All allegorical art and poetry in every age and time enshrines such symbology, and we are now called on to interpret and lift it from the outer casing which always covers it. Symbols are manifold. They can mean several things and on each level can express truth. The work-a-day story can be taken at its face value or it can be analysed psychologically or spiritually. You take your choice. There is never any constraint to believe, but if a symbol holds life-enhancing significance for you, who dare tell you it is not true simply because to him it means something else. If the great body of mythology and much art and poetry has its esoteric symbolism, how can we exclude an art so brilliant and colourful as heraldry, born in an age which had the idealism to mount the Crusades and build the great Gothic cathedrals? All art is in a deep sense One, as all life is one, and heraldry MUST be included in the general pattern.

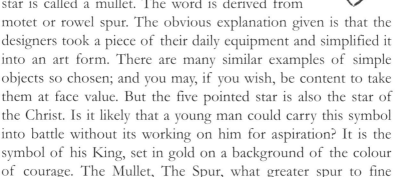

So to return to our young knight in vigil before the altar. Let us suggest his shield bears three golden stars on a red field – in the language of blazon: 'Gules three mullets or'. The five pointed star is called a mullet. The word is derived from motet or rowel spur. The obvious explanation given is that the designers took a piece of their daily equipment and simplified it into an art form. There are many similar examples of simple objects so chosen; and you may, if you wish, be content to take them at face value. But the five pointed star is also the star of the Christ. Is it likely that a young man could carry this symbol into battle without its working on him for aspiration? It is the symbol of his King, set in gold on a background of the colour of courage. The Mullet, The Spur, what greater spur to fine action could a young knight bear?

Let us now use our imagination on the assumption that deep esoteric meaning has flowed into this strange, powerful art and that it stands as an inspiration to the knightly ardour that is in every young soul of whatever age or speech.

THE ACHIEVEMENT

The full coat of arms is called THE ACHIEVEMENT. It pictures that which the soul is called on to 'achieve' during its journey through the dark forest of life. The factors in the full achievement are Shield, Helm, Mantling, Crest, Supporters and Motto.

THE ACHIEVEMENT

In a short space I must be very dogmatic in stating what these forms mean to me. Others can develop further meanings and this approach offers the opportunity for endless exploration of symbols.

The shield represents the body or personality with which we live out our lives. The HELM is the potentiality of higher thinking; the MANTLING, weaving all around in colour, is the symbol for the aura from which the trends of the soul can be read, the CREST is a symbol for the quintessence of the higher self, the SUPPORTERS are guides or guardians from the supersensible spiritual realms, and the motto in a few concentrated words gives a mantram for aspiration.

THE SHIELD

To return first to the SHIELD. It is normally made up of three factors, the FIELD of a certain colour, on which is set the 'ORDINARY' which is a simple geometrical form, and thirdly the CHARGE which can represent almost anything. The threefold quality of the design of the shield is itself significant since the trinity symbol works into all life.

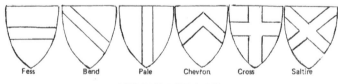

Fess   Bend   Pale   Chevron   Cross   Saltire

SOME OF THE ORDINARIES

The 'ORDINARY' can be prosaically explained as the structure at the back of the shield brought forward to the front as an art form. But the curious name 'ORDINARY' gives another clue. We have suggested that the shield represents the body and personality, but not merely the ordinary self. Heraldry images the potentiality of the higher self. Does the word not suggest the

'ORDINAND', the one who is to be ordained? The right to bear arms was originally granted to those qualified by descent from aristocracy or possession of land. The inner spiritual qualification may be that a man has set his foot on the way of initiation and higher knowledge. As such he is called to inner 'ORDINATION'. The new aristocracy can come from all classes. We shall find that the symbology of heraldry carries through into the future for all who aspire to this inner knighthood. Now consider COLOUR. Outwardly the object was simply to make a splendid show in the lists so that knights could be easily identified. Thus primary colours are set against gold and silver. The 'metals' shine, the 'tinctures' are matt, and in good heraldry are perfectly balanced. Metal is never shown on metal since this would dazzle (the great exception is the cross of Jerusalem, gold on silver). The result is that however brilliant the sun, you can always 'read' the shield instantly. Indeed the stronger the light the better does it tell (another deep symbol). Looking deeper, however, we must recognise the significance of colour as a soul-formative power. Every colour represents soul quality. There will be variations in interpretation, but what matters is to establish the importance of colour on the inner planes. Thus red may imply courage, blue peace of mind, gold is love, silver has divine purity, green is the colour of life working into matter, while purple, more rarely used in heraldry, is the colour of highest religious initiation and development. In astrological knowledge the colours represent the planetary forces. Thus Gold is the colour of the Sun, Silver of the Moon, Red of Mars. The heraldic colours will represent the main planetary influences. Remember always that the symbols in the Heraldic Achievement are indications of the potentiality of the higher self, and are a standing injunction to the personality to lift itself towards higher planes of consciousness and qualities of character. This even links Heraldry with the secret aim of medieval alchemy which was the metamorphosis of the soul. The true alchemists were only outwardly concerned with transmuting base metal into gold. Their experiments were a cover for the inner soul transmutation into the real gold of the spirit. The medieval artists paint the sky gold to represent the living world of spirit. The great feature of the art of heraldry is the harmonious balancing of colour and metal. Often forms are 'countercharged' so that tincture and metal interpenetrate. Can this be seen as an image of the interpenetration of spirit and matter? When argent and sable are in balance, it suggests that mysterious polarity of carbon and diamond, which are chemically identical. Colour is indeed a great mystery.

Then the CHARGES. These can be infinitely varied, but the main examples in medieval heraldry are aspirational in character, as the crescent for the crusader, the escallop for the pilgrim, the fleur de lys, the cross in its many forms. Many are simply puns on names and therefore appear most mundane. Thus Bouchier carries water 'budgets', the leather container on a yoke. Yet could this not also represent the 'water carrier', herald of the Aquarian Age?

Look into any book on heraldry and allow the imagination to play on the Charges, Crests and Mottoes. Some are  of course prosaic, but a current of aspiration and idealism obviously plays through the whole boast of heraldry.

The shield, as we have said, represents the higher aspects of the personality in its earthly life. The CREST, however, represents the quintessence of the higher self which is to be awakened and realised. Often the crests are symbols of great depth and beauty. They are constantly related to the MOTTO which, in three or four concentrated words, expresses the task which the soul has undertaken in descending from the greater life to life on earth.

'Descending into life' – here is the clue. All allegory in myth or fairy tale implies *pre-existence*. The soul was there before it descended and chose to come down into a body. This point is of immeasurable importance, particularly to our thinking today. The descending soul, in need for its further development, recognises that it must go through certain trials and ordeals in the isolation and loneliness of the earth plane. A corollary follows from this, for those who wish to take it, that the 'knight' may several times descend into this dark forest and leave the realm of light, either to compensate for past deeds ill done or in service of his fellow men in a sacrificial and redemptive mission. Thus we find that the idea of plurality of lives or reincarnation is helpful in understanding this mysterious art of heraldry. We must recognise that it deals with evolution of a soul *and of a soul stream.*

THE ANCESTRAL STREAM

When the soul descends it takes to itself a body, that sheath which makes it possible for it to live in this slow earth vibration. But it also must take on an *ancestral stream,* that which has developed in the bodies and souls of its forebears. It is said that before its descent from the Elysian Fields the descending ego is shown its task and urged to 'remember'. It is given a picture of the Achievement, the knightly duty it has undertaken and the soul-setting in which it must work. It has the task of transmuting certain baser qualities of personality and lifting them towards the light. Imagine then, the angel guides, the guardians or *supporters,* showing us the pattern of our lives. They will accompany us through life. They are always there standing invisibly behind us, prompting our efforts and aspirations. The guardian angel is an entity who has taken on the task of helping a soul through life and the sad thing in our materialistic age is that we so rarely recognise this ever present help or give any thanks for it. Does this not give more meaning to the majestic image of two supporters holding up the shield? Look again and see how often they are of spiritual or symbolic significance – a Pegasus, an Angel, a lion rampant, a strong man, a mermaid. Naturally the cynic can always quote very earthly examples in an attempt to debunk such interpretation. The logical intellect can debunk anything and in the struggle towards higher knowledge no one is ever constrained into belief. But if the symbol appeals to you, live with it as a thought. Let it colour your everyday life.

Imagine that the descending soul is shown the ancestral stream he is about to enter, portrayed in the full family achievement. He may perhaps have a special task in relation to his forebears. All carry the same charges and motto. One may after many

127

generations be able to complete and fulfil the common task. Many members of the family may fall short and fail. Through struggle, generation after generation, a transmutation of personality may be brought about. The 'achievement' is then complete and a more advanced soul quality of love or courage given to the world.

Let us here consider the HERALDIC BEASTS. The human soul can be seen as a kind of symphony of all the soul qualities which are spread out in the kingdom of the animals. We can all have in us the quality of jackal or fox, of lion or eagle, of Pegasus or dolphin. The rich world of the heraldic zoo covers soul quality both in this world and the higher realms. The Lion is of course the archetypal heraldic beast Rampant, he represents knightly courage. Passant-guardant he represents alert attention and preparedness. These surely give us the two basic qualities for the fighter. The quality in the 'lion passant guardant' is pre-eminently as that shown in the leopard. Thus the lion of England is called a 'leopard'. He is a 'leoparded lion' – lion leopardi – because the symbol is showing us a soul quality. This essay is no more than an indication of lines for exploration. The world of heraldic beasts begins to speak to us in a new way.

GROUP ENTITIES

Now we must grasp an essential point. *Every human group, spiritually, has an entity.* We must grasp that there is a spiritual being, a group soul, overlighting each group of people. Every family will have a group soul, every nation, every city. Our minds must grasp the vision of a hierachy of beings. The lives of these beings may be long or short. They may be exalted like an archangel, the Spirit of an Age, the Spirit of a country, or, much humbler in scale. They may bring a human group together through inspiration or may be brought to birth by that group. It is essential to grasp the general concept of the entity which overlights each group. The heraldic achievement of a family must therefore be seen as the image of the group soul of that family stream. You are shown this before undertaking the adventure of birth.

You are given the choice and warned of the soul qualities, advantages and limitations which you take on when you enter that blood stream. You recognise what baser inherited qualities you will have to transmute. You see that in some sense you will have to lift out of and beyond that blood stream, but that, to work for the light in the darkness of earth, you need not only the instrument of a body, but an ancestral stream. Now we come to a point of tremendous significance. Heraldry is not ancestor worship. Our present view lifts it forward from interest in the past into the achievement for the future. Man has inevitably had to work in the setting of the bloodstream. He has been born into clan or tribe or family group. In earlier days love or hate were inherent in the blood. The hackles of a Macdonald rose when a Campbell entered the room, because the very vibrations of the blood carried the bond of love or hate. Much more so in Biblical days, when tribal memory, carried in the bloodstream, even extended over several generations.

The essence of the coming of the Christ Impulse into our lives is that love is lifted beyond the blood bond. The individual ego, filled with the Great I AM, the Light of the Christos, is capable of loving other egos, without regard to blood, nation, colour or politics.

Truly we are entering a New Age when the reality of the unity of the human race is being recognised, despite outward conflicts. It is called the Aquarian Age, the age when men may flow together in a new bond of love. This will be characterised by the forming of new groups throughout our society, bound in love to a common vision. There will be no loss of individuality, but rather a lifting of individuality in dedication of free will to group endeavour. Here the new spiritual family will develop, bound by the affinities of selfless and unpossessive love, a polar opposite to the possessive love implied by the old blood bond.

In the old days the retainers and soldiers of a lord could bear his device and share his quarrels as in the rivalry of Montagues and Capulets. In the New Age, with the new law of individuality, heraldry will be lifted forward into a new meaning and significance. All who in the new groupings rally around a leader in dedicated and spiritual activity, will indeed be entitled to carry his arms. His symbol and charge, his crest and motto, will become an inspiration and token to guide and bind his companions in the freedom of dedicated purpose. Thus the tie of blood in the ancestral stream is transmuted into the spiritual brotherhood of the New Age and heraldry becomes not merely a backward looking interest in genealogy and medieval art, but a powerful and living symbol of aspiration in the coming time.

THE FOLK-SOUL

What then of the Folk-Soul of the Nation? Will this not be portrayed in the heraldic achievement? Is the New Britain revealed in her ancient arms? That which makes us Britons is indeed that we are all overlighted by a great being typified in allegory as St George. The supporters of our shield are the English Lion and the Scottish Unicorn. The lion rampant, for the courage of an Imperial race, stands on the dexter side. Dexter, the right, is the pole of action. The negative pole, as in electricity, is the receptive, sensitive opposite to the more active. This is the polarity of masculine and feminine which runs through the whole of nature and in which there must be balanced rhythmic interchange if there is to be health and harmony. For England the receptive pole, 'sinister' only in the heraldic sense, is the Unicorn whose crown has fallen around his neck. What is this wonderful symbol? The Unicorn, a white horse, representing purified intelligence, with gazelle's feet to dance lightly over the earth, has from the point of the 'third eye' on his brow a shining horn representing spiritual vision. The capture of the unicorn is, by tradition, achieved in a remarkable way.

A virgin is persuaded to sit close to the forest and the unicorn then comes and lays his head in her lap and is thus easily taken. The symbolism implies that the soul can so purify itself, cleansing every karmic 'blot on its escutcheon', that it recovers its pristine virginity. Then it will draw to itself its higher nature which can impregnate it with spiritual knowledge. Out of the 'feminine' sensitive polarity new wisdom can come. Britain, no longer an Imperial power, has yet a majestic task in bringing alive spiritual knowledge and new vision into all aspects of life and society. Here we may still lead. The courage of the rampant lion must be transmuted and balanced by the spiritual vision of the unicorn. Our task in the new achievement is to re-crown the unicorn, in the name of St George and all that he represents.

The MANTLING, it is suggested, may represent the human aura. Each of us has around him this colourful etheric structure, visible only to the clairvoyant, and revealing in very precise manner, through blending of colour and light, the soul nature of the individual. In heraldry the mantling is attached by the wreath to the helm. Of course its origin is in the linen which protected the crusader from the heat of the sun. It has been transmuted into wonderful flowing forms, often as of leaves, suggesting that it is to do with the vital forces of what is called the etheric body. Attached to the wreath on the helm, it seems to have connection with the higher thought forces. What indeed does armour represent? The Arthurian knight in his shining armour is an image of almost super-human beauty or perfection. In meditation, higher imagination and clairvoyant vision the advanced individual can be seen surrounded by a film of light This is protective, since the dark forces cannot live in the light. Thus the knightly soul is armed to transmute evil and appears with a shining surround to his head in higher thinking, a breastplate of righteousness and love to protect the heart. He bears the sword of Michael, standard bearer of the Christ, itself formed in the shape of a cross. Thus every part of the coat of arms and the knightly accoutrement takes on a deeper allegory, which is really even truer for the inner striving of the soul today than it was in the days of Chivalry. The very word 'Chivalry' suggests the task of 'gentling' the cruelty and cynicism still all too rampant in the world. The Arthurian knights can still ride forth. 'Heralds' are needed to sound forth the Coming of the King. The legend speaks of the passing of the Arthurian round table to give place to the quest for the Grail. Parsifal, the pure fool, ultimately achieves the Grail through learning to 'ask the question'. Every human soul must in time take on to himself this path to find the

Grail castle and ask the question of the higher worlds, which will give the answer that our age so gravely needs.

This essay is no more than a brief introduction to an approach. Each one can look again at the shields and crests. Let each who bears a coat of arms look and wonder what it may mean for his own task in our age. His place in his ancestral stream may carry with it the need to do some 'doughty deed'. He may find in the 'achievement' an exact image, not of what he is in his workaday personality, but of what he might become if his higher self can be awakened. Then he may lift himself in an almost redemptive act beyond his family heraldic device and allow this to re-form in new significance for the group endeavours that go to build the New Age.

This approach, lifting an ancient art into modern meaning, perhaps suggests why heraldry has such an appeal today for people from all walks of life, including the young. We know how uniforms and symbols appeal. They are necessary for football teams. They are the instrument of dictators. They can be the symbol of aspiration for the free spiritual groups. The group in  Germany who attempted Hitler's overthrow are said to have devised the transformation of the Swastika into the cross and circle, that most holy of symbols.

Our new age is one in which the reality of higher worlds of being has to be recognised. Matter is interpenetrated by spirit. Co-operation with beings on the invisible planes has to be achieved. The symbolism of the new heraldry may become important as spiritual knowledge extends. The idealism of youth will always be inspired to new Crusades and perhaps today, if rightly guided, the knightly qualities will be released to heal our darkened world. Even some of the stranger symptoms in modern youth have their significance. Much of the garb, with pointed shoes and long hair, is suggestive of the medieval squire. The 'tun riders', speeding at 100mph in the dawn hours up the M1, suggest the need for an outlet into an 'act' not unlike the charging of an armoured knight in tourney. It is even significant that now these groups tend to have heraldic beasts displayed on the back of their black and shining jackets. The active idealism of youth needs to be channelled into a new vision of knighthood.

The boast of Heraldry is twofold. The outer aspect is decorative, useful in identification in jousts and tournaments and in display of ancestors on tombs or in stained glass. The inner aspect is wholly ideal and aspirational and enshrines hidden or 'esoteric' secrets. The two are entirely compatible. The hidden stream of knowledge runs all through our art, thought and religion. There is an esoteric stream of Christianity behind the outer rituals and forms of Church worship. It was carried forward in the secret organisations such as Freemasonry, the Knights Templars and the Rosicrucian Orders. The Middle Ages were of course highly religious and the whole symbolism of Gothic architecture reflects the striving to lift beyond the mud and blood, famine and pestilence of life at that period, into sustained contact with higher worlds. Knighthood and Chivalry are woven right through the fabric of the life which produced the great cathedrals. It is certain therefore that the great spiritual symbolism must have entered heraldry.

There is never, be it repeated, any constraint to believe. The art is valid even if the approach attempted here is wholly rejected. This is why every spiritual symbol *must* have its double meaning. If it did not, then it would enforce belief and so violate the Divine gift of free will. Even Shakespeare's comedies are seen as great allegories. *As You Like It* is a morality play down to the smallest action and in every name of every character. But you have no need to accept this. You take the play 'as you like it'.

Thus it does not even follow that the original College of Heralds had any notion of what they were doing. They may have thought they were merely selecting convenient symbols to distinguish one family from another. If, however, we recognise the reality of spiritual worlds and the fact that spiritual beings can, without interfering with our freedom, *suggest* things to us within our own thinking, then the inspiration for the selection of devices and forms may well have come from higher sources. To put this more psychologically – we recognise that the subconscious or, better still, the superconscious, can in a flash of a second, state a truth about the soul nature of a man in a momentary dream or even in an idle doodle. The higher self is always on the alert to speak its guiding truth. Thus what more likely than that the superconscious entity of the family stream should give the flash of inspiration which the Heralds could crystallise into a shield or crest. Perhaps the members of the College of Heralds were sometimes clairvoyant and knew what they were about. The whole of the inner heraldry is *aspirational* from beginning to end, and can be recognised (if the approach appeals to you) as a sign of the deepest wisdom working itself into the outward trappings of a colourful civilization.

Medieval in expression, it speaks absolutely timeless truths about the human soul. Therefore, as with all great allegory in myth and fairy tale, it is deeply relevant to modern life. Indeed it matters *more* to us than to our ancestors, since they knew the truths about the higher world that we, in the arrogance of our mechanistic thinking, have forgotten. It needs imaginative vision to recover the lost knowledge of man's Divine origin and the 'erring pilgrimage' which he undertakes when he descends to earth. Thus symbolic art will play a role of immense importance in the New Age, awakening in us the faculties which can recognise the spiritual truths and advance on the inner path to Knowledge.

15

BIRDS IN IMAGINATION
AND POETRY

'MUMMY, WHAT ARE lions for?' The child's naive enquiry during a zoo visit shows real perception. We adults tend far too much to take things for granted. This essay is an attempt to ask 'What are birds for?' The ornithologist can tell us fascinating things about the habits of birds, the routes of migration, the identification of birdsong and the like. But *why* birds? What are they about?

Look with an imaginative eye at a bird – it is related to the other animals and to man in that it has a backbone, ribs, legs and a head. Yet what a curious shape it presents. Try to think yourself into a bird. Your chest protrudes forward into the great breastbone, your legs become skinny sticks, the forepart of your face is drawn forward into the extraordinary projection of the beak, your arms transform into wings and over all grows the plumage. When we look at the more remarkable beaks such as puffin or avocet we can get a sense that this is a strange distortion of a face.

It is quite valid to try to understand animals by thinking yourself into them, since the whole animal kingdom is deeply related to man.

Intellect divides and separates in order to analyse the complexity of matter. Thus the triumphs of science have been achieved, but at the grave price of losing the sense for the living whole. Three-dimensional thinking leaves us with the impression that the world is made up of an infinite number of separate things. The imagination is the faculty that can apprehend the living whole and experience the truth that life is a great oneness. That which the Imaginative vision of the poets and the symbolism of the myths can tell us, may therefore have truly scientific implications for our time.

We can gain a new understanding of nature if we approach her through the imagination to try to grasp that everything, including ourselves, is a part of a vast living unity. Pope writes:

All are but parts of one stupendous whole
Whose body Nature is a God the soul.

Now let us consider the bird kingdom. Birds are lovely creatures, but we can imagine that the individual bird, having no ego consciousness and no mirror, has no vanity about its own beauty. It experiences itself primarily as a pocket of warm air. From its lungs extend air sacks which penetrate even into the centre of the bones in place of marrow. Its volatile energy generates warmth so that the bird floats in air. The bones are brittle and almost ash-like in quality, as if the body had been through a heat process. There is very little blood, and no great intestine. Thus the digestion of the bird is rudimentary, as if it were unconcerned with the metabolism of earth. Since it is really an entity of warm air, it must feel the rest of its physical body to be an encumbrance. It really belongs to the ethereal light-filled realms, hardly touching down into that heavy frequency we call the earth.

Tennyson expresses this in his brief poem, *The Eagle*:

He grasps the crag with hooked hand,
Close to the sun in lonely lands
Ringed with the azure world he stands.
The wrinkled sea beneath him crawls
He watches from his mountain walls
And like a thunderbolt he falls.

Mythology has always recognised the relation of the bird world to the sun. Many legends link the birds with Jesus, since the Christ is that exalted Being who is Lord of the Spiritual Sun.

Thus in a Swedish legend, the swallow, the bird of consolation, flies around the cross crying 'Svala, Svala' which means 'console' and pricks himself on the thorns so that the blood still shows on his ruddy chest. The oyster catcher in Celtic legend guided St Bride, the foster mother of the boy Jesus, when she took Him in a small boat to the Western Isles. The cock missed the Star of Christ and is always waiting its reappearance, calling at dawn, 'Star, star are you there'. He is also dedicated to Apollo, the Sun God, and his red comb depicts the Sun on earth. Space does not allow for multiplying of such instances, but of all the sun myths that of the Phoenix is the most important and illuminating.

The Phoenix is the most marvellous of birds. Its feathers can be compared only to the lustre of precious stones. It has a wonderful long tail, scintillating with reflections of purest gold. It has shining gold and blue on its neck, a crown of colour upon its head, purple wings, a glint of gold and silver in all its feathers. It has the hooked beak of an eagle, the grace of a heron and the most wondrous voice which neither the notes of the nightingale nor the flute of the Muses can equal. No wonder that no ornithologists have been able to place quite what the Phoenix is or where it is to be found. The truth is that the Phoenix takes the best of all species in existence. It never was an earthly bird because clearly it belongs to an astral realm. Imagination has taken the finest qualities in all the birds and put them together into this archetypal bird, embodying all possibilities out of which the whole bird kingdom was formed.

The main feature of the legend is the connection of the Phoenix with the Sun Fire, the elements of warmth and light. This bird of the Sun lives out its long life in the seclusion of the sacred forest of the Sun as the attendant of Phoebus, Overseer of the Groves. It is, so to speak, a priest of the wood where the Sun Temple is found. Each morning he flies on wings of flame to perch on the top of the highest tree in the forest and there, turning nine times towards the rising Sun and bowing, he awaits the first rays. As soon as these touch the threshold of his brilliant palace, a warm wind springs up with the new day and the Phoenix shakes himself, throbs and trembles, and suddenly, in a transport of enthusiasm, he sings. With the rising Sun, the glory rises in his own heart and expresses itself in sound., and the sound of his harmonious voice, far more mellow than any nightingale's, floods the forest as new light floods the earth. They say that the lion roars in response and all nature joins in the concert and Heaven and earth are united in love.

At long intervals of time the Phoenix has the urge to leave this abode of delights and go to the country where reigns the empire of death. The immortal bird is now concerned with nothing but dying. He builds himself a nest, using aromatic herbs and the most precious spices. He then yields up his life; his nest becomes his tomb. A fermentation, a heat process, starts in his body, he is consumed from within in his aromatic sarcophacus. The process of fermentation produces the fire which is associated with the legend. He is burnt to ash, but within the pile of ash appears the new Phoenix, a tiny bird of identical form. The death carries with it the torch of life; the nest once a sarcophagus becomes a cradle, and the fire which consumed the ancient body will rejuvenate it. The little bird grows rapidly in splendour and, when he has matured, his first concern is to pay honour to the ashes, the remains of his former self. He therefore constructs an egg-shaped chalice, collects the ashes and bears them away in his talons to the ancient Temple of the Sun. He deposits it upon the altar, where with pomp and majesty the chalice is sacrificed by the venerable priest. Then the reborn Phoenix takes over the same duties as his 'father' before him. Yet though we use the word 'father', be it recognised that it is always the same Phoenix born again to the eternal light.

What then of the plumage of the bird, its real splendour? Here we must sense that the bird is the centre of some immense artistic activity. The individual bird obviously is not the artist. Some wonderful creative imagination is using the whole field of bird plumage to work out its designs. How very inadequate to think it is merely done by chance and by survival of the fittest. Look at the 'eyes' on the peacock and wonder whether this is merely developed for survival. Look, still more, in a museum, at the Malay Great Argus, its plumage and great tail covered with hundreds of wonderfully decorative 'eyes' which glow as if they are little spheres of light, real shining eyeballs. The individual bird never made these. We are looking at a point where a great cosmic artistic activity is manifesting itself. Note the important point that the design in the plumage is always a whole. It is not that each feather is coloured, but that the design is, so to speak, stamped upon the whole field of feathers from outside, the patterns running from one feather to another,

We have to imagine the shapes and colours streaming in on to the photographic plate of the birds plumage and impressing themselves. The bird is the tiny focal point of a huge artistic activity and we thus have to see the *bird* as a partly supersensible entity. Here it is worth stressing the scientific fact that the cells of the feathers in the embryo are formed from the outside inward, suggesting an influence pouring in from the periphery.

It is helpful to look at the cases in museums where the more fantastic plumage is shown. We so much take for granted the colour of starling or robin that the marvel is lost to us through familiarity. But the humming birds and the ruffs and all the fabulous imaginings that come in the exotic plumage suggest a creative realm of sheer delight, far beyond utility. We are looking through into an artistic workshop of design and into the sheer joy of forming with cosmic light and shining colour. Imagine free unembodied colour, before it is impregnated into matter. Imagine some way in which this cosmic colour and light can, with the least weight of matter, be brought down into manifestation on to our plane. Would we not see this in the butterfly's wing, the golden sheen on the poppy, the feathers of the kingfisher? The eye is here allowed to behold that which the imagination can innerly enter – the glory of light invisible. Every bird as it flies is a praising of the Lord. The entire realm of plumage which surrounds the earth is a point of praise. No wonder we are constrained to represent angels as bright winged. The Heavenly world flashes down into our consciousness in plumage. Our love of bird plumage is not a matter for more curiosity. To many it is debased merely into a means of bird identification. Rather is it a challenge to us to grasp imaginatively the fact of Divine design and continual delight in creation.

This approach gives further clue to the nest building activities. Once again, choose to study the more exotic nests and see the architectural fantasy of the bird kingdom. We must surely see that the habits and instincts of nest-making are 'built-in' to the particular bird from the outside. It is a focus for instreaming creation. The simplest nest is moulded to the shape of the bird's body and can therefore be seen as an extension of the physical bird into surrounding nature. The really complex nests suggest a delight in sheer architecture of moss and twig and leaf.

The sense that the bird's activity is integrated with the Great Whole of Nature comes when we study the bird form in relation to its activity. Consider the gannet, floating a hundred feet above the sea, sighting a mackerel many feet below the surface, plunging down, closing its wings the instant before it hits water so that its form becomes a flashing stream-lined torpedo. Somehow this is more than mere natural selection for survival. This is Design. Gannet and fish are an integral process and have no meaning unless they are in relation to each other. Can we put it that the group-soul of gannet and of mackerel are allied in the great unity? Light returns in the end to light. The flashing fish and the diving bird, are part of this redemptive process. The concept of 'nature red in tooth and claw' is not the whole answer.

Then consider the song of birds.

Here also there are two ways of looking. We can rightly use song for identification of species and be content to leave it at that. Or we can use it to awaken wonder, that source, as the Greeks knew, of all knowledge. An apocryphal saying of Jesus runs:

> Cease not from your search until ye find; finding, ye shall wonder; wondering ye shall enter the Kingdom, and in the Kingdom ye shall find peace.

The Kingdom is everywhere, but on a higher frequency which normal looking does not touch. We have to lift our thinking to imaginative perception and see beyond the immediate appearance. Then at every point in nature the kingdom can be entered. Perhaps we have here the answer to our first question 'What are birds for?' They are to awaken wonder, the key to the Kingdom.

Bird song is explained by the scientists as a means of identifying territory. Every willow warbler sings to define his established territory and will fight any invading male. This is true enough and quite undeniable, but like every allegorical symbol it has a double meaning. The more prosaic explanation emphatically does not ever debunk or preclude the more imaginative.

Consider again that all life is One. The earth is a great organism. Life on this plane is an image of its creative counterpart on supersensible planes of higher frequency. 'Alles vergangliches ist nur em Gleichniss,' wrote the great scientist-poet Goethe. 'All that is passing is only an image, a 'reflection'. Music is the stuff of soul-forming, part of the whole creative pattern. On our plane it has profound formative power. So what of that burst of earth music with the first light of dawn, that miraculous moment when the first cheep is answered by another call and in a few minutes the entire concert is shouting to the glory of God in a torrent of celestial sound? Goethe showed that where darkness meets light, colour is born. The active conflict of light and darkness produces colour. He called it 'the deeds and sufferings of light'. From this arise the colours of dawn, which in imagination we may see moving in a belt around the turning world. But at the same point music is born. Where the shadows of night are first met by the light, the larynx of the Earth pours forth bird song. Over the temperate zones a moving wall of song rises as a crest to the advancing wave of light. Must we not feel that, whatever the ornithologist may rightly say about territory, the phenomenon of the dawn chorus is part of the Divinity of the Earth, manifested in a giving back of melody to the creative Heavens.

Our approach suggests that the kingdoms of nature are an integral part of a great living whole. For those who can accept this view a new light is thrown on the possible explanation of the mystery of bird migration. In our age of separatist and mechanistic thinking, the tacit assumption is often made that, since the bird finds its way incredible distances, each bird must possess some intricate built-in navigational mechanism. Science has so far failed to find such route-finding device, or offer any adequate explanation of the amazing phenomenon.

A different possibility is seen when we acknowledge the earth as a living organism and manifestation of realms of higher being. The bird kingdom, with every other kingdom of nature, is an integral part of a vastly complex organism. First we must grasp the idea of the group souls of the animals. Each species represents a group soul. The ego of the individual beasts does not descend into incarnation as in man. This makes the difference between man and animal. In man, a spiritual being, the ego or eternal core, has descended. In the animal, the group ego on a higher plane controls every member of the species. Thus the group ego of the Swallow controls all swallows. Imagine the individual swallows to be your finger nails, your arm connected with your brain to be the invisible supersensible group-soul. All you have to do is to think your hand from one point to another and the nails move there. We do not need to seek for direction-finders in our individual nails. So with the migrating swallows. The group ego 'thinks' them from England to Africa. They are also sensitised to the warmth currents of the earth and are able to move with ease along these 'etheric' currents.

Is it not easier to 'think' this explanation, than to 'think' a complex direction-finder into the mind of each swallow? Since all creation is thought, a basic indication of truth is likely to be whether we can really think a thing.

A further question – what is the explanation for the extra-ordinary interest in birds in so many people today? Why this great love of them? What, indeed, is our affinity with the birds? The bird kingdom hardly touches down to earth. It is a part of the realm of nature which belongs to the upper spheres of light and colour. We sense that our lifted thinking is akin to the bird world. Thoughts flash into our heads as feathers flash in the birds. The immediate thoughts have some counterpart in the plumage of birds. The head of man is so poised that the brain is lifted out of gravity, even to the extent that it floats in liquid and therefore has no weight. Thus it is open to the thoughts of the cosmos and can be shown in symbol thus.

We touch a great secret which Steiner has given us. The bird is Head metamorphosed. All animals have a skeleton modified to meet their special nature. In the bird the lower systems are rudimentary. Think of the skinny sticks which are the legs, albeit the claw or talon is developed into a splendid tool. Realise that the bird has no great intestine. Digestion is at a minimum and food is passed through at extraordinary pace. All the animals are related to the human pattern and with the eye of imagination the bird must be seen as a head transformed, hovering above earth and touching the realm of colour in its feathers as man touches the realms of thought. We know well that some people think like sparrows, some like magpies or peacocks or eagles. It is a very true symbol that ladies wear feathers round their hats and not round their middle. The plumes of Aztec warriors decorated the head. Only Papageno in *The Magic Flute* is covered with feathers all over his body and he by nature is volatile and birdlike. This imaginative view is helped if we switch our vision to the cow. Contemplate a herd of cows grazing in a meadow. Feel how they are given over to the weight of gravity, in contrast to the bird lifted into the spheres of 'levity'. Look at the placid slow almost inward gaze in the depth of the huge dark eye of the cow and compare it with the flashing of the eye of the eagle, penetrating to its prey from enormous heights. Realise that the cow and the kindred beasts, the ruminants (what a suggestive name) are given over to the great and marvellous task of metabolism, the breaking down of matter in digestion. They are indeed a huge digestive system. As bird is head transformed, so is cow digestion transformed. This explains why Hindu religion reveres the cow, since it has in nature a holy task of bringing spiritual forces down to earth.

Now make another comparison. Think of a lion and listen to the kind of noise it makes when it roars for food and ravenously tears its prey to satisfy hunger. The lion is a great chest system metamorphosed. The chest is hugely developed and accentuated by the great mane, while the stomach is reduced to leanness. The chest or heart system, standing between the head system and the metabolic or limb system is the point where blood and air are in balance. The weight of the blood in the cow is greater than in any other animal. In the bird, blood is at a minimum. As we have seen, it is little but warm air in a case of brittle ash-like bone. The lion stands between bird and cow as heart stands in man between head and metabolic system. No wonder the rampant lion is the archetypal heraldic beast representing heart courage. These three are the beasts of the Evangelists, the fourth being the angel form of man. Together they represent the Human Archetype.

The imagination of the poets may give us a vision of nature which is truly scientific. Indeed, Shelley says 'Poetry is the breath and finer spirit of all knowledge. It is the impassioned expression on the face of science.' Wordsworth recognises that without imagination a kind of death results. When intellect is divorced from imagination the vision of the life of the whole is lost.

> Sweet is the lore which nature brings.
> Our meddling intellect
> Mis-shapes the beauteous form of things —
> We murder to dissect.

The poetical vision always penetrates to the being of things. The greater life within things is the source of inspiration and must often be conveyed in symbol. Thus the poetry of birds constantly endows them with spiritual being. In our age we tend too easily to treat this as so much fantasy. It may prove to be the great truth we have to rediscover if we are to take the next step in understanding.

We will close with two short poems. The first is by Julian Huxley, that great scientist with vision of the whole.

EARTH AND BIRDS

> To most of us, a bird's a feathered song
> Which for our pleasure gives a voice to spring.
> We make a symbol of its airy wing
> Bright with the liberty for which we long.

Or we discover them with love more strong
As each a separate individual thing
Which only learns to act or move or sing
In ways that wholly to itself belong.

But some with deeper and more inward sight
See them a part of that one Life which streams
Slow on, towards more mind – a part more light
Than we; unburdened with regrets or dreams,
Or thought. A winged emotion of the sky,
The birds through an eternal Present fly.

Gerard Manley Hopkins sees the Christ within all nature, and to
Him dedicates his sonnet on the falcon (or more correctly kestrel).

THE WINDHOVER

To Christ our Lord

I caught this morning morning's minion, kingdom of daylight's
    dauphin, dapple-dawn drawn Falcon, in his riding
Of the rolling level underneath him steady air, and striding
High there, how he rung upon the rein of a wimpling wing
In his ecstasy! Then off, off forth on swing,
As a skate's heel sweeps smooth on a bow-bend: the hurl and
    gliding
Rebuffed the big wind. My heart in hiding
Stirred for a bird, – the achieve of, the mastery of the thing!

Brute beauty and valour and act, oh, air, pride, plume, here
Buckle! AND the fire that breaks from thee then, a billion
Times told lovelier, more dangerous, O my chevalier!

No wonder of it: sheer plod makes plough down sillion
Shine, and blue-bleak embers, ah my dear,
Fall, gall themselves, and gash gold-vermilion.

'I caught this morning' – meaning that I really saw, perceived,
what the Bird was, and my secret heart stirred in response to the
deity within it. 'Buckle' here means bind, to lock together. The
so-called bird is a focal point for soul and spirit qualities, entering the earth sphere through the vehicle of bone and feather.

Thus, brute beauty and valour and act, air, pride and plume are buckled together in the splendour of the hovering falcon.

We must come to look upon the birds with a new awe and wonder and allow our poetic consciousness to lift us to understanding, so that we may look beyond this marvel of nature into the ethereal realms of creative spirit. Each manifestation of nature can become as a 'magic casement' for looking within and beyond. Then we shall find that the whole of nature is interpenetrated by the world of Being, which indeed shapes its myriad forms. Thus Hopkins is right in discovering the Christ, the Lord of Light, his 'Chevalier', hidden within each natural form, so that Divine light will break even from clay furrow or dying ember.

16

MAN IN NATURE

OUR THEME today is nature and nature study, but we shall try to stretch our thinking somewhat wider than the usual observation of birds or plants. As twentieth century people, we are somehow always 'over against' nature as mere onlookers. We are watching it from outside. We do not experience ourselves really as part of it. How can this sense of separation be overcome?

Let me quote Wordsworth's sonnet:

> The World is too much with us; late and soon
> Getting and spending, we lay waste our powers:
> Little we see in Nature that is ours;
> We have given our hearts away, a sordid boon!
> This Sea that bares her bosom to the moon;
> The winds that will be howling at all hours.
> And are up-gathered now like sleeping flowers;
> For this, for everything, we are out of tune;
> It moves us not. Great God! I'd rather be
> A Pagan suckled in a creed outworn;
> So might I, standing on this pleasant lea,
> Have glimpses that would make me less forlorn;
> Have sight of Proteus rising from the sea;
> Or hear old Triton blow his wreathèd horn.'

This expresses the poet's deep feeling that our intellectual knowledge is something cutting us off from living nature.

It was not always so. The Greeks knew of the living world of beings whom they could still perceive within rocks and trees and flowers. They called them satyrs and dryads and naiads and they were aware of the elemental living world within the outer forms. It is all too easy to write this off as sheer superstition. Yet we believe that the Greeks achieved a height of culture and civilisation rarely surpassed. Can we in the same breath say that they were among the greatest thinkers and artists in European history and yet were wholly deceived in their major belief about the Divine beings within nature? Is there not another possible explanation – that they still had faculties of perception which enabled them to see what now has become invisible to us? They could still hear old Triton blow his wreathèd horn.

The old people of Ireland and Wales, in the Celtic west, still possess faculties of clairvoyance. They can see the 'little people'. They know of the gnomes working among the roots of trees and the minerals in the rocks, the sylphs forming the flowers, the undines where water and plant are in contact, and salamanders in the flame. These faculties of vision may be recognised as a throw-back which do not belong to our scientific age, yet the 'little people' may truly represent living forces of creative intelligence within nature. Can modern man develop the inner eye in a manner fitting for modern thinking?

An increasing number of people today, from all walks of life, are recording moments of sudden illumination in which they can see nature in quite a new way. Suddenly the rocks and trees appear much more intensely alive, the flowers are seen as if transparent, the colour greatly enhanced, as if a luminous world existed within all the usual forms. Sometimes the colours are even experienced as sounding. A conviction comes that this which is seen is Reality, and that it represents an aspect of a vast living whole. Everything is seen as if it is part of a huge organism, bound together in joy and life and love. This is a glimpse into the Divine world within nature, which could be called the Spirit. The universe is sensed as being not so much a vast mechanism as a Living Presence. The experience may last only a few seconds, but it always leaves a conviction that this is Reality, after which life can never be quite the same again. Raynor Johnson in a book called *Watcher on the Hills* discusses a number of these experiences. They may well represent an emerging of a new kind of vision and consciousness in modern people.

Not everyone is favoured by such flashes of vision. We can all, however, develop understanding and can grasp in thought and imagination the possibility of a living world within matter. It is 'supersensible', in that it cannot be apprehended with the ordinary senses which are tuned-in only on the low vibration of matter. It needs something of a sixth sense to grasp it, but it is no less real for that. Indeed, it is more real than the impermanent changing forms of nature because it is an eternal world. Realise that the outer world of substance with all its fascinating changing forms is but an image of this primary creative world of living formative forces. Goethe wrote 'Alles vergängliche is nur ein Gleichniss' – 'All that is transitory is but a parable'. This gives us the clue that we must try to look on the whole Earth as a Great Living Creature, with what we call 'Nature' as a kind of skin around the rocky skeleton, which itself in ages past was really alive. Man, then comes to be seen as an integral part of the whole pattern, and not a chance accident of evolution. He is that point where nature becomes conscious of himself. He is the thought organ of the living Earth and therefore profoundly responsible for the care of the Earth. Grasp in thought this concept of a World of Living Intelligence or 'Spirit' which can think itself into appearance in the ever changing shapes of nature. A new way of looking emerges in which we can approach the supersensible inner reality by imaginative perception. This, when developed, goes far beyond what we ordinarily mean by 'nature-study'.

The keynote for our imaginative 'reading' of nature is this transformation or 'metamorphosis', a perpetual process of 'dying and becoming'. In this nature reveals her secrets. Forms every-where flow into each other in a perpetual process of refining and lifting from the coarser to the more delicate. Everything is working in rhythms of metamorphosis, some infinitely slow, like the folding of the mountains, some almost visible in the plants, and some so fast that we can watch them in the changing clouds. We shall in time come to see it as a great process of redemption in which human thinking has a part to play.

METAMORPHOSIS IN THE PLANTS

Now let us in this light look at the kingdoms of nature. First the plant world. You will have noticed that at times a tulip throws a petal by mistake half an inch too low. This shows itself as half coloured petal and half green leaf. It is not just a 'sport'. It is a sign, in which nature reveals her chief secret. *Petal is leaf transformed.* The plant indeed is all leaf, but it transforms this organ into root or petal or thorn or stamen. Set certain leaves into the soil and they grow roots. Take a plant to bits and lay the leaves in a series, as they have grown from lowest to highest. Buttercup is most illuminating. You will see that the forms progress, reaching in about three steps what is obviously the maximum splendour and then gradually refining and finally fading into a mere little shoot. Then the miracle happens which the eye of the imagination can see. Leaf moves over, first into calyx, then into petal. Some plants hide the secret, some reveal it. In the rose the outer petals show a little crinkle at the edge. Move inwards and this becomes a yellow cyst, a central rib hardens and pollen begins to show. You find the stamen is nothing other than petal transformed. The true plant is not the appearance that you see at any one moment. It is a supersensible, invisible cycle of metamorphosis, moving from seed through leaf expansion, through corolla, through fruit expansion and into the final contraction of the seed again. You must learn actively to 'think with' the plant through its whole life cycle and it will begin to tell you its secrets. The real plant, you may say, is an Idea. It is that which catches mineral and substance from air and light and water, and holds it tenuously for a brief while in a miraculous form which is always changing.

Then it dies. But does it?

Petals fall from the faded rose but then the life has concentrated in fruit and seed. The petals fall and are broken down into humus, the body of the living earth. In nature there is no death, only metamorphosis of form, the discarded sheaths returning to the living body of the whole. Always matter is lifted towards more etherealised delicate forms, as if a continuous process of redemption were taking place, lifting darkened clumsy substances back towards the Light.

Man is integrally part of the whole. In him too *there is no death* in the sense of extinction. There is the discarding of the worn out sheath to be given over to earth or fire, but the core of man is eternal and belongs to a plane of widened consciousness. The soul of man can metaphorically be free from the leaf stage and expand into corolla and petal. Our love of flowers arises because they tell us (subconsciously) that everything is lifting and returning to a realm of light and colour from which it descended. This redemptive process runs through the whole of nature, though in man it is largely turned inwards into a soul-changing process. Goethe, the great poet-scientist who first developed the thesis of plant metamorphosis, said 'You want to know the secret of life? That which the plant does unconsciously, do consciously.' No wonder we need to cultivate our gardens.

BUTTERFLY METAMORPHOSIS

In this light look at the symbol of the butterfly. A splendid caterpillar develops and proudly crawls. Then he wraps himself in a cocoon, spinning silk around his body. Inside it he turns into a nasty sludgy grub. If he could be conscious he would feel he was a failure, looking back at his great days as a caterpillar. Then the miracle happens. Just as leaf changes through calyx to corolla, so caterpillar changes through pupa to butterfly. The two meta-morphoses are comparable. The form of wings are impressed *from outside* on the body of the grub. In a few days it transforms into the glory of coloured wing. If any physical substance is Sunlight caught and held into matter, it is the butterfly's wing, glinting with gold. Gold we know is the metal of the sun. No wonder man hungers for it. Silk is (if we can grasp it) spun out of light. No wonder woman adorns herself with it. Butterfly is earth matter lifted back to the living spiritual sunlight. Butterfly and plant metamorphosis are akin. Butterfly is flower animated – flower is butterfly enchained to matter. Not chance natural selection, but kindred Divine process makes them alike.

MAN AND THE ANIMALS

Man's deeper relation to the animal kingdom is so big a subject that it will only be possible to touch it briefly. A whole new approach to zoology begins to open up. Man, we know, as a physical body, appeared last on the earth and in relation to the aeons of evolution is only a late visitor to this planet. Yet we are told he is made in the image of God, who made him only a little lower than the angels. Man as a being of thinking, feeling and willing, of head, heart and limb system, is central to the pattern of living things which walk or swim or fly with skeletons. Last to appear, in the sense that in him the pattern is at last realised to perfection, he is first an idea. Although the present human organism is not the last word and will surely be carried in the far evolutionary future to something more beautiful, it does undeniably show a harmony of parts and faculties which no other earth creature has achieved. As bearer of the ego of Man, as a mechanism which can harbour consciousness and compassion, the human organism seems to be a kind of symphony bringing together all we see spread around us in the animal world. We are bedevilled by the assumption that man's ancestor was an ape. For the present argument, hold firmly to the view that Man, as an Idea in the Imagining of God, is there from the very beginning in the exalted realms of spirit. Step by step the pattern has to be realised and translated into the gravity field of earth matter. In order that man in a skeleton frame may walk the earth, a highly complex environment has to be built up. Use your imagination to see that before the completed body of man can emerge from the creative logos, its parts, in a kind of experiment, begin to emerge first. Fragments of the melody are set down and tried out, as in Beethoven's Choral Symphony, before the completed theme is sounded. Thus each animal species can be seen as an early specialisation for some specific purpose, of a part of man, while he himself is held back until the moment has come for God to 'breathe the spirit into him so that he becomes a living soul'. Each is a metamorphosis of some organ or part of the central structure of man. Thus the idea of hand is turned into that superb but very limited tool in the eagle's talon. The cow is to be seen imaginatively as the digestive system adapted and given over to the earth. The teeth of the wolf are shaped specifically as a perfect instrument adapted to satisfy hunger through hunting. The gannet in all his glory of movement is entirely shaped to dive for fish. The lion seems to be an exaggeration of the chest system of man. The creatures which gallop and run show the pattern of the skeleton given over to the horizontal axis, performing their specific function grandly but without the infinite adaptability of the human skeleton, which alone is perfectly adjusted and balanced in the vertical axis. The birds, seen with the eye of imagination, seem to be creatures in which the lower parts of the skeleton are shrunken and undeveloped. Legs become curious sticks, digestion is virtually non-existent, bone is like brittle ash, air sacks replace marrow and indeed the whole body of the bird is like a warm air pocket to rise above the pull of earth. These volatile creatures, centres of dynamic activity, live in a sphere half out of earth gravity. The bird seems to be a metamorphosis of the head system, and a wild and beautiful clue is then seen – that the gorgeous plumage compares strangely with the flashing of thoughts. It is a true symbol that women wear feathers in their hats and not around their middles, since the bird kingdom is innerly related to the head and thinking part of man. In the beauty of plumage and in the ingenuity of nest making, we must see an artistic activity beyond the individual bird, pouring into appearance upon earth.

The clue is that each animal species can be seen as related to some specific part of the archetypal pattern of man, adapted to some particular function in living. The animal kingdom is the human organism spread over the face of earth. Man is a symphony of all animal forms. Each animal is necessary for the environment that makes man's survival possible. Each species therefore, in a sense, has sacrificed itself into a constricted function in the service of man, the Divine archetype. This debt we owe to the animals. Our love can therefore go out to cow and bird, dog and snake, in a new way. Man as the perfected organ of consciousness on earth has a great task in lifting and redeeming nature. The luminous world of spirit, hidden within the forms of nature, is an age long process of release and redemption and as we love and study these forms, whether in plant, animal or crystal, we are helping in this great process. Many people are quite convinced that flowers grow more beautifully if they are loved and looked at. And what of the loved animal? Even if only dimly we can grasp our place in this enormous wholeness, we awaken a new sense of relatedness and responsibility to the natural world.

The human kingdom is not separated from nature but an integral and central part of the whole pattern, and each of us has our conscious part to play in lifting a creation which 'groaneth as in the pangs of childbirth'. A new approach to nature study emerges with this sense of kinship with all created things.

Now all this could easily be written off as so much poetic fantasy quite unrelated to the harsh and very practical world in which we live and struggle. Think again. Is this really so? Is the so-called 'practical man' who prides himself on being down to earth with no imaginative nonsense really in possession of the full truth? Does not this vision of living wholeness have its direct bearing on practical living?

Consider man's relation to the animals nowadays. Factory farming has been developed by our generation as a direct outcome of the assumption that animals have no real feelings and can validly be used as machines for producing food. They are mere protein machines, egg-laying mechanisms, veal producers. So we are prepared to crowd the hens together in darkness and. fix the calf so that he cannot lie down while he is artificially fed. Those who are prepared to do these things laugh at the sentimentalists that hold the antiquated view that animals are ensouled and Divine creatures.

We are degrading the animal nature and by so doing we degrade ourselves. It is an attribute of very 'male' thinking that we can ignore the feelings of animals and feel that we are perfectly free to do with them what we like, so long as it pays. The feminine in our nature (whether we are actually woman or man) is protective of life and can grasp that we have a very different responsibility for animal welfare. It is remarkable that, as if in answer to the mentality that can tolerate and practice some of the extreme methods of factory farming, a new relationship seems to be developing between man and animals which is based on sympathy and respect.

This is shown in a number of deeply moving books. These suggest that our love of the animals can break through their natural timidity and establish a new intimacy with them. When this happens we open up fields of study of the real nature of the animal which are hidden when we merely observe its instinctual behaviour patterns. Thus Maxwell revealed in *Ring of Bright Water* the incredible playfulness and sense of fun in the otter. Len Howard, in *Birds as Individuals*, describes the astounding confidence the wild birds develop when they know they are loved and welcomed. Elma Williams, author of *Valley of Animals*, found that animals began to adopt her and describes how they live together and thrive in her Welsh sanctuary. Boone, in *Kinship with all Life*, describing his relations to a very remarkable dog, gives incredible revelations of animal intelligence. Though in no sense a mystic, he became convinced that a contact can be made with something much deeper than the thinking of the individual animal. It is as if each creature can be a window into the greater thinking of the species or what has been called the animal group-soul. When this contact is established we could indeed learn from the animals about the mysteries of life. It is contendable that an animal does not really become its true self until human love breaks the barrier of reserve and the new confidence is established. Then both men and animal are lifted in dignity.

Individuals like St Francis have, through the centuries, had these powers of contact with animals. What is now remarkable is that many ordinary people seem to be developing them. It represents a flow of love from the heart of man to the animals, and this is reciprocated. Such an attitude has a healing and redemptive quality. As it spreads, the pleasure in the blood-sports will fade, and a revulsion will come against such things as bullfighting.

Thus we must recognise that the basic attitude we take towards the kingdoms of nature works right down into practical policies and lines of action.

If the earth is really an ensouled creature, then it may be that those methods of agriculture and industry which wholly ignore the unitary life of nature may result in a counter-attack. We may seriously have to envisage the anger of the earth, the reprisals by the elemental forces, thrown out of balance by the blind interference and avarice of man, who feels that nature is something he has to 'conquer' and do battle with. Some are coming to feel that the disturbances so notable in our time are a sign that we are drawing the wrath of the earth upon us.

The view we have tried to consider is of course unorthodox, but more and more thinking people are prepared to give it consideration. It leads us to recognising the arrogance of man when he treats nature as an insensate mechanism to be exploited solely to his own advantage. We wake up to the solemn fact that we are stewards of a living earth imbued with spirit and Divinity. Blake wrote: 'Every rock is deluged with Deity'. What have we done with our stewardship?

On the positive scale we have developed such skill and knowledge that human intelligence could now control and direct the life of the earth, and make the deserts blossom as the rose. The marvels of scientific investigation have opened up the mysterious workings of the infinitely small and the infinitely great. Teilhard de Chardin, that great scientist and seer of our age, writes that 'The time has come to realise that Research is the highest human function, embracing the spirit of war and bright with the splendour of religion'. The prospects and possibilities

156

are tremendous. All the more urgent is it that man honours the earth as a living organism. When he fails to see this, he is led into a thinking which too easily concerns itself with the particular, and is tempted to get quick results without due consideration of the effect on the balanced working of the whole. This directly leads to practices which are not consonant with man's task of stewardship.

Thus we are degrading the dumb animals as if they were machines. In our belief in chemicals, we are ignoring the cycle of life and the ancient principles of organic husbandry by pouring artificial fertilisers into the soil and by reckless killing of predators by toxic pesticides. There is now mounting concern that we may be so lowering the vitality of the living soil that great tracts of the earth may ultimately become infertile. The very air we breathe is becoming noxious and the waters in our rivers and oceans are becoming polluted, so that the wastes flowing into the sea are killing the fish. It appears that our great reservoirs, held up by huge dams of which we were so proud, may become quite dead and develop putrefying algae. Our bird and butterfly populations are dying through reckless spraying of poisons and the insect world is developing immunity to DDT.

Finally, there is the pollution by nuclear fall-out and the possibility of the ultimate human folly of nuclear warfare. Many are convinced that the high-altitude explosions have the effect of so rending the protective etheric envelope of the earth that harmful cosmic radiations may pour in. There is even concern that the very axis of the earth may be tilted, which could have devastating results. Thus if we feel that spiritual worlds exist behind the realm of matter, we may be sure that the earth is being watched with concern, lest its wayward inhabitants, in their pride and recklessness, overstep the borders of sanity.

All this arises from action on short-term views, in an attempt to get quick results on the assumption that nature is merely a mechanism. We may well be compelled by mounting disaster to change our view and, at whatever cost, learn to take the long view and to serve the earth. We have the skill and knowledge to enter a great new stage of human endeavour and research, in working with the life of which we are an integral part. There is a debt to be repaid. We can each begin by learning to look with a child-like wonder at nature as a vehicle in which a mysterious world of creative life is at work.

17

REPAYING THE SACRIFICE
OF THE ANIMALS

OUR MINDS today are influenced and conditioned by the prevailing mood of materialistic thinking. This leads in our generation to the too easy assumption that the earth is essentially a dead speck of dust in the vast mechanism of the Cosmos, that man stands over against a nature wholly indifferent to him, and that the animal species, of which he is the crown, have evolved through the chance of natural selection.

This view of evolution leaves us the apparent right to use and exploit the natural kingdoms to our own advantage. Intellectual and male thinking sees it as so much sentiment to bother about the feelings and 'soul' of animals. If we can turn them to our advantage we are fully justified in doing so.

Change the basic world-view and you change the attitude, since the latter is the outcome of the former. Consider the alternative picture which, it must be remembered, has in broad outline been held by every other culture but our own. Our modern materialism is essentially the product of the thinking of only three or four generations.

See first in imagination the Infinite Being of God, Absolute Consciousness. See that worlds are then imagined into being. Our earth is the product of Divine Thought. First it is formed as Idea which then through the aeons is realised into the plane of matter. The Book of Genesis very clearly indicates two stages of creation, first in Idea and then into substance. Grasp the primacy of Spirit, that physical substance is the final step in cosmic processes, an end product deposited out of higher insubstantial planes. Too readily do we take for granted that matter is primary and spirit some vague sort of emanation therefrom.

Take as our postulate that Man is the central and first Idea of God in forming Earth. He is the purpose of Earth, which is a stage or setting upon which a spiritual being, man, can grow into self-awareness and thus to moral freedom. In order that this particle of God-consciousness, the human ego, can incarnate in the gravity field of earth, a suitable vehicle, the body, has to be evolved over long ages. We are not our bodies. Soul and spirit have their own line of evolution, leading down into the bodies prepared by physical evolution. Man and his complex body are 'made in the image of God', the physical basis for the soul powers of thought, emotion and will. Last to appear in physical form, Man is there from the beginning in Idea. Man is the Archetype which initially included the whole pattern. 'Man know thyself and thou shalt know the universe'. The human form is the microcosm which mirrors the macrocosm. All natural forms are included in the Archetype. From Man, in this sense, all other natural forms have separated, and in this thought we discover his profound relationship to the kingdoms of nature.

At first sight this difficult thinking seems to take us far from the practical problems of animal welfare. It does, however, give us the basis for the new and, I believe, true view of the animals and from it will flow new love and sympathy through an understanding how man is closely related to the animal kingdom.

To repeat, Man, in Idea, was there from the beginning and all was included in this archetype of Divine Imagining. The animal species may be seen as aspects of the whole which chose to hurry into incarnation and specialize themselves as vehicles for certain desires and instincts. Every animal can be seen as a specialization of some organ of the human body, with an accompanying distortion of the balanced pattern of the whole.

Thus in the bird the face has been drawn forward into that superb tool the beak, beautiful in its functioning but extraordinary when seen as a distortion of the primal pattern. The claw is a wonderful tool in comparison with which the hand appears as an embryonic, almost baby, organ. Here is our clue. Man has managed to hold back from specialization and thereby kept close to the archetype. Therefore he alone is fit to receive the incarnation of the spiritual ego. This Being can then use the body, as the perfectable tool of Spirit and Thought. The hand thus can be developed to infinite skill in making and using tools by the very fact that it has not specialized. The cow is the digestive system set into an earth form. Its whole nature is developed so that it may placidly spend its entire time breaking down grass that it may turn into humus. Contemplate the great inward-looking eye of the 'ruminant' as it 'ruminates' and compare it with the royal flashing of the eagle's eye, perfected as a hunting tool. Consider the elephant. Surely here the idea of nose and upper lip have been developed with an organ of extraordinary sensitivity, and with it the upper teeth have been specialized into the strength and beauty of ivory tusks. In comparison with these organs the rest of the huge elephant body seems somewhat clumsy as if it were an unfinished job! Snakes and worms are like the guts, made into independent creatures. So every organ can be seen as the basis of an animal species. Find the organ that compares to the species and you have the basis for the new zoology. Man is a symphony of the whole created world. The animal world is the human organs spread out over the face of the earth and perfected into specialized functioning. The body is all the animal kingdom.

The being who managed to hold back in evolution and therefore remain nearest to the archetypal idea is the one which can receive the incarnating ego and soul. The animals, whatever their degree of individual intelligence, are not egos in the sense that each man is an ego. Rather must we recognise that each whole species is the expression of an exalted being, the group ego, who does not actually come into incarnation but works through the instincts of each single animal.

Most of the animals have developed skins which, in their many variants, are more or less loose casings to the body. Hair or scales, spines or armour, they all serve the special function of the species. Human skin alone allows the blood, the carrier of the ego, to shine through. It is an organ in which inner and outer meet and, thus it becomes a vehicle for soul expression, revealing emotion in blushing or blanching. The human face can smile and radiate light or express agony of soul as can no other creature. So also, for man the conscious ego, the arms have become means of gesture. Lifted out of gravity, they are free to wield all implements with intelligence or to convey the feelings and meanings of the actor. Thus the human organism and countenance, pliable and infinitely adaptable, can express the divinity of soul within him and become a channel for the world of art. The human head, furthermore, is lifted right out of gravity, whereas the animal head, terminal to a horizontal spine, is always bound by gravity.

Thus man can open his thinking to the higher worlds. The very shape of the head has maintained its cosmic roundness of form. At the other pole the human leg, alone among the higher animals, is given over wholly to gravity. Even the leaping jaguar in his splendour cannot straighten his hind leg into the earth. Thus Man alone can truly dance. This may be parodied in the animal circus but no other earthly being could produce ballet. Hence man, standing vertical, presents the true and perfectly balanced channel between earth and heaven.

Now if this be truly seen, can we honestly think that man has evolved out of the ape? The thought is not really thinkable. Rather we must see in the ape a creature who nearly achieved manhood, who just failed to 'hold it' long enough to become man, who allowed himself to fall into specialization and hardening just too soon. In this light there is something almost pathetic in his nearness to man. The head of a young chimpanzee is strangely like that of a human baby. The brow is finely rounded, the lower jaw in human proportion, but in the first growing year he appears to fall back, age rapidly as the forehead recedes and the jaw thrusts forward to become typical ape. It leaves us with a sense of pity. You cannot honestly 'think' an ape into a man, but you can think a falling away from man downwards into the ape. What is 'thinkable', in this sense, is probably a clue to finding out truth.

162

This brings us to a tremendous step in our thinking. It becomes ever clearer that the primal human form was creation's first handiwork and that animals represent physically fixed deviations in the direction of some limited specialization. Man is nature's first-born child and he stays human just because, in the long story of evolution, he finds it possible to hold in check those impulses that lead to the modelling of the various animal forms. A helpful image here is that of a balloonist floating over the ocean, who keeps losing height and is threatened with submersion. To avert disaster he throws out ballast so as to remain in the air long enough to get to land. In the same way man, faced with the danger of premature hardening, threw the animal kingdom out of his being. Thus he rid himself of a large part of his instincts, passions and desires, which then incarnated in the shape of beasts. The hyena nature, the wolf nature, has to be overcome in order that we may become truly man. Legend tells us that the horse is the last to leave the archetype enabling man to step forward into conscious intelligence.

Hence perhaps the great bond that exists between man and horse. Here also may be the meaning of the victorious battle between men and centaurs. We owe to the animals our development into human beings. This must be seen not merely as a mythological imagination but a real truth when evolution is considered from a spiritual viewpoint. It gives us a clue to many symbols in mythology. It may throw light on the enigma of the Sphinx, half lion, half man.

Not for a moment does this imply that the nature and instincts of any animal are not noble in their right setting. Even scavenger hyena is doing a very necessary job. But when lower animal instincts are still rampant in the human soul they delay development and progress. Modern myths like Orwell's *Animal Farm* indicate the way man may go, and Ben Jonson's *Valpone* is a Renaissance imagination of the fox in man taking control.

We can see man now at a turning point. In his developed free-will he can chose to reunite with the divinity within him, lifting himself towards union with his spiritual self, so as to evolve towards higher manhood. If he does not do this he may descend into a new animality, a bestiality which will have none of the nobility and splendour of animal instincts functioning in their rightful sphere. This would be the New Fall. Man could degenerate into extremes of sensuality or, more horrible, we may be beginning to see human beings appearing all will and intellect but without heart, soul-less creatures capable of every cruelty in their lust for power. These are distortions of the human archetype within living man, very different from the specialized incarnation of its aspects in the animal species. There is something especially bestial about the revival of torture in our self-conscious days after a century of humanitarian thinking.

Man ever dominated the creative plan as an archetypal spiritual form. This becomes clearer the more we open ourselves to the thought that man and earth with its animals, flowers and rocks, are a single indivisible community, that nature's kingdoms are part of our very being, genetically linked with us, belonging to us in mutual dependence. Thus, morally speaking, we are responsible for them. To feel deep obligation to redeem them is not sentimental, for they fell in order that we might rise to human stature.

Now how does all this relate to problems of animal welfare? In this way. So long as we do not feel we have any real relationship to the animals, we may feel justified in treating them with indifference, as machines or means of profit, or as objects for cruel experiment. When we, even dimly, grasp that in the broad view they are part of our nature, and that only by their sacrifice have we risen to true manhood, then we look on them with new vision and new love. Dumbly they look at us, often with fear in their eyes. Here is soul-quality set into limitation for our sakes. We owe them the ultimate debt of gratitude for enabling us to become man. Furthermore we are all together in a great process of redemption of the earth. As man strives to rise to understanding of the spirit, he can lift the animal and natural kingdoms with him. The very purpose of life on earth is that a being of free-will can rise consciously towards Divinity. If his life on earth is dependent on the sacrifice of beings into the forms of attendant nature, then he in return must by love and service lift these creatures back towards the divine. A new love floods towards the animals. As the great vision of Man awakens in us, it becomes simply impossible to maltreat an animal since all life becomes sacred. This view is seen not as so much sentiment but as the absolutely essential step which human consciousness must take if it is to progress towards the Light.

In this present spiritual crisis in human history at the opening of the Aquarian age, man will find that progress of soul and spirit is debarred to him if he chooses to ignore and degrade, maltreat and exploit the animals. This is not to say that he is not to use them and collaborate with them. While we are in matter we must use and develop it to the Glory of God. What is essential is a true attitude towards the living whole, so that we may develop towards a higher manhood through recognising our kinship to all life. Every deed which furthers animal welfare is part of a great redemption now taking place on the earth in which man, in co-operation with the forces of Light and Love, has the opportunity to repay his debt to nature and the animal kingdom. It is not unrealistic to think big thoughts. Without them, we shall not arrive at true understanding.

18

THE POLLUTED PLANET
AND THE LIVING SPIRIT

SPACESHIP EARTH, let us admit it, is in a bad way, and it is we men who have upset the balance. It seemed to us that the resources were infinite. Now we wake up, aghast, to the fact that we are using up 'capital' at an alarming rate. We are using up the world and polluting it into the bargain. We are becoming aware of this sinister fact and have seen the 'writing on the wall'.

The purely materialistic view of life is having to acknowledge apparently insurmountable problems. Yet against this outlook stands what can be called a spiritual world-view which emerges in our time and is bringing to many people a sense of mounting optimism about man's future. This view sees that the universe is shot through with living Creative Intelligence and Being. Creative Spirit is seen as the origin of all things, and from it the material world is derived. We recognise the reality of a great oneness of Absolute Being which has divided its unity into hierarchical levels of being. These provide the archetypal ideas from which the material world has been poured into manifestation. 'In the beginning was the Word …'

So many people tacitly assume that matter is the primary reality and that the universe is a dead mechanism. Now into our consciousness floods the opposite view that spirit is primary and that the great Oneness interpenetrates the temporal world in all its diversity.

This basic hypothesis can obviously be applied to any aspect of life. So let us now look at the great threat of our age – pollution – in the light of the spiritual world-view.

The astronaut Edgar Mitchell described his experience of seeing Earth again as he emerged from passing behind the moon:

> There have been few of us privileged to experience the mystical and soul-rending feeling of floating through endless space and looking back to see home, the beautiful jewel of earth. After months, and years of perfecting and testing an immense system of man and machine which would place me there in space – all of that was but a foreshadowing of my realisation of the place man has in the scheme of the universe. We are part of a universe of consciousness. I sensed this out in space. I devote my life to the discovery of what this means for me and for all humankind.

We can also, more simply but quite validly, explore space by reaching up in imaginative meditation. In inner stillness lift the consciousness above the atmosphere of earth. Move up, into the velvet darkness of the sky beneath the 'majestical roof fretted with golden fire' and, floating in orbit beyond the pull of gravity, look down upon the turning earth in its beauty. It is not difficult to feel its organic life. See it as a creature of the cosmos, an organism imbued with life. Conceive it as a living Whole, capable of inhaling and exhaling the life forces and energies of space, with a bloodstream of magnetic and etheric currents, and points of power and light like glands in its surface. Every cell has its core of energy and spirit, and the whole earth has its consciousness and is full of being. Yet in the layer of highly evolved consciousness which surrounds it, that 'centre that we call the race of men', evolution has become conscious of itself. Mind in man responds to Mind in the universe and has been brought into being by it. We men, integrally part of our Mother Earth, are her thought organ. Mankind has reached that stage in evolution when consciousness can be expanded so that thought blends with the higher intelligence. This is what, in our small way, we are approaching in meditation and creative imagining. Indeed it seems unlikely that we can imagine anything which does not on some level already exist as a precipitation of Divine Imagining.

Thus we can as a mental exercise create a higher plane. In our tenuous subtle body we can walk in a landscape of equally tenuous substance, beautiful and light filled. In meditation we move in those regions which the soul visits in sleep and in which it sojourns after death. Space is filled with an infinite number of levels of Being and Consciousness, all interpenetrating. 'In my Fathers house are many mansions'. To conceive it in this imaginative way starts us with the vision of Earth as an organism within ever greater organisms and the Whole alive. Everything is spirit in different conditions of density. Space exploration in our Space Age need not only be in rockets but can be through lifted consciousness across the frequency bands.

Now from the viewpoint of a spiritual being look down upon Earth. What is going wrong? Why is it so dark? Why can the higher worlds no longer make contact? Because man in his intellectual development of the last centuries has cut himself off from the Whole to which he truly belongs. He has lost all knowledge of the reality of higher worlds and of the hierarchy of planes of Being. He has lost Spirit and God. Thus the planet to our watching has become dark and silent. Intellectual, self-conscious, self-sufficient man has lost all sense for his real purpose on Earth. Cut off from his spiritual source, satisfied with the brilliance of his investigations into physical nature, he becomes a denier of the spirit and believes the universe to be a vast dead mechanism. Conceiving himself to be a chance accident in evolution, he feels entitled for his own advantage to exploit what he deems to be the dead mineral body of earth. He has lost all sense that this is his Mother Earth, an ensouled creature, and that he is part of it, as a blood corpuscle is integrally part of an organism. Failing to apprehend the miracle of interrelatedness in the complex balance of all nature, he rapes the earth in his greed and ignorance and arrogance.

Looking down from our spiritual heights we can experience the marvellous harmony of earth life. We can see the incredible complexity of the pattern and how in all its diversity it is a working unity, delicately poised in its constant movement. It has been said that Earth is a planet of Wisdom, and that it is the task of man in the coming epoch to turn it into a planet of Love. When we compare the chaos of our emotional life with the beauty of the working of natural law, we must admit we have a long way to go! We can see how man is integrally part of the one-ness of nature, yet we watch him acting as if he were completely alien in a nature wholly indifferent to him. We watch him polluting air and water and soil and recklessly planning to release radiations which he will never be able to control, yet which he knows may do irreparable damage to life.

From our high viewpoint, a spiritual being among other beings, we know by direct vision that the harmony of the complex life pattern on Earth is not an isolated phenomenon but is part of the life structure of energies in the cosmos. The whole solar system is a spiritual organism. From the galaxies energies can be released which are instilled with intelligence and with love. We can therefore sense that a man-made catastrophe upon Earth would be retrograde for the cosmic life. Man we know as a great experiment of the Divine World, a project for developing a spiritual being who can carry the responsibility of free will and evolve into a co-creator and friend of God. And now we watch with anxiety lest, so near his goal, he destroys himself, unable to pass beyond his egoistical greed. We see the culmination of an epoch, now that the step into widening consciousness is possible. Individual men begin to recognise their true spiritual nature and to strive towards union with their higher selves. As this happens and the cry for help and contact with spirit rises upward, the darkened planet begins again to glow in points and centres devoted to meditation and the glorifying of God. Through such centres the power of the living spirit can be earthed. Their light amounts to an invocation to the redemptive forces of Light.

We can grasp the idea that the High Intelligences of the universe are working for the harmony of all life, and will not tolerate the condition of an errant Earth full of discord, hatred and negative emotion. Therefore there is the readiness to make contact with man wherever and whenever he shows himself open and awake. Communications intuitively received from high sources of Intelligence indicate that energies are indeed being released, and could lift and transform individual consciousness and vitalize a society built on values of harmony and love. It appears that 'Operation Earth' has been launched, but its success depends on man's awakening to the infinite creative strength which would follow on his blending of thought with the higher intelligence. Furthermore, if we can accept the evidence for continuing consciousness and individuality after so called 'death', we shall realise that our friends who were concerned with the movement for conservation while on earth will still be capable of throwing their weight into the rescue operation from the 'Beyond', through telepathic influence on our thinking. This factor must be remembered. The work continues from both planes and the whole movement is strengthened when some influential figure moves on to operate from a level of widened consciousness.

In facing the problems of pollution let us never lose sight of Earth's place as a living organism in a living universe. The new science of ecology comes to explore the intricate balance of life. Here intellectual understanding begins to grasp how it works as one in all its complex diversity. The ecologists reveal to us the appalling things we are doing to the planet. We need not describe them here. Read Rattray Taylor's *The Doomsday Book*. As a leading ecologist he shows in terms we all can understand how easily the delicate balance of life and atmosphere can be disturbed. He shows for instance how we might bring down upon ourselves a 'heat death' which would turn temperate Europe into an arid desert, that is if we have not brought down a new ice-age. Either is easily possible, and within the life span of our children. As he warns us, the book reads like a horror story.

The ecologists know that our salvation lies in learning how to *think wholeness*. But this we are not yet trained to do. Technology is quite incapable of doing so, for it is not in its nature. If a new invention can be launched, it must go ahead. If a new machine can fly faster, fly it must. Economics cannot think wholeness. The test of worth is whether a thing pays; so long as profit is the primary value, the mind cannot turn to wholeness. And anyway we have lived two centuries of intellectual rationalism and have got so imbued with the experience of separation that the very concept of 'the One' is an alien metaphysic.

How then do we think into Wholeness? Who is qualified to do so? The answer is given in those who have achieved initiation into higher knowledge, whose intuition has been so developed that, as seers and sensitives, they can blend thinking with the world processes and thereby expand consciousness to become one with the widths of spirit. This is a new quality of human thinking which can speak directly from the Whole. It speaks not about the spirit but from the spirit through direct experience. Thus this higher knowledge can provide a genuine touchstone as to what we may or may not do to the living planet. It is known that certain sensitives in this country, at the time of the first high-altitude nuclear tests, cabled the President of the United States to warn him that by rending the etheric envelope of the atmosphere we should allow the entry not only of radiations dangerous to life but also of dark and evil beings who could attack the very soul of man. Thus we can foresee that there should be co-operation between the leading ecologists and the mystics who can supplement scientific discoveries with spiritual investigation. This could give a measure as to how far we dare go in our treatment of the living Earth. Meditation is thus seen as an adjunct to science of paramount importance if our planet is to be saved.

We have tried to conceive the Earth as a sentient being, a living organism. We have seen what man, in search of profit, has done to it. He is polluting the rivers, lakes and seas, filling air with noxious fumes, recklessly destroying the tree cover, poisoning the soil and damaging the life cycle of the plant world by his blind use of chemical fertilizers and pesticides. Is it not likely that the Living Earth will hit back in retribution? How long will this great being tolerate the rape by the leading repository of intelligence on her surface? For man who was given the task of stewardship has shown instead his greed and ignorance.

To quote one paragraph from Dr. Schumacher's most important and readable book, *Small is Beautiful*:

> The continuation of scientific advance in the direction of ever increasing violence, culminating in nuclear fission and moving on to nuclear fusion, is a prospect of terror threatening the abolition of man. Yet it is not written in the stars that this must be the direction. There is, also a life-giving and life enhancing possibility, the conscious exploration and cultivation of all relatively non-violent, harmonious organic methods of co-operating with that enormous, wonderful incomprehensible system of God-given nature, of which we are a part and which we certainly have not made ourselves.

We men are violating the living body of the Earth to which we belong and she is writhing under the treatment. But earth is also part of a universe of living pulsating energies imbued with life. The Whole is a great spiritual organism. We men are not each an isolated mind but are a pulse of the universal mind experiencing the illusion of separation. Here is the factor we are ignoring in all our thinking. Communications from the higher intelligences warn us that we shall never solve our problems if we continue to think of the earth as an isolated unit in a huge dead mechanism of the universe. It is an integral and important facet of the greater pattern of consciousness and there are energies now released which can assuredly redeem the pollution we have caused. It is likely that we have gone so far in our evil and ignorant ways that even if we repent (the Greek word is *metanoia* which means 'change your thinking') we shall not be able without the help of higher power to redeem the damage. But that power exists and is alerted. Herein lies the tremendous hope.

Read Roberto Vacca's book *The Coming Dark Age*. It shows the quite appalling catastrophes that loom ahead and are inevitable if present trends continue unchecked. Yet we can at the same time hope for the coming of a new age. It may be a 'near run thing', as Wellington said of Waterloo. God seems to play the game of 'brinkmanship'. There is still just time, if we can learn collaboration with these energies of the Light.

Conceive them pouring invisibly over and around and through us. They are backed by the vitality of the Creative Source. They are alive and intelligent and filled with Love. Resisted, they could sweep away obstacles like a river in flood. Where accepted through the instrument designed for their operation, namely man, they will bring vision and creative power,

In other words the old society and the old methods may simply be losing vitality. They may simply run down, deteriorate and die away. As this happens the 'new' will manifest, precipitated into form by universal impulses working for harmony. It would seem axiomatic that there must be ample energy to meet human needs, energies connected with the spiritual sun and therefore not carrying the desperate dangers of nuclear power. We are in an energy crisis, yet it contains this new vital factor. These new and saving energies may prove to be working in close affinity to the Creative Intelligence of the universe. If, therefore, we were to use them for selfish greed, financial profit or war, it could lead to further chaos through the Creative Intelligence withdrawing the influence and refusing to co-operate.

Here is a strange possibility that we need to face. We may simply be compelled to admit that spiritual forces and beings are involved and are a reality. If and when these changes begin, it may be necessary to explain to a bewildered public what is happening. Television may here be important and top political authority may have to speak out and admit that it recognises the reality of beneficent spiritual powers from outside the planet. A revolution in thinking could rapidly come about as soon as events begin to take place which cannot be explained away 'rationally', for we must remember that living ideas are continually pene-trating our minds and breaking down the barriers of resistance so that ever more people will find themselves ready to accept a new and spiritual vision.

This picture is not one of blind optimism which chooses to ignore present trends and assume that all is well. It must indeed recognise the appalling and almost unthinkable calamities which could overtake us if the present structure breaks down. Yet we have the assurance from high sources that though catastrophes come, the in-flooding of the transforming vitalizing energies of the new age will follow quickly. 'Operation Earth' is perfectly timed and all is known. The great hope lies in the concept of a 'Higher Command' working for universal harmony. There never was such a drama. It is indeed a living saga or myth in which we are all involved and have our role to play. So bad are the present prospects that we must strive to 'think wholeness' in order that the ignored factor may be understood and our forgotten and invisible allies brought into full operation. 'Look up, for your salvation draweth nigh'.

For since by man came pollution, through man must come the redemption from pollution. Man is the bridge between the two worlds, material and spiritual. Since he is the point of self-consciousness in the body of earth, he must be the instrument to channel the cleansing power of earth, he must be the instrument to channel the cleansing power of the Light. Since he has freedom of choice it is for him to decide whether that power shall flow. A re-orientation of attitude within man opens the floodgates. First he sees his position in the very soul of the Cosmos. Then he takes on himself the task of involving the high energies of the forces of Light. There must be no false modesty arising from our sense of inadequacy. With humility we must accept the responsibility of calling on the creative intelligence. The initiative is with man. Nor does it need an enormous number of men. We are watching the diffusing of a living energy which instantly permeates the whole organism of Earth, like an injection into the blood stream. There must, as at the fall of Sodom, be a sufficient number of dedicated groups and individuals.

We are concerned with an impulse from the spiritual sun which can transmute and activate every cell. We give the name of the Cosmic Christ to this power, which can *be* in the whole universe and at the same time within the core of each atom. Surely this is the power of the Solar Logos which in nuclear fission we release in a downward direction in uncontrolled destruction. If we could but tap it creatively by lifting consciousness into its supernal field, then that which is polluted could be

175

redeemed. Mary Fullerson, in her inspired book, *The Form of the Fourth*, suggests that risen thinking will enable the individual man so to enter and accept the fire of the spirit that physical cells will be transformed and we shall be able to move untouched through a polluted environment. Techniques of cleansing and catharsis prepare a man to receive this 'ordeal by fire'. So also it must follow that the Christ power could, by Divine dispensation, enter the very heart of matter to transmute and cleanse polluted earth, air and water by molecular change.

Through human agency pollution is destroying the life on the planet. It is as if there were an anti-life impulse, a diabolical influence using the human instrument to undermine the harmonious unity of life on earth. The chief spur is obviously greed and the insatiable passion for big profits. This is bound to be, so long as the primary motive for action is assumed to be economic gain. Thus truth is being constantly sacrificed to economic advantage. This implies a most sinister pollution of mind and character. The satanic forces do battle with the Living Christ on every level. Our pollution problems must be tackled positively in that we must stop doing the things which threaten life, but we must also include in our planning, as a perfectly realistic and practical process, the channelling of the Christ Light and Love into the body of the Earth. Thus we initiate a chain reaction of healing against which the decaying forces of pollution and death will not be able to stand. It is with this vision and backed by this Power that we must take our stand against the practices causing pollution.

Organic husbandry has recognised that the soil is a very complex living organism, and that there is a cycle of life in plant growth from seed through leaf and flower and back to humus and new seed. This cycle is broken and ignored when artificial fertilizers are used, with resultant danger of lowering soil fertility. Going further than the teachings of the Soil Association is the recognition that elemental beings and nature spirits are indeed a reality. What our Celtic forebears knew as the 'little people' represent forces of living and creative intelligence working in the plants. The 'devas' appear to be angelic beings who are in effect the architects of plant design, and the nature spirits are the 'craftsmen' working to fulfil the life cycle in individual plants. Modern clairvoyance rediscovers the reality of the elemental world in nature and it appears that we no longer dare to leave this factor out of account.

Is it purely fanciful in these serious days to speak again of the nature spirits? A single example may be taken in answer to this question. At Findhorn in Morayshire a remarkable experiment in co-operation between man and the invisible worlds has been undertaken.[1] Findhorn is a new age community in which all aspects of life are dedicated to serving the Divine will and purpose. At its inception a dozen years ago, Peter Caddy, the founder and custodian of this now large and flourishing community, settled on a caravan site in barren wind-swept sand-dunes which could grow only spiky grass and pine trees. His wife is a very remarkable sensitive and with him also was a friend with developed powers of clairaudience.

They had 'guidance' that they must start growing vegetables, an apparently almost absurd task on such ground and with no experience of gardening. So they turned and asked the devas for help and Dorothy got a clear and instant telepathic response. Following this lead they went into action. In three years a thriving garden of glorious flowers, magnificent vegetables and many broad leaved trees and shrubs was growing. The sandy waste is now completely transformed and the garden is of outstanding beauty. The quality of vegetables and plants is unsurpassable. In those early years there was no explanation as to how it had happened except the claim of co-operation with the nature spirits. No artificial fertilizers were used. Soil experts with long experience of organic husbandry looked into it and declared that compost alone in such a setting in so short a time could not have brought about the transformation. The phenomenon simply cannot be explained away.

The implications are of profound importance. In one of the devic messages the phrase was used about Findhorn that 'one

1 See *The Findhorn Garden Story*, Findhorn Trust, Forres, Morayshire.

garden can save a world'. The whole unified field of consciousness of the nature spirits knew at once that a group of men had
made contact and was willing to co-operate with them. Man
working with the nature beings could truly turn the deserts into
blossoming gardens and overcome the pollution of the planet.
This fantastic adventure is open to us. Clearly it needs spiritual
vision united with science and practical skill to take the step. The
way was indicated in Steiner's Biodynamic system of horticulture
and agriculture, and now recent researches in America have given
scientific demonstration of an astonishing sensitivity in plants,
hitherto not conceived. The remarkable and enthralling book
The Secret Life of Plants by Peter Tompkins and Christopher Bird,
surveys all these developments. Thus if we're to feed mankind
on food which maintains vitality and quality it looks as if
co-operation with the spiritual worlds may prove a first essential.

There is something fabulous about this new vision of our
relation to the plants. It is as if a new realm of subtlety is
opening up. Human thinking and emotion seems integrally linked
with the plant world, and these new findings suggest how
terribly crude have been so many of our dealings with nature.
We have thought we were battling to conquer nature. Now we
begin to see that we are ourselves part of its delicate complex,
and are intimately connected with all its kingdoms. In the
'onlooker consciousness' of our intellectual age, we have thought
man to be a chance accident in a world of nature wholly
indifferent to him. Now, with the discovery of the etheric field
of vital forces working within every form as a complex unity we
find that we are a responsible factor in the working of the whole.
On a deeper level the entire sweep of evolution, is reflected and
experienced in us.

So too with our relations to the animal kingdom. We now
begin to see that the archetype of man was there from the very
beginning as a Divine Idea and that it is reflected throughout the
whole animal world, as if every species is a facet of the human
organism specialised in adaptation to environment. In this sense
man has risen to his true manhood through the sacrifice of the
animals. In the larger and more spiritual view they are us and we

them. Our present treatment of animals stands as a karmic blot in human evolution and until this debt is paid the spiritual advance of man will be impeded.

The Earth is polluted by us, physically, morally and mentally, for man uprooted from his spiritual background is a creature of violence, smashing his subtle environment to satisfy his desires and passions. So he thinks himself at war with nature.

We began this essay with an imaginative picture of the earth from a viewpoint in the cosmos. Let us return to this. Intuitive communications through friends in the Beyond tell us that an etheric mantle of light is being gathered around the Earth from the finer and purer vibrations of the cosmos. 'And I saw a new Heaven and a new Earth'. This field of subtle life-filled force is to impregnate the whole earth and the Spirit of Earth rises to meet it. As the event happens human consciousness, as an inseparable factor in the earth consciousness, will inevitably be lifted towards another dimension, and then there will be a blending in thought between those on both planes (embodied or disembodied) who are linked by the greater love. We are urged that there is no time to lose, since this extraordinary process is apparently happening now and the inconceivable blending of the timeless with time is taking place. In other words the polluted world is being cleansed on the etheric level and every man, in his freedom of choice, is invited to be a part of the event. Teilhard expresses this in his experience of the Mass on the World in 'Hymn of the Universe':

> It is done. Once again the Fire has penetrated the earth ... the flame has lit up the whole world from within. All things individually and collectively are penetrated and flooded by it, from the inmost core of the tiniest atom to the mighty sweep of the most universal laws of being; so naturally has it flooded every element, every energy, every connecting link in the unity of our cosmos, that one might suppose the cosmos to have burst spontaneously into flame.

Is this picture just so much poetic fantasy? Perhaps so ... and perhaps not. A 'wild hope' (in Teilhard's phrase) 'that our earth is to be recast'?

To summarise all this very briefly: To overcome pollution in all its aspects the Christ energies from the Cosmos must flow into the body of the Whole Earth as well as into the bodies and souls of man. And man himself is the necessary link and instrument which will make all this possible. This redemptive flow has already begun and its working is apparent to those who are perceptive. Ultimately nothing can stand against it.

19

THE NEW PILGRIMAGE

PILGRIMAGE – a new concept of modern pilgrimage seems to be emerging and it may prove to be of deep significance for the spiritual awakening in our time. In mediaeval centuries hundreds of thousands of pilgrims streamed between the holy centres and shrines. What was the motive for this extraordinary phenomenon? Across all European frontiers they came, walking or riding, like Chaucer's Canterbury Pilgrims, along established routes to reach a centre made sacred by the relics of some saint. Thus, the hope was to get healing of bodily ills and salvation of soul by actually going to a holy spot to pray and to give alms to the monastery or cathedral. In the Age of Faith, many were still actively aware of the Guardian Beings, the Angelic Presences of the Shrine. To them, the pilgrims came in mood of worship and of wonder.

We may imagine a holy man settling as a hermit in his hut, built on a spot in which he found he could make the break-through in consciousness to the Higher Worlds. After his death, a shrine or chapel is built and, since healing power appears to be active, this may later become a church or cathedral, guarding the holy relics which are believed to have supernatural power. When the pilgrim stream grew, it brought wealth to the monastery or minster and it became the goal of penitent Christians to make a pilgrimage for salvation of their souls. Often such a journey would have been undertaken as a penance for wrong-doing. On the recognised routes, stages of the journey are marked by hostel-ries and churches. Thus, the great pilgrim route to Compostella has on it a wonderful series of Romanesque churches with

181

carvings which must have filled the pilgrims with wonder and delight. The serving and exploiting of the pilgrims became a source of profit for many, just as the tourist industry has grown up in our time. Canterbury and Chartres, Glastonbury and Rosslyn Chapel, Bourges and Vezeley, Durham and Lindisfarne, Mont St Michel and St Michael's Mount, Westminster and Ely – Europe is covered with a network of pilgrim routes. The steps to Becket's shrine in Canterbury are worn hollow by the knees of the innumerable pilgrims who had achieved their goal. And, of course, the ultimate pilgrimage was to the Holy Land and here the impulse grew into the Crusades.

With the change in consciousness marked by the Renaissance, the impulse to pilgrimage fades. In our time, once again, innumerable people stream through the churches. So many millions come to Westminster Abbey and Chartres that it becomes a problem of how to control and channel the flow. But what really on a deeper level is moving them all? Tourism has debased pilgrimage in an age which is largely agnostic and on the quest for pleasure and diversion. This is a picture of our state of consciousness. But that consciousness is undergoing the most notable change which is truly epoch-making in its significance.

The 'Holistic World-View' is emerging in our generation, a veritable reversal of the materialistic, mechanistic and reductionist picture of the universe discovered by our grandfathers. The materialistic interpretation of life is dissolving to give place to a revival of the Ancient Wisdom, which grasped that the Universe is an affair of Mind, a vast harmonious continuance of Thought poured out from the mind of the Creator. The Whole is Holy. It is something hugely more than the mere sum of its parts. It is alive – we must stretch our minds to conceive and experience a vast ocean of Life and Thought, of Love and Will, existing on an ethereal plane beyond time and filling all space. From this realm of Creative Idea, the physical world of matter and nature is expressed – pressed forth into form. Thus, the Earth is seen as a living organism with its own breathing and bloodstream, its glands and sensitivity and its own intelligence. Mankind, so far from being an accident in natural selection to whom nature is wholly indifferent, is seen as integrally part of Nature, the point where nature becomes self-conscious. Therefore, he is clearly the steward of the planet. Indeed, the human race is seen as one of the great experiments of God in evolving a being 'a little lower than the angels but crowned with glory and honour', who can learn to carry the divine gift of free-will and become in due time a co-creator with God. Thus, Earth appears as the training ground for the 10th Hierarchy. In Blake's words:

> We are set on Earth a little space
> That we may learn to bear the beams of love.

The Hermetic Wisdom recognised the basic Law of Correspondence: as above, so below. Microcosm reflects macrocosm. The human body is thus the microcosm, reflecting the greater organism, as every fragment in a broken holographic plate shows the entire picture in miniature.

You don't get a living organism floating around in a dead mechanism. Thus, the solar system is seen as a greater organism, the series of planets corresponding to the endocrine glands in our bodies. These glands relate to the Chakras or psychic centres through which living energies flow from the cosmos into the body.

Now our imagination grapples with the discoveries about ley-lines and centres of light and magnetic power in the earth. Dowsers can now research into the flow of earth energies. Alfred Watkins, first discoverer of ley-lines, thought them to be track-ways and had no adequate explanation of their purpose. Now we recognise that they can represent the lines of the living earth energies, linking centres of power. Grace Cooke, a clairvoyant and sensitive, in her book *The Light in Britain*, describes how she saw Avebury and Stonehenge as temples in which, by ancient ritual, spiritual light was stored, to flow in healing along the lines marked by standing stones. Truly, they compared to our electrical generating stations from which the power is carried to remote parts by the lines of pylons.

We grasp now the concept of a network of Light Centres covering the country like a grid. As Watkins showed and modern dowsing reveals, the Christian churches are constantly built on crossing points of ley-lines or other focal points of power. It would be fascinating to make a map of Britain showing the ancient sites and the Druidical centres placed upon them, then imagine this overlaid with a perspex sheet with all the Christian churches, cathedrals and monasteries marked on it, and see how often they overlay the pagan centres; then make another sheet of New Age centres and we should see how frequently the centres of the Alternative Life Style, springing up all over the country, actually fall on the points of light and power. Those who are dedicating their lives to New Age work seem frequently to be led by invisible guidance to settle on significant spots where the energy flows.

Indications have been given from the High Sources that we are called on to do all we can to strengthen this grid of Light. We all foresee the coming of moments of great tension in the Armageddon battle between the forces of darkness (the Beast of the Apocalypse) and the Heavenly Powers of the Archangel Michael. The supreme hope which can fire all our hearts with courage is that, in the moment of ultimate tension, there may be an inflooding of the power of the Living Christ. Light could be poured through human souls and bodies. Those who reject it will be battered and overwhelmed by it. Those who can open their hearts and attune to the angelic energies will be lifted with strength and joy. It is something of a science fiction picture – but why not? The alternative is a nuclear holocaust which, to say the least, is sensational!

The implication is that the grid of light centres, power points and holy mountains may be used for flooding spiritual light with transforming power through the whole country. If Nature is to receive this inflow of energy – raising the very frequency rate within all matter – then obviously the chief channel of inflow will be that point in Nature which has become self-conscious, namely MAN. The human heart can receive the inflow of Divine power. Earth energies may be activated in a cleansing operation to de-pollute the planet.

Now we see the meaning of the New Pilgrimage. Since Mankind has been given free will, it is certain that the Heaven

184

World will not interfere and take over to the detriment of human freedom. Disasters still leave us free, and may be necessary if we do not wake up and change our evil ways. But if a sufficient number of human beings can see what is happening and consciously attune to the forces of the Living Christ and His Regent, Michael, then the great Operation Redemption can fulfil its purpose.

We are called on now to devise ways of linking and activating the dormant light centres, each of which has its angelic guardians. Let us go not merely as tourists, but as Pilgrims, recognising a conscious task of preparing the way for the inflooding of the Light when the great moment comes. Whenever we enter a shrine, church or holy place, we should greet its Guardian and pray for the incoming of the Healing Light. Simple rituals of perambulation, poetry, candlelight, dance and music may be devised where appropriate (respecting the feelings and convenience of other tourists). New rituals can validly be invented. They will often be given to us, born in our minds with a strange certainty, since they come from our higher self or the angels who speak with the still, small voice within our own thinking. As we leave the place, we should always give thanks and blessings to the Guardian. As we travel the countryside we should make our journey into a conscious pilgrimage. We are integrally part of Nature and the Being of the Earth and, when we rejoice in the beauty of scenery, we are Nature herself coming awake. All life becomes poetry and the Earth herself is not quite the same after we have journeyed over her in this pilgrim mood. We are part of the Awakening.

Thus, we are rediscovering the holy mountains and the landscape temples. By 'temple', we mean a structure which enables a Divine Being to operate in the heavier density of the Earth plane. Thus, the Greek temple was a point where Apollo or Athena could touch down without being contaminated by the coarseness of matter. The Egyptian temple has clearly the same pattern of chakras as is found in the human body, and the same is true in the Gothic cathedral: microcosm and macrocosm again. We see that the human body with its psychic centres is truly a temple into which the Divine Spark of the immortal, imperishable Ego can descend to operate with creative Will on earth.

So we begin to discover and explore the landscape temple, etheric structures which manifest the same pattern of base centres, solar plexus, heart, throat, brow and crown centres. These are not man-made structures but antedate man, as part of the living organism of the earth. They may be great or small. Thus, Britain is a heart centre of the Earth, but London is a heart centre of Britain and many landscape temples may be a few miles long, lying along a ley line. They are visible to clairvoyant sensitivity which can see the inflow of Divine Angelic Light.

Here is a new field of exploration. It really means learning to work with the Energies of the Earth and it may have an important part to play in the coming changes. PILGRIMAGE here takes on a new and vital function. As we in our groups under-take pilgrimages with dedicated intent, we shall be establishing and encouraging the flow of healing light and power, and linking up the Grid of Light Centres, that it may be strong enough to hold the flow of the Christ Power when it comes sensitives can see the flow of energy in a cathedral. There are apparently definite lines of flow which can be detected by dowsers. If these can be consciously channelled, it would release spiritual power. Already we see signs of attempts to turn the stream of tourists into something of a pilgrimage. Think what it would mean if all the thousands who steam through Mont St Michel had taken on the conscious task. The breathtaking loveliness and wonder of Chartres, which often moves one to tears, comes very close to a real pilgrim impulse. It only needs a little change of emphasis to illumine the enthusiasm for art with a sense of the living and present reality of the Angelic Being, portrayed in stained glass and sculpture. The awakening of the spiritual worldview gives us this necessary vision and we may go to the great works of ancient art, knowing that they speak directly to the soul of the reality of Higher Worlds and the coming of the Christ Impulse anew in our time.

In our cathedrals we could easily invite people to feel themselves as pilgrims and follow the ancient routes within the building used by the pilgrims of mediaeval days. Already the attempt is being made to encourage meditation as we move around.

Consider how favourable is the climate of our time for a revival of Pilgrimage. There has been a wonderful impetus towards art and architectural history given since the war through the lead of the great art historians and the publication of beautiful books with modern photography. This is heightened by the development of tourist facilities and the delight of 'going places'. When these two factors link with the awakening vision of the spiritual nature of man and the universe, then 'Pilgrimage', in a real and true sense, must begin again.

This spiritual worldview calls for *interpretation*. In each of the great arts we discover that the Angelic Wisdom, expressing the great truth of Man's spiritual nature, has in its own symbolism told the story of his descent from the heavenly spheres into the struggles of Earth life. In Blake's phrase he has passed from Innocence through Experience to Imagination. All the arts will be re-interpreted and a new creative inspiration will come as men and women awaken to spiritual vision and, as we open to Fourth Dimension awareness, more and more people will begin to see the angelic beings in the holy centres. Already those in whom these faculties are awake begin to take guided tours to Greece and Egypt, the Holy Land and the great Cathedrals. The 'esoteric' tour is becoming a function with wonderful opportunities. It is a true aspect of the revival of Pilgrimage.

But more than this, we enter the last two decades of the twentieth century and stand on the threshold of the Aquarian Age, when energies for the cleansing of the planet are flooding through the Earth. It is a dramatic time, an Apocalyptic time. We all know that if mankind continues in his folly, greed and ignorance, that the living Earth, of which he is the errant steward, will react against him in earth changes, earthquakes, storms and floods. Faulty thinking is a factor in causing these great disturbances which threaten us.

If mankind is to survive as a species, he must learn to work with Gaia, the Goddess of Earth. The human race, integrally part of Nature, is an aspect of the consciousness of the living Being of the Planet. At present, industrial man is 'bleeding' the Earth of her living energy and heart by massive entropy. (See Kit Pedler's remarkable book *The Quest for Gaia*.) The alternative lifestyle now emerging on a wide front represents the many movements working for conservation, for harmony of all life and for a new society, based not on competition and violence, but on co-operation. To take part in these activities calls for a love of Nature and a feeling for the kinship with all life as a great Oneness working in harmony. If, in addition, we are drawn to the great holistic concepts of the spiritual nature of man and the universe, we shall see that the New Pilgrimage is a vital factor in the very salvation of the Earth. We are making a constructive contribution to the cleansing and depolluting of the planet. Since human freewill must always be respected by the angelic beings in their operation for redemption of the planet, we may feel that conscious pilgrimage amounts to a form of invocation and prayer, attuning to the higher worlds and inviting the inflooding of the forces of Light. It serves a vital function in the coming time of change.

Bunyan's great hymn takes on greater meaning for us:

> He who would valiant be
> 'Gainst all disaster
> Let him in constancy
> Follow the Master.
> There's no discouragement
> Will make him once relent
> His first, avowed intent
> To be a Pilgrim.

20

TOWARDS AN ADULT EDUCATION
FOR THE SPIRIT

MY FIELD OF ACTION has been Adult Education – not merely further education or vocational education but the new and peculiarly English movement for the Short Term Residential Colleges. This is something much more exciting.

There was a wide realization after the war of a need for a new sort of Peoples' College to which everyone could come in a setting which could lift them out of hum-drum surroundings and in which peacetime values and interests could be revived. What better use for an English Country House? These houses had been centres for social life and culture for centuries, but for the upper class families. Why not make a metamorphosis of the country house party by devising short residential courses open to every-one from all walks of life?

This idea was pressed by the great educationalist Sir Richard Livingstone. I may modestly boast that I was fired by it even before the war and in 1936 toured the Scandinavian Folk High Schools to find their inspiration. Here the great Bishop Grundvig in the 1840s had seen that in the depressed and broken Denmark after the Napoleonic Wars there was need for a real revival of the Folk Soul of the country. So he devised colleges to which the young farmers were brought for five or six months to learn not farming, but Danish history, folklore and literature. He insisted on what he called the 'Doctrine of the Living Word'. Lecturers were forbidden to use notes. They must speak from the heart straight to the hearts of their students, and were free to shape their own curricula wherever their enthusiasm lay. It was a question of 'enlivenment' as well as 'enlightenment'. The result was that the young people went back as better Danes and therefore better farmers with a new sense of meaning to their lives.

For us it was not a question of copying the Folk High Schools, but of taking something of their original fire and inspiration. We in England had a unique possibility in using our country houses as residential centres running continuous programmes of short courses on every conceivable subject so as to stir people's imagination and awaken enthusiasm. This was a real and live movement and impulse in our adult education, and after the war some thirty colleges were founded with wardens or principals promoting and devising their own programmes.

I was greatly privileged to be appointed in 1947 as Warden to Attingham Park, the Shropshire Adult College, the fourth of the group to be founded and the finest of the houses, built in 1785. I nailed my flag to the mast on the concept of the country house used as a cultural centre, concentrating mostly on the 48 hour weekend course on every imaginable theme, with summer schools and midweek courses as well. The short course is a very important educational instrument in its own right, an opportunity to present integrating ideas which will illumine a subject.

In our Attingham programmes, offering weekends on every imaginable theme, I began to include such courses as 'The Expansion of Consciousness' or 'Death the Great Adventure' or 'The Quest for the Grail in Our Time' and found that there was an astonishing response. Here was clearly a field for adult education practically untapped. People responded to the need for recovering a sense of meaning to life. My governors were some- what suspicious of these spiritual courses, lest they drew a bad reaction from ratepayers! Was this valid academic education? But they assuredly packed the house and brought in necessary funds.

Looking back now I see that in the 1950s and 60s this series of courses really made history in the movement for spiritual awakening in Britain, for very many people working in this new field came together and met each other in this open setting which was not affiliated to any particular dogma or doctrine. So I saw the importance of an adult education concerned with the spiritual nature of man and the universe, presenting the general 'holistic' world view. Thus when I retired in 1971 I founded the Wrekin Trust to continue with this work, now free to come out in my true colours and concentrate all efforts on adult education for the spirit.

Here I might add to Grundvig's Doctrine of the Living Word what might be called 'the Doctrine of the Living Idea'. The Vision of Wholeness teaches us to see that this is indeed an ocean of Wisdom and Living Creative Thought and that Ideas are veritably living thought beings who long to engage themselves with human thinking and thus become operative on the material plane. This is why crude argument about things spiritual should always be avoided. It is like tearing a living flower or butterfly to pieces, and is very painful and profitless. A University of Light must indeed incorporate the Doctrines of the Living Word and the Living Idea.

In so far as we are dealing with spiritual beings and impulses in the form of adult education, the setting and presentation is of vital importance. Beings, whether human, angelic or elemental, need to lower their vibrations to come into co-operative contact with us and we must in response raise ours. Where the presentation is dull, heavy, over-cerebral, inartistic, overloaded, they will have to withdraw because of the painful density of the vibrations. We must take it as an absolute (and glorious) fact that, through telepathic contact our conferences dedicated to spiritual knowledge will draw many from the Planes of Light. This has been well born out by sensitives in our conferences. Thus we owe it to them, if we wish their co-operation and inspiration, to make the setting as gracious and beautiful as possible, and plan the programmes so that people are not jaded by over-intellectualism. Here again for this purpose the country house is perfect (though I must admit that after some conferences in bleak modern universities the very bricks have been vibrating and glowing with warmth and light by the end!). Thus such a setting as the Findhorn University Hall, bravely and beautifully decorated, offers a splendid channel for bridging the two worlds.

Inevitably in the achievement of building the Findhorn community the cultural side has to some degree had to lag behind the more practical and creative aspects. Now we come to a time when this should be made good. Here we can speak out of the vision of the Essenes, for in many ways Findhorn is comparable with an Essene community, and this impulse is very much alive today. The Essenes, through their life style and their daily communions with the Angels of the Heavenly Father and the Earthly Mother, achieved an extraordinary inner strength and harmony.

Their teachings and meditations culminated in the noon contemplations of the Sevenfold Peace – peace and harmony with the body, the mind, the emotions, with humanity, with culture, and with the Kingdoms of the Earth and Heaven. Their including of 'peace with culture' is of special interest to us. They say that the masterpieces of art and literature were inspired from the Ocean of Creative Wisdom and Being, channelled into form through the genius of master minds. On the eternal planes the thinking of these great ones still lives and they have crystallized something of their experience of the Divine One-ness into great drama or sculpture, architecture or painting, dance or poetry, myth, epic and fiction. If we could learn to resonate with their thinking we should lift consciousness on to these planes. The Essene peace, or harmony with culture, enabled the soul to attune to the thinking and feeling of the creators of the master-works.

Now such is the pressure of life and events nowadays that people have not got time to spend in much academic study of literature or the arts, yet we must admit that the Wisdom Tradition in the West has poured itself into the arts and is there to be found if we can get the clue and the right approach. Esoteric knowledge, driven underground as heresy, is enshrined in the symbolism of the great works. Symbols are many faceted: Truth never constrains. You are free to interpret on all levels, physical, psychological, spiritual. Thus in our time we need a new form of interpretation in the light of the spiritual world view. This would open vistas of new vision which would strengthen us in all that we are doing. The Romantic Movement in English painting and poetry – Blake, Turner, Wordsworth, Coleridge – is a channel for neo-platonic ideas, and through it we may understand what Keats meant by saying 'I am certain of nothing but the holiness of the hearts affection and the truth of imagination'.

We are all taking part in a spiritual awakening. We shall be greatly strengthened in receiving and handling this impulse if we can attune rightly to the arts and literature. The world picture of man's spiritual nature and the redemption of this planet is so tremendous that it cannot but express itself in new drama, new ballet, new painting, poetry and sculpture. And a new mythology, for the myths and legends and fairy stories were the way in which the spiritual truths were made acceptable to the general public who were not yet evolved to the stage of undertaking the initiations in the mystery temples.

Thus in Findhorn as it develops the Arts must play a great part and the University must include a new approach to study of the master works of culture. This will not be purely academic – there is not time for that. It will involve re-interpretation – of Shakespeare, Michaelangelo, Dante, Homer, Greek Myths, poetry, painting, history of architecture – in the light of the holistic world picture. The clue to history is that consciousness evolves, with everything else, and we are now watching and taking part in the greatest step forward into cosmic consciousness. Here the right lead is needed to help people in study, to select poems, guide reading, interpret paintings, show the development of architectural style as an image of evolving man. It could be immensely exciting. It has never really been done before, since the age of the logical intellect has put us over against things and forms as mere observers. This mostly holds good in the academic as well as the scientific fields. It is of the analysing intellect. Now we need to learn to blend in consciousness with the being within forms, re-awakening the faculties of the intuitive feminine right-hand hemisphere of the brain.

In time, perhaps soon, it will be recognised that here is a new and valid field of adult education, calling for a very different form of tutoring. Courses based on this 'Living Idea' thinking now just begin to be included in general adult education. In due course the Open University should become interested. It offers, to my mind, the clue for Findhorn's cultural effort. It does not involve a lot of academic study for which your dynamic activity leaves little time. It calls for an approach to the Arts and to Literature, beginning quite simply from where we all are, to learn how to go beyond the mere 'onlooker consciousness' and blend with the being behind and within the master works, and this should be a part of everyone's life.

Perhaps the clue lies in that remark of Whitehead, reminiscent of Plato:

> *Moral education* (i.e. true adult education) *is impossible without habitual vision of greatness.*

21

LIVING IDEAS IN
ADULT EDUCATION

I WRITE OUT OF the experience of twenty-three years as
Warden of Attingham in Shropshire, a centre for adult
education running short residential courses on very varied
themes and open to all. Attingham was founded in 1947 and was
among the first of a group of colleges, now numbering nearly
thirty. The movement of the Short Term Residential Colleges,
as they have come to be known, was one of the most fruitful
experiments in adult education after the war. It arose as a
spontaneous development, meeting a real need of which many
were aware in those years when we were striving to recover peacetime values. It was realised that there was a need for a new kind
of institution offering short residential courses from a weekend
to ten days in length, in surroundings which would lift people for
a brief spell out of the rush and worry of their ordinary lives,
allowing them time to plunge deeper into new interests.

Such 'People's Colleges' are a new and very English contribution to adult education. The essence is that the Warden is
responsible for the promotion of courses and the development
of the programmes and is therefore exploring in the field through
his personal inspiration and enthusiasm. Anyone is welcome, no
qualifications are asked for and no sort of credit is given. The
courses are therefore sheer education with no secondary motive
and this often sweeps away the customary English reserve against
showing enthusiasm. The colleges are united in developing
the idea of the short course, but each has very much his

own character. Some are closely associated with local authorities and some are independent. The nature of the house and setting, the local demands and possibilities and the leadership of the Warden and his team all develop the lively difference in the movement. Attingham, with its seventy beds, is among the largest of the colleges and is privileged to be in a most beautiful eighteenth century mansion. Perhaps it is nearest to the vision of the country house used in a new way in our changing society. The setting in fine architecture and parkland is of enormous importance.

It can be a rich experience for people to come together in a tranquil setting, there to meet a group of kindred spirits as a house party, all drawn by love of music, or history, archaeology or astronomy or whatever may be the theme of the course. All who have taken part have known the sense that time does something strange. Forty-eight hours seems to last for a week.

I had a lecturer who, on the Sunday morning, said, 'As we heard on the first Friday night ...' and then checked, realising that we had only been together for a day and a half. Naturally and rightly a large proportion of our weekend conferences are given to the liberal studies and the arts. This is particularly suitable for the country house setting; but there are also conferences which have definitely launched some line of thinking and action on important social problems. Attingham has on a number of occasions provided a gracious and neutral meeting ground for the protagonists in some contemporary issues.

Whitehead once wrote the phrase which could well have come from Plato: 'Moral Education is impossible without the habitual vision of greatness'. This could well be our motto for Adult Education in these days when so many standards are slithering. It is of vital importance to rest our minds on the great achievements of the human spirit in art, literature, history or heroic endeavour. This can be the real purpose of the short course.

THE SIGNIFICANCE OF THE SHORT COURSE

The longer we go on the more convinced am I that the short course in residence in a fine setting is something of supreme importance in our time. It is an instrument for education in its own right, not simply a watering down of university teaching. It is a powerful educational form if used rightly, and a form peculiarly adapted to the world we now live in. We are all in a hurry and under pressure in a society in which men and women are called upon to adjust at a pace never faced before. We are rapidly moving into a world society and problems must be met on a planetary scale. Human 'know how' is such that no problem is ultimately insolvable. Human intelligence is perfectly capable of feeding the world populations and transforming society.

Yet we are up against so many problems which if handled wrongly could lead to catastrophe. Hence the urgent need for thought provoking conferences and also for the cultural courses in which the mind can rest in something more permanent than current affairs and interests. As Yeats wrote:

> Caught in that temporal music all neglect
> Monuments of unageing intellect.

We have to envisage that in some sense Ideas are living things that can enlighten and flash into our minds. We must admit that every revolution on any level has been brought about by ideas flaming in one mind and leaping to others. This applies not only to the French Revolution or the Industrial Revolution, but also to all social, educational, artistic or religious revolutions. It has been well said that 'there is nothing so powerful as an idea whose hour has come'.

Whether we are to survive as a society depends on the ability to apprehend new ideas which lead us into unknown and unprecedented social conditions. Einstein wrote: 'If man today does not find a new way of thinking, humanity may well be doomed to extinction'.

197

Now, if we can take it even as a poetical concept that ideas are alive and need to strike then in what circumstances would we expect them to do so?

Alas, they do not often strike in the churches nowadays. I make no immoderate claim for the adult colleges, but I would stress strongly the value and purpose of the short course in this connection. It is of prime importance that thinking people should come together, removed for a short time from the demands of daily occupation to discuss and get illumination on important aspects of life and society. Where could that be better done than in the atmosphere of a gracious country house, in a surrounding of fine architecture and the tranquillity of nature and the wide parklands. In such a setting things can happen – and do happen. The short course can be a very remarkable experience. It is far more than the imparting of knowledge from a lecturer to his pupils. It is truly a group deed, an act of group thought and imagination.

We may in our time state what could be called the Doctrine of the Living Idea. We may well feel that a course is dedicated to enlightenment by the mystery of the living idea. The setting is offered so that the flash of inspiration may come. An idea having once been thought becomes somehow available on the wavelength of general thinking. We have assuredly had the experience that ideas have flamed in discussion and that out of them something has grown as an aftermath to a course, which might really make a lasting contribution to our social pattern and thinking.

We should here do honour to the memory of Grundvig, founder of the Danish Folk Highschools. The great movement of the Folk Highschools was launched through the vision and leadership of Bishop Grundvig in the 1840s. He found a Denmark broken by depression after the Napoleonic wars and saw the possibility of revival through bringing the young folk together for six months in a new form of college, not so much to teach them to be better farmers as to be better Danes. Thus he taught them Danish literature, history and folklore and sent them back inspired to their farms. This movement did much to revive Denmark as a great democracy. Grundvig declared what

198

he called his 'Doctrine of the Living Word'. Lecturers must speak from the heart straight to the hearts of the hearers, and the object was 'enlivenment' as much as 'enlightenment'. Furthermore he insisted that they should not speak from notes, but must give out those thoughts which they had really made their own and about which they minded deeply.

Although in our English colleges the courses are short and are open to all who care to come, we link with the Folk Highschools in our aim of enlivenment and enlightenment and the ideal is certainly that 'lecturers' should follow the doctrine of the 'living word'. A course is a challenge to lecturers to find and present those ideas which will fire the interest of our very mixed audiences. Thus to Grundvig's Doctrine of the Living Word let us add the Doctrine of the Living Idea.

THE CREATIVE IMPULSE

Now to say something of the real springs of adult education. There is a drive within everyone which is basic. We all know in our hearts that the real fun is the heightening of skill and discrimination in some direction or other through the mystery of some new knowledge or technique. This need not be a highbrow affair. It can be the mastering of bee-keeping or chrysanthemum-growing, or the taking of a vintage car to bits and re-assembling it. It can be the identifying of birdsong or acting a Shakespeare play, mastering a language or a creative craft. The same inner drive can work on refined and ever subtler levels of achievement, touching delights of intellectual understanding. The delight is to be involved with some subject which enlarges the limits of the personality. When we have, over a weekend course, tackled Brahms's Second Symphony and cracked our brains over its analysis, that symphony is to some degree in our blood. We are bigger by that great work. In a course on architectural appreciation our sensitivity extends out to the buildings, and a weekend on the night sky lifts our consciousness among the constellations. The passive pleasures such as lying on the beach in the sun assuredly having their place, but this active delight in mastering and developing the creative power is the basic joy of man and this needs to be recognised. Further, it is a drive that comes from what you might call the higher self. We have been bedevilled by the Freudian suggestion that all the drives in man come from the lower self, and that our artistic and religious aspirations are a sublimation of the sexual instincts. We recognise that there are indeed drives which come from the dark unconsciousness but there are also impulses arising from the light-filled superconscious.

The aspiration to master creative powers and wider interests is to be seen as a basic delight and joy for the human being and can be a real lead given by his higher nature.

It can begin at any age. In this sense adult education begins whenever the young discover the flame of enthusiasm within themselves. Every young thing has this flame which will flare up when it meets the interest or person with whom it has affinity, for its essential nature is love.

The lucky ones are those who are led through by the flame into adult activity. The young Schliemann had the vision that perhaps Troy was real and the Iliad true and this led him through to a lifetime of great archaeological discoveries.

The finding and keeping alive of the flame is of all things the most important. The tragedy is that so often the young get discouraged in meeting the cynicism of the adult world. Our task is to watch the flame and revive it again, even in maturity.

RECOVERY OF MEANING

The awakening of enthusiasm is thus one of the major tasks for adult education. Shortly after the war Prof. Ashby gave a great lecture of 'The Pathology of Adult Education' in which he pronounced 'the law of diminishing enthusiasm'. He recognised the passing of the golden age of the Workers' Educational Association, under the inspiration of leaders like Tawney, helping working men to find their place in society through study of economics and sociology. He looked back to the pioneering days of the Mechanics Institutes where men on the way to the factories came in for lectures at 5.30 am. The whole front has now changed. The spur is now within each individual whatever his walk of life to discover himself and widen beyond the limits of his personality into relationship with the greater whole, thereby heightening his sense of the real meaning of life. This is an inner quest and exploration. One might say that the basic purpose of adult education should be the recovery of meaning in life in an age when so many are discouraged and disillusioned. The Austrian psychologist, Frankl, after the war, found that many of his patients broke down precisely because their lives seemed without point or meaning and he developed what he called 'Logotherapy' or healing through recovery of a sense of meaning. In an enquiry he found that 80% of students in American Universities at the time declared they saw no deeper purpose in life. Against this is the recent enquiry by the 'News of the World' which revealed that out of 700 young people interviewed 67% declared belief in God as the meaning of life, but saw God as universal consciousness, a primal oneness underlying all manifestations of life. To them sense of meaning is restored, often with joy. Such is the present trend. Thus in our generation we restate 'the law of mounting enthusiasm'.

YOUTH

Let me read a quotation, the authorship of which I cannot be sure of, though I have been told it may be from Schweitzer.

> Youth is not a time of life. It is a state of mind. It is not a matter of ripe cheeks, red lips and supple knees, it is a temper of the Will, a quality of the imagination, a vigour of the emotions. It is a freshness of the deep springs of life.
>
> Youth means a temperamental predominance of courage over timidity, of the appetite for adventure over the love of ease. This often exists in a man of fifty more than in a boy of twenty.
>
> Nobody grows old merely by living a number of years. People grow old only by deserting their ideals. Years wrinkle the skin, but to give up enthusiasm wrinkles the soul. Worry, doubt, self-distrust, fear and despair, these are the long, long years that bow the head and turn the growing spirit back to dust.

Whether seventy or seventeen there is in every being's heart the love of wonder, the sweet amazement of the stars, and starlike things and thoughts, the undaunted challenge of events, the unfailing childlike appetite for 'what next' and the joy and game of life.

You are as young as your faith, as old as your doubt, as young as your self-confidence, as old as your fear, as young as your hope, as old as your despair.

While the central place of your heart receives messages of beauty, hope, cheer, courage, grandeur, and power from the earth, from men, and from the Infinite, so long are you young.

When the central place of your heart is covered with the snows of pessimism and the ice of cynicism, then you are grown old indeed, and may God have mercy on your soul.

That gives one of the aspects of adult education!

We live in a very intellectual age, and the gigantic and thrilling achievements of science and technology show how far the analytical intellect can go in great group effort, but there is another faculty which can apprehend the living whole and that is the Imagination.

There is a polarity between the dissecting intellect and the creative imagination, and the atrophying of the powers of imagination in its true sense may prevent a man from grasping the reality of the great unity of life. Every subject can be seen as a magic casement through which we look into the reality of the stupendous wholeness of things. In every subject we can try to find the integrating ideas which relate to the whole of life. Perhaps this is the key which binds our very varied courses.

It must of course be recognised that there is romance and great imagination behind scientific achievement.

Teilhard de Chardin sees research into the deeper reality of the universe as the drive which unites science and religion and gives us an experience of adventure which is the true alternative to war.

There is no need to stress the part that the Adult College can play in the future when the automaton has given much greater leisure. In the new society it may be recognised as a virtue to withdraw from the scramble for jobs in order to develop some creative talent or intellectual interest which will bring tranquillity and joy into our lives. In an affluent society new financial attitudes and arrangements will encourage this and the whole tone of our lives will be the better for it.

THE LATER YEARS

Many people come to Attingham when they are facing retirement and advancing age. Ours is the first society in human history in which most are given a dozen years free at the end of their career or after the launching of the family. Previously, life, broadly speaking, consisted of nurture and training followed by toil till worn out.

Many fear retirement, failing to see it as a challenge and a freedom in which the riches of life experience can be harvested.

It is perhaps not mere chance that this phenomenon has appeared in our society now. A new society of mature citizens could begin to form, freed from the demands and anxieties of making a career. Naturally there may be straightened circumstances but there should be delight in developing a creative attitude to these last years of life.

I quote here from Yeats' *Sailing to Byzantium:*

> An aged man is but a paltry thing,
> A tattered coat upon a stick, unless
> Soul clap its hands and sing, and louder sing
> For every tatter in its mortal dress,
> Nor is there singing school but studying
> Monuments of its own magnificence;
> And therefore I have sailed the seas and come
> To the holy city of Byzantium.

Byzantium was to Yeats not only a great ancient city but a symbol of a higher state of consciousness touching the ultimates of things. Our ageing may be a time of preparation when we can stretch our minds to wider and deeper understandings. Many are beginning to realise that consciousness is by no means limited to the human brain on the earth plane, but that there can be extended fields of consciousness. If we can accept that the being of man is eternal, then it follows that it was there on some higher plane of consciousness before coming down into the limitations of the body. It did not begin at conception, but was in existence in a wider sphere before birth. This is a profoundly important thought if we are to understand the meaning of life.

Wordsworth knew this and it is good to consider with fresh eyes the well known lines in his *Ode on the Intimations of Immortality*:

> Our birth is but a sleep and a forgetting:
> The Soul that rises with us, our life's Star,
> Hath had elsewhere its setting,
> And cometh from afar:
> Not in entire forgetfulness,
> And not in utter nakedness,
> But trailing clouds of glory do we come
> From God, who is our home:
> Heaven lies about us in our infancy!
> Shades of the prison-house begin to close
> Upon the growing Boy,
> But he beholds the light, and whence it flows
> He sees it in his joy;
> The Youth who daily farther from the east
> Must travel, still is Nature's Priest,
> And by the vision splendid
> Is on His way attended;
> At length the Man perceives it die away,
> And fade into the light of common day.

Wordsworth in later disillusion virtually denied his intuition.

It is for us to revive the 'vision splendid', realising that as there is no death without rebirth, the death of the vision in manhood may lead to its resurrection in age, bringing a new and profound joy, delight and hope. If it be true that there is in each of us an eternal core of being, there before birth and returning to its 'home' after the discarding of the worn out sheath of the body, then truly can we say that there is no death.

The core of man is eternal as all life is eternal and it is only the outer sheath that falls away and decays.

We are considering a factor which may indeed change our thinking and above all our whole attitude to our last years of life. Birth is seen as a descent of an eternal and spiritual being into the limitations of the body, striding across mountains, swimming in the seas, mastering creative crafts and skills, but we are not our bodies. Rather do we live into and through them and, as this necessary sheath begins to wear out and run down, the eternal spirit strives even more for release into wider understanding. In the later years this becomes increasingly important and the deepening vision should develop as the bodily energies fade. 'With every tatter in its mortal dress' the soul can expand and consciousness move into greater light, until such time as it can discard the worn out coat and be released back into the realms from which we came.

THE VISION SPLENDID

Adult education in this sense could be called 'the vision splendid', and our whole attitude towards retirement and our later years should be conditioned by this view. Broadly speaking, how-ever, in our materialistic age we move on into the realms of wide consciousness totally unprepared. We must recognise that the conscious cultivation of our faculties for creation and the under-standing of human achievement in the arts, sciences and thought, is really building something which we shall carry through with us wherever consciousness goes. It is not a question for the older person of merely finding diversion when the time hangs heavily, but rather the beginning to deliberately equip himself for an exploration to which there is no end. Adult education is literally endless. We may in a true sense be preparing for what might be called a University of the Spirit, and much that we do here in cultivating the vision of wholeness may thus bear fruit on differ-ent planes. This to some may seem mere flight of fancy. Please yourself and take it 'as you like it'. It is no dogma to be imposed but a way of thought which all are free to accept or reject.

But it is very clear that many minds now are questing for deeper meaning and a new understanding of the great oneness of life. This has been shown at Attingham. Whenever I put on a course concerned with the 'eternal verities and the divinity of all life' the house is packed. Some two- or three hundred people apply and come from all over the country. I would submit that here is a field in modern adult education which must be taken seriously. It is not to be treated merely as a personal fancy among more sound academic courses.

In all the width of adult programmes there is now a place for courses touching on the meaning of life and what might be called the spiritual picture of Man and the Universe. In our generation many people, young and old, are thirsting for a world-view which lifts them beyond the materialistic outlook so common today. Indeed, it could well be that now in a new phase of Adult Education a group of colleges will grow up wholly avowing the primacy of the spirit, but demonstrating this in a variety of topics.

In an age when so many are frightened or bored, disillusioned or cynical, there is a surge of new hope, zest and love, a new feeling that every subject is a symbolical link with the oneness of life which we are only now beginning to apprehend. We begin now to see how the timeless truths are hidden within the allegory of so much mythology, legend and fairy story the world over, and are expressed in hidden form in much great art. Modern spiritual knowledge opens new possibilities for interpretation and understanding and we see that the great physicists are coming strangely near to the mystic in showing that life and the universe may be ultimately of the nature of thought. The response to these courses shows, I submit, that there is now need and a thirst for discussion of what life is truly about. Adult education is very exciting. It is, to use our very English word, fun! After certain courses we are left with the sense that somehow life will never be the same again. We gather in our house parties, for the course is truly a metamorphosis of the old house-party, directing our thought and endeavour towards some creative purpose, and the true reward is often that something happens which inspires people afresh with a new sense of the infinite significance and value of all life.

22

THE CASE FOR
UNDAUNTED OPTIMISM

T HIS COURSE is one of a series. Each term we run a
conference on the spiritual world view of life and of
man. A little while ago there was 'Frontiers of Reality',
and that was followed by one in which we invited the higher
worlds to descend in a course called 'The Working of the Spirit
in Social and Economic Life'. And then we had what you might
call a return match, for the next one was 'The Expansion of
Consciousness' and we went up over the frontiers of reality in
the other direction. This was followed by 'The Primal Oneness
in Diversity', and that great theme has led us through to 'Hope
in Man's Future'. The final one of this series while I am at
Attingham is going to be 'Living into the New Age'.

Well – 'Hope in Man's Future'. We live in an age when
obviously many people are relatively in despair. There frankly
doesn't seem to be much hope. The news is of nothing but
wars and confusion, strikes and trouble centres, earthquakes,
starvation and pollution and all the ghastly things that seem to
be happening, mostly as an obvious and direct result of the way
that man has treated the world and his fellow men. The exercise
of man's self-will is leading, frankly, to confusion, individual and
collective. It is very difficult to deny this. Naturally we struggle
to solve the problems, but something is all going wrong.
Inflation is probably upon us. It seems impossible to control the
release of hate, anger and rivalry, and meantime overshadowing
it all China works at its nuclear bombs. The world is a sinister

place. Where is there any hope in man's future? As Yeats wrote, 'The best lack all conviction, and the worst are full of passionate intensity ...'. It is easy to say it's a very bad world, and therefore there is practically no hope – any of these problems are virtually insoluble as man proceeds along the path of self-reliance upon the intellect and upon his own self-will. That is why it is of immeasurable importance to meet and to discuss the theme of hope in man's future along another line which is still ignored or denied by the great majority of our fellow country-men. This lies in the possibility of a redemption of man through cooperation with higher planes of consciousness. This holds a hope so great that we indeed talk about the coming of a New Age. The Aquarian Age is breaking upon us and we have the honour of being born in this generation so that we can in some degree serve towards this great enlightenment that may be coming to mankind.

Here lies hope in man's future, but this great and divine ally is one we wholly ignore in facing our problems. Put simply, we leave an ever-present God out of the picture. The changing of vision that has come in our time reflects what Oriental wisdom has seen for centuries. It has seen behind the world of appear-ance a great, unitary world of absolute Being which is absolute consciousness, absolute life, ultimate energy, the primal source of creative power. The east called it 'That' because it was un-nameable. We may now recognise that there is this great One-ness of life, of spirit, from which all matter in its myriad forms is derivative, and therefore spirit, God, permeates every atom, every plant, every crystal, and every human soul. We are faced simply with the atrophying of the organs of perception, which in earlier days were still open so that they could see. In Greek days, even perhaps in the Middle Ages, they could be aware of the reality of higher worlds. Those faculties died on us, of neces-sity, in that man's evolution demanded mastery of the world of matter, and a development of intellect. Hence the development of scientific thinking, and the price paid was the atrophying of the organs of perception which enabled man to realise and work with the higher worlds. The result is that we have entered a materialistic civilization and that we even in our superiority deny the existence of God, the world of the hierarchies and the world of the elemental beings working in nature because we cannot see them. We recognise the crown of intellectual development in Athens in the fifth century, and yet we say, 'Oh yes, their belief in their gods and thy elemental beings working within nature is just so much superstition; we know better.'

Now we come to a stage when the scientific mind is beginning to expand its focus, having narrowed it to matter so closely that it ultimately has learned to disintegrate the energy within the atom. We now reach the stage when the mind of the physicist draws close to the mind of the mystic. As soon as man disintegrates the spirit frozen within the atom, the very power of the Logos, he has done a god-like deed, and has taken upon himself an immeasurable responsibility. Until then we were playing with toys. Now we have gone beyond toys, but we are still, alas, playing with them. Therefore the higher worlds are profoundly concerned with this planet, because the whole spiritual organism of the solar system is in danger of disturbance and disruption, if we should blow this planet off its course. It is not a matter of indifference to the divine worlds, and therefore, from what we gather, there is intense interest on higher planes, and readiness to cooperate if man will but send out his invitation. This is the fundamental point to see, that the spiritual worlds, the forces of light, the forces of Michael and of the Cosmic Christ, may not intervene against the principle of free will. Man is the great experiment of God in developing a creature of free will which even the angels have not got, because they are closely bound into God's will. We are free.

We are now waking up to the supreme fact that if we will but invoke the forces of light they can in response flood human consciousness and are actually beginning to do so. Therefore with the full clarity of our scientific thinking we may take another step in consciousness, recognising that higher planes are a reality, that space is not just dead and empty, that this planet upon which we walk is a living creature. We are the consciousness point of this living being of the earth and we can send up our cry for redemption to the forces of the Cosmic Christ.

When confusion becomes absolute in human society the Avatar descends. It would seem to be principle of history, that a rescuer is sent down to earth from the planes of higher consciousness for the redemption of man, for putting him right again when he has done too far wrong. This has happened through the ages. Here are two verses from the Bhagavad Gita, the greatest of all Indian mystical teachings:

> Whenever there is a withering of the Law, and an uprising of lawlessness on all sides, then I manifest myself.

This is Krishna speaking to Arjuna.

> For the salvation of the righteous, and the destruction of such as do evil, for the firm establishing of the Law, I come to birth age after age.

This is to be taken seriously. Seers the world over are fore-telling the reappearance of the Christ, not incarnating into a human body but as the Cosmic Christ who is present everywhere in every human soul. The great and supreme hope arises in His comment, 'I am with you always, even to the end of the earth's cycle.' The Christ is present in every human heart on the etheric level, on the level of the lifeforces of the earth and man, and therefore can be awakened in us. Therefore we can 'come' the Second Coming, if one may put it like that, in our own hearts. What seems to be happening is that spiritual forces of light are being released from the hierarchies of heaven so that those groups and individuals who lift heart and thought toward the light can be flooded with a new understanding and new qualities. This is the immeasurable thrill of the coming of the New Age. This seems to be the new dispensation. This is the pouring out of the Aquarian waters, the waters of light over the earth, and it begins to happen in this generation.

It is not a question that possibly in the next 25,000 years something may happen. We have got to recognise that if we invoke now, the event could take place. I read from the Bhagavad

Gita, written 3,000 years ago; now I read from Teilhard de Chardin in his epilogue in *Le milieu Divin* giving us a contemporary expression of the same hope.

> One day, the Gospel tells us, the tension gradually accumulating between humanity and God will touch the limits proscribed by the possibilities of the world, and then will come the end. Then the presence of Christ which has been silently accruing in all things will suddenly be revealed like a flash of light from pole to pole. Breaking through the barriers within which the veil of matter or the water-tightness of souls has seemingly kept it confined, it will invade the face of the earth. Like lightning, like a conflagration, like a flood, the attraction exerted by the Son of Man will lay hold of all the whirling elements in the universe so as to reunite them, or subject them to His body. As the Gospel warns us it would be vain to speculate as to the hour and modalities of this formidable event. But we have to expect it. Expectation, anxious, collective and operative expectation of an end of the world, that is to say of an issue of the world, that is perhaps the supreme Christian function, and the most distinctive characteristic of our religion. The Lord Jesus will only come soon if we ardently expect it. It is an accumulation of desires which would cause the pleroma to burst upon us. We Christians have been charged with keeping the flame of desire ever alight in the world. What have we made of our expectancy? No doubt our prayers and actions are consciously directed to bringing about the coming of God's kingdom. But in fact how many of us are genuinely moved in the depths of our hearts by the wild hope that our earth is to be recast. Who is there who sets a course in the midst of our darkness towards the first glimmer of the real dawn? We keep saying we keep vigil in expectation of the Master. But in reality we should have to admit, that we were sincere, that we no longer expect anything. The flame must be revived at all cost. At all cost we must renew in ourselves the desire and the hope of the great Coming.
>
> Let us look at the earth around us. What is happening under our eyes among the mass of the peoples? What is the cause of this disorder in society, this uneasy agitation, these swelling waves, these whirling and mingling currents, these turbulent and formidable new impulses? Mankind is visibly passing through a crisis of growth. Mankind is dimly becoming aware of its short-comings

and its capabilities. It sees the universe growing luminous, like the horizon just before sunrise. It has a sense of premonition and of expectation. The world can no more have two summits than a circumference can have two centres. The star for which the world is waiting, without yet being able to give it a name or rightly appreciate its true transcendence or even the most spiritual and divine of its rays is necessarily Christ Himself, for whom we hope. We must try everything for Christ. We must hope everything for Christ.

The critical moment has been reached in human history when either we smash ourselves and the world, or we wake up and open our hearts to cooperation with the New Age, which is nothing other than the flooding of spiritual light into human souls. This could happen like a chain reaction shooting over the face of the globe. There is nothing that could not be achieved once this began.

Hence the importance of every gathering such as this. This whole gathering is an invocation, a lifting of expectancy and hope, and not a sterile sort of hope but a passionate expectation that the divine world could begin to cooperate within our own thinking. Now what is necessary for this? Here lies the purpose of all meditation, whatever the variant or method – that we should pull ourselves out, if only for a precious half hour of the day, from the rattle of action and the disturbance of our concerns, and that we should turn around completely and move inwards as if we are moving into a secret chapel. Then we can purge the disturbance that is in heart, thought and solar plexus, until absolute stillness is achieved. It is as if we move deeper and deeper on to subtler planes of stillness, until the soul is absolutely still, like a silent pool, with the surface reflecting, and all mud in the water having settled to the bottom, so still that even the breathing has ceased and nothing but the silence remains. Then we are approaching the moment when we are actually touching this world of Absolute Being. This is the gateway. We have come through and are beginning to be one with the Oneness. It is here that contact can really begin to be made within this little point, which is one with the whole sphere of the spiritual sun. As we create this little chamber of absolute stillness, in imagination we can become luminous in a new way, which is really the vibration of the spiritual sun working within us. It isn't that we have to go anywhere; the spiritual sun is there, the sun of Christ is in the heart. We are the spiritual sun.

It is at this point that we begin to discover the qualities of the soul which are the inevitable result of this experience. We have achieved absolute stillness, absolute silence, but not a dead silence. It is silence that is vibrating; we can almost begin to hear the silence. The silence begins to sound. The world of being begins to sound through the silence. We hardly have organs of perception to hear it. The most we can do is listen to the silence with alert attention, and then there can descend what is called bliss consciousness, with the sense that when the soul is in relationship with the world of Being, this is where it is meant to be. This is home. The world of confusion that we have left is not home. We are living for the moment in bliss, in great stillness, in joy, in absolute tranquillity, in courage, in hope and in love. These are attributes of the Higher Self. When in meditation we have touched this moment of stillness and of joy, these are like light, absolutely part of us, and we part of them. Where there is light there cannot be darkness. We realise the unreality of the darkness. Once we have this condition in heart and thought there is no darkness in a soul. In other words the negative emotions of hate, fear, jealousy, resentment, regret, anxiety are just not present. These are the attributes of the lower self. They are all concerned with either the past or the future. 'Oh my Beloved, fill the cup that clears today of past regret and future fears …'. So wrote Omar Khayyam. The cup, of course, is the chalice of the soul, the grail chalice of the heart held up for the Divine Wine, not the earthly wine as it is so often thought.

This is our problem. The present moment is very rarely intolerable, however difficult our situation may be. Be honest about that. What is intolerable is the sense of past regrets and future fears. They bedevil and dog us in this instant moment. There is no moment but now, and it is like a knife-edge passing on to the next 'now'. The problem of entering the New Age is

213

to learn how to live in this 'now', because this absolute moment is the point where the Christ walks. He has undertaken to carry our burdens, but he has not undertaken to carry all the rucksacks full of heavy weights of past journeys. He enables us to let go that load like Christian in *Pilgrim's Progress*, to live in this moment and to be clear of past regrets and future fears. In so far as we can do that we are not capable of the negative emotions. If we can live in the consciousness of joy, love, and absolute tranquillity which we experience in meditation, at that moment the dark emotions are not capable of coming in. Hence the immeasurable importance of entering into this condition in meditation once or twice a day, so that we may then plunge back into the world of action, with the whole soul coloured by these qualities.

And what are those qualities? The poets have always known that these higher attributes are beings. Hope! This description by Manley Hopkins in *The Wreck of the Deutschland*: '... Hope had grown grey hairs. Hope had mourning on. Drenched with tears, carved with cares. Hope was twelve hours gone ...' Hope as a being has withdrawn. 'Patience on a monument, smiling at grief ...' These are qualities, but are also beings. We know who the Lord of love is, obviously. So also Courage is a being. It is a very significant phrase that, 'take courage'. We 'take thought'. Right you are. 'Take hope', 'take tranquillity', 'take love', take the lot of them. They are yours for the taking. We are called upon actively to take them, and the way to do it is simple. We draw them into our soul in this instant, this eternal moment, and we resonate courage, or hope, or tranquillity, recognising, that just as our stillness was actually part of the sphere of the spiritual sun, so our resonated courage is part of the great planet, perhaps of Mars, in its vast sphere. All these qualities pick up a response on a higher frequency level in the spiritual world. Thus the creating of these attributes in the soul and carrying them into action is itself an invitation to the world of higher being; to stream in and augment that which is being manifested by any human soul. The soul is part of the whole oneness of things. Therefore we can become conscious points at which these attributes of the higher self, created consciously in the stillness of the heart, are then expanded and augmented by the inpouring of Being and beings, and so the individual ought to be able to carry himself, light-filled, into the darkness of the earth, and the confusion of society.

This is our contribution to the coming of the new age. We are bringing in the New Age by learning to live in this way. It is a question of carrying the eternal moment down into action. In the old days when the ancient wisdom was taught in the mystery temples of Epidaurus and Eleusis, the candidates for initiation were led through their ceremonies, through the darkness, through the maze, up to the point of light, and if they went through their ordeals there came the moment of illumination and ultimately imitation. The days have changed when the selected candidates for initiation were able to go through the experience. The ancient and ageless wisdom now pours itself into the world again, but open to anybody prepared to take it. It pours out in books, in lectures, in scientific wisdom, but where is the temple? Where is the ritual that leads to this moment of ecstasy? The temple surely is each human body which can house the spirit, just as the Greek temple was a chamber into which the god could descend upon earth.

So in the heart do we create a chamber for the descent of the Spirit into the temple. This is our mystery temple. And through the mazes of darkness within the personality and the body we at last come through as candidates of initiation, to this holy of holies, this stilled centre of the light, and there experience the ecstasy, the bliss-consciousness which the candidate for initiation at Eleusis also experienced. Then the problem is to walk into society with that light in the heart still flaming.

This now presents us with a technique which we have clearly got to begin to learn. I said at the beginning that when society is in absolute confusion, then we may expect the Avatar to descend. There is ample evidence that this could happen any time now. There is already being a flooding of light and there could be a real entry of the Christ and Michaelic powers into human society and the stream of earth evolution.

We live in an apocalyptic age. Of course there is confusion; an apocalypse is not comfortable, but it is profoundly exciting.

215

What is the right attitude to take towards it? All our lives are in confusion more or less. I have no doubt that there are 150 insoluble problems present in the personalities in this room, overwhelming difficulties of one sort and another, reflecting the confusion that appears to be in our outside society, and there is every evidence that this will get a great deal worse. 'Hope has grown grey hairs ... Hope has mourning on ...' as far as society is concerned, 'drenched with tears, carved with cares ...'. But we see this supremest of all hopes that has ever faced man. Even now, even in our time, the power of the Christ can flood the human heart.

Now, how do we carry this timeless moment? If confusion comes, still more if the higher worlds flood the consciousness, we shall be faced with human situations totally without precedent for which we have no brain track. All our past brain tracks are habits of the lower self, and into these we react. If we are faced with a completely new circumstance we have nothing to react with but a set of old habits, old reflexes, and may be thrown into bewilderment. So what then?

We are suddenly faced with a situation for which we have no precedent. Remember, if we are living in the moment, the past regrets have simply fallen away. First of all we recognise that we are the total cause of what we are in this moment, we are absolute and total cause; we have made ourselves by our blunders and our successes and this is the thing we are carrying into the future, to the glory of the Lord. If we are faced with such a moment, what can we do? We can use the creative imagination. We conceive how our higher self would react.

When we have seen the flash of what the higher self wants in our imagination, we then, as an actor, act that imagination and take a step forward. It is really a faculty of acting into the higher self. It is not for nothing that England is the great nation of amateur actors. We don't necessarily need to act Shakespeare now; we need to use this quality to play this supremely exciting drama. We can't learn the part before hand, but in the great adventure, moment to moment, crisis to crisis, we lift ourselves to our higher self and step forward. If a man could do that in

216

the moment of crisis, it could well be that panic would be averted. 'If I be lifted up, then all men will be lifted with me.'

So to adventure into the unknown is a faculty which all of us have to develop, and to develop it with joy, knowing that it is leading us through the maze into the world of our higher self, the world we touch in meditation. When we start moving this way we find our fellows. Do we not all know that we are meeting those who are on the same wavelength. Any soul who has in any degree taken this inner step will recognise the same quality in the others whom he or she meets, and will love them for it. This is the real love. This is the love of the god that is in you for the god that is in me. The divinity in you, the divinity in me, loves itself because it is one. In other words, instantly, when this path is begun, souls begin to come together in a new society, in new groups. The New Age is forming under our eyes. It is actually running together in human souls who are uniting in new groups, fired with this new vision. There never was such hope in man's future. The real hope for mankind is coming out of these souls uniting into new groups, resonating the positive attributes of the higher self, and really thereby forming a new society. We need not ever oppose anything. We just hold to the light, and step by step work towards it. There never was so thrilling an activity or occupation for mankind.

23

THE RECOVERY OF MEANING

ONTINUALLY we move forward into a new moment. Perpetual new birth. The future pours into manifestation through the living forms of Nature. We are each a point to receive the future as it becomes present. New spring comes with tender green shoots. Yet behind this delicate flowering is an irresistible power.

Each man is a point of consciousness, free to control this inflow with harmony or to spread confusion and waste. Here within nature is this extraordinary human kingdom which, having free will, has no obligation to work with the beauty of the Natural Law. Each man is a vortex point through which the creative power of the inflooding future is canalized. But as self-conscious egos we can all too easily concern ourselves with the satisfying of desire rather than serving the need of the Living Whole. Just consider the wisdom working within the body of man. Consider the harmonious working of nature's law. 'Who hath put wisdom in the inward parts?' With such absolute certainty and balance within the Whole does nature work. To our dawning consciousness we realise that the Earth itself is a living organism, within a Cosmos itself shot through with creative intelligence all working in a delicately poised harmony. Integrally part of this Living Unity is the 'centre that we call the race of men'. Man is a creative point within the order of working of God's Law. What a responsibility. We are that point where evolution becomes conscious of itself. Therefore we are the stewards of the planet, and what have we done with our stewardship? We have in our greed to satisfy our desires, polluted the lovely Earth and wastefully squandered the energies working in the balanced whole. Man is a spiritual being, a droplet of the Divine Source, incarnated into a soul-sheath which gives him emotional relationship to his fellow creatures, and a beautiful physical body which is really a part of Earth and links him firmly with the laws of substance. Compare the chaos of our emotional life with the order of Natural Law. In this Planet of Wisdom, as it has been called, man, the repository of consciousness, seems to be the instrument for spreading confusion. What wonders would develop if we could bring the same order into our life of desires. Here lies the supreme possibility. If our undying Ego, our Higher Self, could take over our lower desire-self and bring it into order so that it could, in our field of influence, work towards ever greater harmony in meaningful action, then the face of the planet would be transformed.

Meaningful action – that is the key-note. How much of what we do is meaningless, wasteful, inharmonious. 'Let Light and Love and Power restore the plan on Earth.' It is all very well to send up this invocation, but it will not be fulfilled by some higher source. It is we men who must consciously achieve it by bringing the Law into this living moment in our own lives and so blending with our Higher Self. Then could come a flooding of creative energy. The human individual could become a creative point for increasing the meaningful and right working of the energies of the Whole. 'How do I increase meaning significantly in the place where I happen to be?' This is Ted Matchett's formula in his important work of training for creative action. This simple question has profound significance for *us now*. The greatest creative force is the *will to meaning*, the active will to re-unite our own activity with the vital Unity from which the world of substance is derived. We have to conceive of a vast living continuum of Being, a structure of Self-supporting Thought and Meaningful Energies, shot through and through with creative intelligence. In and through this the Creative Imagining of God works. We watch the continuous working of Divine Law as it flows in an endless stream out of the future into this living Now. The Eternal Worlds flow into time through Natural Law.

And within this structure an organ for free creative action has been evolved. Here is Mankind, a hierarchy of spiritual beings, given the earth as a field of action and of training, to learn the responsibility of free will, that Divine Gift which could make man a co-creator with God. It seems as if the All-Knower, loving His Creation, wished for a point within that Creation which, developing the self consciousness, could become creative and so reflect back to God his own achievement. What you might call 'Creation Mark II' begins when man begins to act in freedom within the Pattern of Meaning.

By *meaning* is meant the fulfilling within the moment of the needs of the living active whole which works in harmony. The intersection point of the timeless with time is everywhere and always. The whole human layer with its myriad points of consciousness constitutes the web through which the future is born into time every moment. Thus each of us within our own field of influence is responsible for realising *meaning* to the maximum. 'Thy Kingdom come, thy Will be done on earth.' Clearly this implies that His Will is not being done on earth. All the kingdoms of nature are automatically geared to the fulfilling of His Will, except errant man. All the angelic hierarchies are axiomatically serving that Will since they are God, subdividing His Unity into spheres of activity and Being. The angels do not need free will, since their delight is to serve God. Mankind alone, that great concourse of droplets of Being, has been given free will and has taken over the gravity field of earth in which to be trained in this great responsibility. Man is the great experiment of the Gods, for it is only through experience of separation from the spiritual worlds and from God's Will that we can develop to real freedom. Hence the power and truth of the Parable of the Prodigal Son. We descend so deeply into matter and the gratification of the desires of self that we reach the point of feeding on the husks of the swine. Then we 'come to ourselves' (awakening to the reality of our Higher Self) and say 'I will go back to my Father'. Of course He welcomes this willed return

221

with joy, for each of us is potentially a companion and co-creator with God.

Man has been called the Tenth Hierarchy. Whether incarnate on earth or sojourning in the eternal between lives we are all bearers of self consciousness and free will. Whether we make the grade or are dragged down by the greed of our lower self into meaninglessness is the ultimate decision of each of us.

'When I consider the heavens, the work of Thy hands which thou hast ordained, what is man that thou art mindful of him or the son of man that thou visitest him, for thou hast made him a little lower than the angels and crowned him with glory and honour.'

We see the long evolution of man as the great adventure into higher consciousness. The present epoch is the time when the greatest step forward can be achieved. Man is called on to take

> The longest stride of soul men every took.
> Affairs are now soul size,
> The enterprise is exploration into God.

No wonder that the spiritual worlds appear to be deeply interested and concerned about the immediate future of the planet. If we by our folly really damage the precious web of life on Earth then the whole spiritual organism of the Solar System will suffer. It is touch and go whether enough men awaken to their spiritual responsibility and potential before human avarice and ignorance brings catastrophe.

Indeed much apparent outward catastrophe is now inevitable if that which is meaningless is to be sloughed off. The meaning-less is dead and we must reject the corpses and the husks of the past. Yet we know that there is no death without rebirth. The two processes are inseparable and a new spring now floods into human consciousness, bringing harmony and light and rejecting what is inharmonious and dark. As the personal instruments for this channelling of light, each of us is playing our part in the greatest saga which ever took place in human history. We watch and we take part in the birth of a New Age, a great operation of Redemption to restore meaning to life and re-establish the broken link of our communion with the beautiful worlds of Creative Spirit to which we really belong.

As we enter the changes of the New Age we shall find that all answers come from an understanding of the spiritual nature of man. This is the essence of the recovery of lost knowledge. The universe is spiritual in nature and man in his essential being is part of the great Oneness. His problem, as a being of self consciousness and free will, is the re-aligning or re-attuning with the whole. His extravagant wasteful and meaningless activity directly arises from his sense of separation, which puts him out of touch with the living spiritual worlds so that he comes to feel that the earth is just dead mineral and is his for the exploitation. Incidentally the word extravagant means 'wandering apart' as when the ghost of Hamlet's father says 'the extravagant and erring spirit hies to his confine'. All sin is sundering, a cutting off from the Whole. Once he recovers the lost knowledge of his own imperishable spiritual being and realises his responsibility to the whole, a new range of conduct will result. He will strive again for meaningful action.

We now enter an age of change and tribulation. The present breakdown is the direct result of man's wasteful and meaningless activities (i.e. activities unrelated to the serving of the meaningful whole). There will be enough for all if we learn to waste no time, no food, no energy, no words. By cutting out the wasteful and the meaningless we realign with the whole of which we are integrally part. Supposed wants would be abandoned and that which is dead and past, jettisoned. It seems then axiomatic that the need of the moment would be met. There must always be enough to meet the real need, but there emphatically will not be enough for extravagant want. We must learn now to prune drastically. Economy is the key-note but on every aspect of living. Yet paradoxically it appears that for those who really are asking 'in His Name' for needs to be met, there can be abundance. In God is abundance but God plays the game of brinksmanship and allows no hoarding. When it is required and not a moment before, energy is released to meet the need. In this context we see that money rightly used represents spiritual energy. Here is hidden the secret of manifestation.

What steps do we take for recovery of meaning? To cut out what is meaningless in our lives involves a change in character. Rudolf Steiner has said that the great esoteric law of development is: for every step into higher knowledge take three steps in development of character. Interestingly our quest for meaning seems to link us directly with Buddha's Eightfold Path. This is natural enough, for the great truths are timeless. Thus Steiner in his remarkable and basic little book *Knowledge of the Higher Worlds* describes the same eight functions or attributes of the soul which must be mastered if the throat chakra, the so-called sixteen-petalled lotus, is to become active. It is this that opens the pupil to clairvoyant vision. When we consider these attributes they appear quite logical to show us the stages for recovery of meaning

Right thought. We must think ourselves again into time relationship with the Whole in the moment to moment emergence of the future into the present. We must learn to see what is meaningless in our activity.

Right Resolution. We must develop the 'will to meaning', taking over conscious direction and control of the self.

Right Speech. Recognise how much psychic energy is wasted in meaningless words. We can watch ourselves, to cut out idle chatter. This does not mean austere cutting off from companionship, but a control of a wasteful expenditure of energy in unnecessary speech.

Right Action. We can strive that what we do at each moment shall be meaningful, fulfilling the need of the immediate situation. Then, since we know that the Living Oneness of Being is being precipitated into form each moment, we may know that the energy supply is infinite and all needs will be met.

Right Livelihood. We must survey the pattern of the activity on which our livelihood depends and see how far it conforms with meaningful activity. We are consciously thinking ourselves into service of the whole, and we may know that such are the forces now being released into our lives from this Whole, that extravagant and meaningless activities will be swept away in the coming storm.

Right Endeavour. This involves striving to achieve what the Buddha called 'harmlessness'. In our violent society we condone and even practise things which hurt life. Our very survival as a society turns on our personally achieving new values which cut out the cruel and the wasteful on all levels.

Right Attention or Recollectedness. This attribute as Steiner describes it involves our learning to stand outside ourselves and survey our life's pattern, and also to try to learn all we can from life, the great teacher. It is only our illusion that events seem to follow each other in meaningless chance. We now recognise that life on earth is the greatest training ground and we are being meaningfully led through events and experiences as soul trials and ordeals.

Right Contemplation. The Buddha described this as the Rapture. This phase implies the experience of the greatest of all joys when the soul truly blends with the living Ocean of Meaning and Being from which it came and to which it, in its very nature, belongs.

In the coming epoch man is called upon to work upon his emotional nature, his 'astral body' so as to bring into this chaotic and volatile area something of the harmony and order of natural law. Then he begins to bring to birth a new and higher self or faculty in his being. This is called the Spirit Self. This earth has been called the planet of wisdom; Right Endeavour on man's part will turn it into the Planet of Love, and meaning will be restored to life.

There is surely no joy like being possessed by creative purpose and action. This is known to the mountaineer or skier when every faculty is heightened in adventure, by the musician or actor in performance, by the craftsman completing some critical process which is the culmination of days of preparatory work. In all creation comes at times the sense of giving the entire being to the service of some end far greater than ourselves. In the moments of exaltation we are lifted into the meaning of the whole and are filled with energy. The pause for sleep and food merely serves to keep body and soul in action. As in the individual, so in the Group Soul of a nation, when the sense of great purpose calls for total sacrifice. An example is the energy released in the French Revolution when an untrained citizen army stood against the combined Grand Armies of Imperial Europe and threw them back, or when the dispirited French army was led by Joan against the English at Orleans.

Enthusiasm – the word in its Greek origin means 'possessed by a god'. How precious an experience, bringing colour and zest and creativity into a life at a time when many are bored and cynical and have an overshadowing sense of lack of meaning.

It is, of course, all too true that much purposeful drive is by no means to be identified with 'will to meaning' in the sense used by Matchett & Frankl. Yeats indicates this in his lines:

> The best lack all conviction and the worst
> Are full of passionate intensity.

But the ultimate truth and goal is surely summarized in two verses in St John's Gospel (Chapter 15, verses 4 and 5):

> Abide in me and I in you. As the branch cannot bear fruit of itself, except it abide in the vine, no more can ye, except ye abide in me.
> I am the vine, ye are the branches. He that abideth in me and I in him, the same bringeth forth much fruit, for without me ye can do nothing.

To close, here is the quintessence of this thought in T.E. Brown's little poem, *The Shell*:

> If thou coulds't empty all thyself of self,
> Like to a shell dishabited
> Then might he find thee on an ocean shelf
> And say 'this is not dead'
> And fill thee with himself instead.

> But thou art so replete with very thou
> And hast such shrewd activity
> That when he comes he'll say, it is enow
> Unto itself, t'were better let it be
> It is so small and full
> And has no need of me.

24

MAN AS FOCAL POINT FOR CHANELLING THE LIGHT

W E ALL KNOW the experience of waking in the early hours with a sense that in sleep we have been filled with forebodings. The Victorians had a saying: no man is solvent at four o'clock in the morning. The heart sinks and the pit of the stomach seems possessed by anxieties. If you can consciously transform this it can become a very significant experience. This is in fact the very best time for meditation. One can rarely drive out the devils while cuddling up in bed, but one can get up, light a candle, wrap oneself in a warm cocoon of blankets and forget the body.

The problem is to clear out the anxieties which have taken possession and create a centre of inner stillness. This is the first object of all meditation. First become quite still physically with spine erect and check through your body to see that you are not tensing brow, jaw, neck, shoulders, hands or legs. Enter the inner chapel and sweep out the cobwebs and drive out the bats of disturbing thoughts. Quietly watch the breathing rhythm and note how it gets ever more gentle until you are in absolute inner stillness. You may feel that you are, in a sense, 'being breathed' by the universe. It is as if your heart were breathing. You can in your imaginative experience inhale spiritual light down through the crown of the head, impregnating the body, filling the heart, to be breathed out in love for all being.

You have created something that was not there before, a protected centre or chamber of stillness and tranquillity. It is like a cathode ray, a vacuum which begins to glow when an electric charge is passed through it. You have, in the surrounding psychic field, made a glowing point of stillness defended against attack by dark emotions. In time the alarms and fears are just not there any more. One begins actively to experience the qualities or attributes of the Higher Self which are, basically, stillness and tranquility, courage and love, gentleness and joy.

A variant in this imagination is to see yourself as in a chalice like an opened flower. You are a point of consciousness in this flower, opened up to receive the light of the spiritual sun streaming down from higher worlds. Bask in that sunlight. Every fibre of your being can be impregnated by the light. Just as there can be no more darkness in the room when we turn on the light, so the dark and negative emotions of the Lower Self cannot enter at the same time as the positive attributes of the Higher Self. They are a polarity.

In Omar Khayyam we find the wonderful lines:

> Oh my Beloved, fill the cup that clears
> Today of past regrets and future fears.

These are the negative time-ridden emotions of the lower self. Since man possesses the faculty of looking before and after, he will be hounded by remorse and anxiety and self pity. The animals of course do not suffer in this way. As human beings we are bedevilled by such emotions and meditation is a way of lifting above them. Lift this chalice of the self until it floats like a water lily on the surface of the psychic atmosphere of earth. See the blue heavens above. We are lifted into stillness, out of time. We are touching the eternal in ourselves. We have indeed become an 'intersection point of the timeless with time', and we are discovering in inner experience our real being, our Higher Self, a Self which is free from the ravages of time-ridden thinking.

We are sounding positive soul attributes within ourselves; we are reaching up towards the spiritual worlds. We are creating by our own initiative the attribute of tranquillity within the heart and thus expelling anxiety. Against all odds we can sound courage in the heart.

We begin to discover the great truth known to the Greeks – 'Man know thyself and thou shalt know the Universe'. We begin to sense what this means, sitting in that cocoon in the early hours when all is still before dawn. By now beautifully warmed so that our body is forgotten, the worries are dispersed, we are open to the penetration of the light and can begin to sound the qualities in the heart.

Just as when you strike middle C on the piano, the note reverberates in response in higher octaves, so we can innerly attune to higher planes to which the soul attributes belong. Actually these are the attributes of the great spheres of the planets. The old notion of the 'Crystal Spheres', still held in Shakespeare's day, becomes acceptable again in our time. Venus is not just the shining orb we call the morning star. The crystal sphere is the great area round which the planet makes its orbit and this represents the field of its 'sweet influences'. Each of the planets has its sphere and they all interpenetrate, the earth lying more or less in the centre of them all. Thus the sphere of influence of every planet is in this room, the cosmic soul attributes are all here, Courage from Mars, Joy from Jupiter, Love from Venus. They are also within our own soul. When, like sounding Middle C, we sound Courage, it reverberates up on to higher levels and draws down a response from the spiritual worlds. This is the mystery of *Attunement*.

Since man is the measure of all things, we discover the universal quality in our own souls and deliberately sound it up into the planetary spheres to call forth an answering response. In so doing we blend with the Whole. We experience in this secret hour of meditation that we are truly part of this eternal and timeless world of Spirit, and that we can build the qualities of our higher Self into our lower self. By now perhaps it is a quarter to five and you may be approaching the stage of wonderful inner stillness and tranquillity, which the East calls 'bliss consciousness'. The dark possession is wholly evaporated and you can safely come back to earth, unwrap the cocoon and return to bed with light and love in the heart and peace in the mind. Then sleep, and awaken to carry these qualities into your environment of daily activity.

We are really doing a remarkable task in overcoming the anxieties of the Lower Self in order that the Higher Self possess our being. This is our cosmic duty. We do something to dispel the darkness of our world. For this man comes to earth and can thus begin to influence his environment, channelling and radiating light into the whole area touched by his life activities. For every man is a focal point for the inflooding of the eternal powers of the spirit.

What do we mean by that word 'eternal'? Here there has been much misunderstanding. We are still bedevilled by the heritage of medieval belief that we suffer 'eternal damnation' because of some evil done in our earth life, or enjoy praising the Lord to eternity as a reward for a good life. But this concept of eternal suffering or joy is itself a time-ridden idea, for it is assumed to mean time without end. We must change this thinking. The eternal worlds are simply the spheres of being outside time. The realm of Absolute Being, the Divine Creative source, is everywhere, interpenetrating everything, but beyond Time. When substance and form are created, then Time has to come to birth as well. In solid matter events must appear to move one after another.

Thus when a spiritual being wishes to become active in a solid planet like the Earth it has to enter the field of Time. We are spiritual beings. We are able to return to source, to revisit the Timeless or Eternal planes to which we belong. You can drop back into them for an hour, a day, or a hundred years. You move into the Eternal in sleep, leaving the physical and etheric bodies on the bed. During that time you are free to range in soul-travel, though we mostly do not possess faculties of perception to know it. The great adepts have developed what is called 'continuity of consciousness' and can therefore know of their sleep experiences. This is a great source of spiritual investigation. In meditation we again get in touch with the Timeless World and of course re-enter it when we discard the physical body at so-called death. A spiritual being can move freely anywhere in the Timeless field, moving instantly wherever thought is projected and of course returning instantly to the waiting body when this is necessary.

When we discard the physical body at so-called 'death' we are released back into a world of much greater life. There can be no extinction for this droplet of the Divine source. Thus fear of extinction at death is removed if we can grasp the great concept that *man is a being of Spirit, Soul and Body*. The reason for the wide fear and doubt about death is that we have mostly lost the understanding of this great truth. In the centuries following Christ's descent and of course earlier in the teachings of the mystery temples, it was known and understood that man was a spiritual entity in a universe spiritual in its essential nature, and that in order to live upon earth he had to take to himself a physical body. This consciousness was gradually lost, and the date 869AD may be seen as a kind of watershed. In that year at the Council of Constantinople, the Pope decreed that henceforth it was heresy to speak of men as body, soul and spirit. From now on he was body and soul, soul having certain spiritual attributes. This really opened the possibility of the materialistic view of death.

The New Age vision is now, so to speak, reversing the Council of Constantinople by recognizing once again that man is not his physical or astral body, but that these are the necessary sheaths which make life and activity possible and effective in the limitations of the physical plane. The true entity of man is a spiritual being, ageless, eternal and indestructible. If this could be destroyed it would undermine the whole concept of a 'Creator'. The spiritual being in you always was and always will be.

Let us follow through with this thought. Firstly, it means that survival is axiomatic. Of course you survive, since you are evolving through an endless evolution with further life and wider consciousness. But the more important implication is that you were there before you were born. We have to conceive this condition of unbornness or pre-bornness – pre-existence. It implies that we enter birth as an already developed soul. As a timeless being we choose to enter Time at birth.

Some people have actually experienced this consciously. The seventeenth century poet Traherne possessed the faculty of remembering back into the womb, and beyond, and most of his poems are concerned with this knowledge. Here is a verse from the poem he calls *The Praeparative*:

> Before my sinews did my limbs unite
> I was within
> A House I knew not; newly cloath'd with Skin.

The verse describes the embryo before the body begins to form and goes on ...

> Then was my Soul my only All to me,
> A living endless Ey,
> Scarce bounded by the Sky,
> Whose Power and Act and Essence was to see;
> I was an inward Sphere of Light
> Or an interminable Orb of Sight,
> Exceeding that which makes the Days,
> A vital Sun that shed abroad its Rays;
> All Life, all Sense,
> A naked, simple, pure Intelligence.
> Without restriction then did I behold
> The pure Ideas of all things.

Consider the tremendous implications of this possibility. The tacit assumption of a great many people, arising directly from the loss of vision of the spiritual nature of man, is that you begin at conception and that your character and qualities are built up solely from family inheritance and of heredity and the impact of your environment. Thus it is felt that our limitations can be explained away and excused on the ground solely of our heredity and upbringing. Our defects are not our fault but misfortune.

The counter view, arising out of the belief that an eternal spiritual entity is incarnating, lifts our thinking on to a different scale. It is said that Bach, a great spirit who was the Being of Music, needed the absolutely perfect physical ear in order to bring down heavenly melodies to earth. He therefore chose to incarnate at the end of fourteen generations of musicians. He chose an ancestral stream which would give him the tool for great music to pour through. This view would explain why Genius so often comes at the end of a line. The postulate of pre-existence implies that we actually choose our parents and the environment into which we are going to incarnate, in order to get the setting the soul needs for developing faculties and undergoing the great training experience of life on earth.

Now first of all this means, if you can accept Traherne's testimony, that it is a mistake to think of the newborn child as a 'tiny little soul'. It is possibly a great and mature soul beginning to incarnate into a tiny little body. The soul is still expanded in the widths of the universe and begins the astounding process of narrowing down into the growing body through a series of seven year cycles, until at twenty-one the Ego can be fully incarnated and 'comes of age'. Entry into a body must be an appalling limitation for a free-ranging spiritual being, something like the entry into a sarcophagus. Birth is thus a kind of death, and death more truly a rebirth into a greater freedom.

We begin to see that what Wordsworth expressed in the great *Ode on the Intimations of Immortality in Early Childhood* is indeed the truth. It is for us within the New Age movement to revive the 'Vision Splendid' and as we get older to prepare for the release of this ageless, immortal and therefore ever youthful entity from its worn out body. The body is obviously a temporal thing, subject to the ravages of time. The soul, though maturing through earth experiences which may even appear shattering, will be released back into a world in which it knows that it is eternally young. A man can only be rightly called a 'poor old soul' if he has identified his soul with his ageing body, and its aches and pains.

Listen to W.B. Yeats in the poem *Sailing to Byzantium*:

> An aged man is but a paltry thing,
> A tattered coat upon a stick unless
> Soul clap its hands and sing and louder sing
> For every tatter of its mortal dress
> Nor is there singing school but studying
> Monuments of unageing intellect,
> And therefore have I sailed the seas and come
> To the holy city of Byzantium.

There is a challenge to the lot of us. That is the text for unending adult education. We can rejuvenate the eternal being in its ageing body by 'studying monuments of its own magnificence' and equally by grasping the future prospects opening to us as the soul advances into wider planes of being. Yeats was convinced of the truth of re-incarnation. This earth is what Keats called a 'vale of soul making'. We undergo soul trials and ordeals in order to develop qualities and attributes before returning to the eternal realms between death and a new birth.

This field of gravity upon earth gives the experience of drastic limitation and of being separated from the will of God. The result of this is that we develop free will, that Divine gift. Thus man can evolve to inner freedom. It is all a vast experiment that man may learn out of his free decision and his own work upon himself to overcome the greed of his lower ego and unite with his Higher Self.

This transformation takes a long time. You cannot hope to pass your A Levels and enter a university by dropping in to school for one term in the third form. Every class offers new teaching. In every historical epoch the consciousness of mankind evolves. It seems obviously necessary that the human being should pass through the whole 'School of Earth', learning the lessons of each epoch. We carry history forward in our own souls. We have all, however humbly, played our part in the age of Greece and Rome or the Middle Ages. Therefore 'studying monuments of its own magnificence' means studying in a certain sense achievements of our own souls through history. What memories would lie in each of us if we could but look back through the corridors of time. Steiner tells us that one of the purposes of the present age is to develop our consciousness far enough so that in the next life we shall be able to remember back into this present one and beyond. How the study of history would then change, for we all are history.

I know of a doctor psychiatrist who uses hypnosis to discover the point of lesion in the memories of his patients. Often this is found in an earlier life. In one case the patient described a naval battle in Nelson's time, and in this memory was found the moment of soul damage which reflected itself in mental breakdown in this life. Apparently Mountbatten heard of this and asked to borrow the tape to play to his admirals and naval historians in order to hear a first hand account of a naval battle. This suggests that high authority in this country recognizes the truth and significance of reincarnation.

Naturally all guessing or speculation about past lives is useless and undesirable, but to grasp the general principle can be very strengthening. We can validly note which periods of history we are specially drawn to, knowing that a deep affinity may be showing itself. We may also recognize that souls tend to incarnate in groups. This means that our special friends, our colleagues in work and our relatives are probably beings with whom we have been in incarnation together in earlier lives. In these important days, it is the more likely that we are being drawn together again of intent and for real purpose. We are in these years finding our spiritual families, which thought gives us strength to meet personality difficulties in our lives and to hold a deeper respect for those souls with whom we are linked.

Man is being called upon to wake up to his responsibility as the organ of consciousness in evolution. We are being prepared for entry into the Aquarian Age when the waters of the spirit are poured out. The great seers have all pointed to the last quarter of this century as the great spiritual turning point for mankind. With the rapid advance of knowledge and consciousness it becomes possible for man to destroy life upon this planet in his folly and ignorance or to take a step onward into cosmic consciousness which could allow the redemption of Earth through a blending with higher intelligence. We are told that cosmic energies imbued with intelligence and love are being released into our sphere from 1975 onwards, and that before the end of the century there will come the greatest spiritual crisis that human evolution has ever experienced.

We are indeed living in an apocalyptic age. If powers of Harmony, Love and Truth indeed began to flood human consciousness it would, to those filled with avarice, greed, rivalry, violence and fear, appear like the outpourings of the Vials of

Wrath. All mankind is now overlighted by the Cosmic Christ, the Exalted Lord of All Light. A new society is being born in the middle of our old and crumbling social structure. It will be made up of those who can receive into their hearts the new love and power for harmony. The emerging society is based more on what men can give than what they can get. It will be the Ark that can float upon the Deluge. Our scale of thinking has to be greatly widened if we are to find real courage to face the coming changes. Such hope is instilled into us if we can think apocalyptically, for after the great tribulation comes the Light. There never was such an age in which to be incarnated. This especially applies to the young, for they have the great task of building the new society in co-operation with the higher intelligence.

Yet, as we have seen, we are each of us eternal souls and therefore however many years we have lived we can carry a young heart. We are all concerned with the great spiritual awakening of our time and it makes little difference whether a man is now in incarnation or working from the freer planes after release from the body. The whole spiritual movement is strengthened by every great soul who moves on but remains in telepathic contact with those still active in the earth arena.

The analogy of war is powerful. We are like fifth columnists in the enemy-occupied country. It is our task to hold a bridge-head in the darkened psychic atmosphere of earth and send up the signal for the parachute troops to drop. It looks as if these great Forces of Light are prepared for invasion. Since they will not violate our free will, we have to invoke them. The initiative is ours. Do not let us be discouraged by all the news of violence in our time. This is but the picture of the Beast in Revelation fighting furiously to drag down the human soul 'because he knoweth that his time is short'. But 'look up, for our salvation draweth nigh'.

236

25

THE OBSERVATORY

LAST WEEK I saw on TV the programme given by Patrick Moore on the world's most sophisticated new observatory, on Siding Spring Mountain in New South Wales. We were shown the huge building rising above jungle trees with its white dome, its body structure, its incredible technology serving the great telescopes. I was a little disappointed that we were not shown much of the stars, but given a great deal about the mechanism by which they looked at them. As I got into bed and composed myself for sleep I 'saw' the whole thing again in a flash. The human body is the observatory. Grounded with its foundation firmly in earth and gravity, it reaches up into the lifted dome of the head, open in the crown chakra along the line of the fontanelle to look out into the realm of the stars, 'that majestical roof fretted with golden fire!' We look at the physical stars with physical telescopes. The spiritual beam of thought goes out into the ocean of Mind from which the visible stars are formed. The rounded skull reflects the great sphere of the cosmos.

Here is architecture. Think yourself into St Paul's. The great dome stands above the drum, this built upon the structure of the processional nave. With the inner eye experience the dome. Run down the ribs from the lantern. Swell out with the great curve. Feel this in your head and know that dome represents the skull and the thinking system. The drum with its vast pillars is then sensed as corresponding to the rib cage, the heart system with the heart as the central altar.

The Renaissance architects were obsessed with the building of centralized churches raised on a platform above the city, the central altar under the lantern (crown chakra) through which the divine cosmic rays poured down in power. You experience that the great columns, still rooted in gravity and holding the structure, metamorphose into the ribs of the dome and become flexible to bend and lock in the rim of the lantern. Wren portrayed the human body with head system, heart system, and the will or limb system. The body is the temple into which the God can descend and touch down into the density of the material world. The architect externalizes his experience of this divine design. Our clue in looking dynamically and imaginatively at architecture is to see the fantastic body externalized around us. Re-experience dome as head. Know that in St Paul's the real altar is invisible and etheric in the centre of the Whispering Gallery. But as you walk beneath a Renaissance dome and step into the marble inlaid circle directly under the lantern, you should tread with awe and a prayer, for you are receiving the inputting of divine energy through your own crown chakra. This is holy ground for pilgrimage, not merely for an academic tourist interest.

So back to the observatory. Become it. Stand above the jungle of the emotional and ego level. Beam up through the fontanelle, open to the stars. Go through into the realm of anti-gravity, ethereal space or levity. Expand with the buoyancy of the spirit. Feel the primary polarity on which body is built – its physical relation to gravity and its openness to counter space. Spirit and thought expand into the ocean of Life and Intelligence. You look not at the physical star, the gaseous body turning in empty space, but to the luminous focal points of being manifesting through the lighted sphere, as spirit reflects itself into form.

> Thus every man
> Wears as his robe the garment of the sky
> So close his union with the cosmic plan
> So perfectly he pierces low and high
> Reaching as far in space as creature can
> And co-extending with immensity.
>
> (Charles Earle)

Now from your observatory come out with me on an imaginative experiment. Look first at the rising of the sun. Put yourself on a terrace among hills, purple dark before dawn. Look how the floor of heaven is thick inlaid with patines of bright gold. See the coming of the first light and the higher mountain tops touched with crimson of the first rays of the sun. Then that majestic moment when the sun first breaks the horizon. Watch it rise. Now pause and think. The sun doesn't rise. That is illusion, obviously. The Sun stands still and the earth turns. Right. Repeat the imagining only this time you spin with the earth. The identical picture appears, but your change in thinking realizes it quite differently.

The intellectual recognition enables you to 'see' earth spinning. In that instant you are one with the whole earthly ball. Roll with it until sun is in mid-heaven and descends again to the western horizon. But now take another and braver step. Release yourself from your body point, the anchorage to Earth's surface. Get into orbit beyond Earth's atmosphere and let it spin, so that your body goes down behind the globe. Suddenly you have expanded in consciousness and Earth now is a beautiful little sphere, shining blue and silver against the velvet dark of the night sky, as Edgar Mitchell saw it when he came out from behind the moon. Now with etheric hands you can hold and love the Earth, that beautiful planet in such need of healing.

You are free to expand again so that you 'see' the family grouping of the solar system, parent Sun and planets in their galactic setting. Know that you are perfectly capable of extending thus into cosmic consciousness. Then contract again, to see the spinning Earth, then plunge out of orbit so that you identify again with the planet and find your own focal point of consciousness, your body. Enter that body and click back into normal sensing so that you 'see the sun rise and the moon set'.

So you are the Observatory. Know that man in all his inventions and technological creations is externalizing that most wonderful of temple structures the body microcosm, divinely and fantastically made to reflect the macrocosm. All creation is contained in this microcosm. We cannot invent what has not already been thought by God. All architecture is an external-ization of what is within the body and, doubtless, a reflection of ethereal structures which the architect has experienced in sleep or meditation. So the astounding complexity within the Observatory in electronic technology, reflects but palely the intricacy of the human brain.

We may even trace the story of our Industrial Revolution as an externalizing of the deeper experience of the body. First the inventors create the steam engine, a structure reflecting the metabolic or limb system which gives the bodily base for the Will. Food in the stomach creates the energy. Coal in the steam engine does the same. Then we invent the internal combustion engine with its subtle interplay of air and liquid. This can be likened to the 'rhythmic system', centred on the heart and seat of the emotions.

And this is followed by our electronic age of the computers, which surely is an externalization of the central nervous system, the basis for the brain thinking of man. What we cannot invent is Life itself. The tragedy of materialistic mechanistic man is that he has now externalized his whole divine body temple into his machines, which now surround and even control him while he, the ego sits in the middle, sometimes terrified at the nightmare of power he has 'created' and left in doubt as to the meaning of his existence.

Spiritual man is on the threshold of taking the next step, realizing his own divinity, recognizing that body is indeed microcosm reflecting macrocosm and that he can now expand from self consciousness into cosmic consciousness of the ALL, of which he is truly part. This is the challenge of the new humanity now emerging. This is the opportunity – to discover the reality of ethereal space, the polarity to gravity-bound space. Here is the new space exploration, counterpart to our physical exploration with our rockets. By entering into the Observatory we can, in Blake's words:

> open the immortal eyes
> Inward into the realms of thought
> Into Eternity

Ever expanding in the Bosom of God
The human Imagination.

All is polarity as the Hermetic Wisdom knew. The exploration of ethereal space, the expansion of consciousness into the etheric ocean of Life and Levity, this is the field for the astronomer within the Observatory.

26

LIVING INTO CHANGE

T HE WORLD is full of a turmoil of anxiety. Change is upon us all. Man is obviously being forced to adapt and adjust at a pace never before experienced in evolution. We rush into a world society through the power of our technology and the population explosion. All problems take on a planetary scale.

A book has appeared in America by Alvin Toffler, a professor of Future Sociology. He calls it *Future Shock*, contending that when the demands of social and personal adjustment are too great, a psychological state is brought about in which people become incapable of decision and initiative. It is a sort of soul paralysis in protest against too great demands.

Thus, since it is clear that tremendous changes are coming on us in the near future, it is of importance to train ourselves to move into conditions for which we have no precedent without being thrown off poise and balance.

Here, in our materialistic age of anxiety, appears a new hope – the phenomenon of the spiritual awakening in our time and the emergence of a spiritual world-view. This seems to be rising like a tide in our consciousness and coming to the surface, bringing a flood of new understanding. Briefly, the new outlook suggests that the universe is not a great dead mechanism but is a shot through and through with Creative Intelligence and Being from which (or Whom) all manifestation in matter derives. The inner kernal of each man is seen as a droplet of the Divine Source, eternal, imperishable and as indestructible as all life is.

Therefore, in the sense of extinction of the individual entity, there is no death. That bugbear is lifted from our consciousness. It becomes clear that there are many levels of consciousness, each more subtle and refined as they rise to the Source of Light, earth consciousness being the densest and darkest. Life upon earth appears, not as a chance accident in evolution, but a field of training for the soul. By taking on the drastic limitations of an ensouled body the eternal entity of man, the 'I am', the 'ego', undergoes the experience of separation from the Divine Will, acquires self consciousness, and learns to use the God-given gift of free will. By passing through grievous soul trials and ordeals he at length discovers that he is not the lonely separated entity he had imagined but is an integral part of a wondrous living Whole. Then he can begin to expand his consciousness to blend with higher levels of being. Then the Prodigal's Return begins.

It appears that mankind is approaching a great spiritual 'crisis' or turning point represented by the entry into the Aquarian Age. The seers and adepts of our time foresee profound inner changes before the end of this century. This may well, for many, involve the opening of 4th and 5th dimensional awareness. It seems that the Higher Worlds are deeply concerned with what happens on this planet, and are prepared to pour in the Powers of Light for the redemption of mankind, if a sufficient number of men will invoke them and call on them to descend. This gives something of an apocalyptic picture, but perhaps this scale of thinking is necessary. After all, we are faced with possibilities of man-made disaster on such a scale that we might as well counter by 'thinking big' about the possibilities of creative redemption and the imminent coming of a New Age. The present swelling turmoil in society may well be a sign of human consciousness beginning to pass into another dimension. If man could truly blend his thinking with the Creative Intelligence on the invisible planes, then nothing is impossible in the rescue of our polluted planet and the transformation of society. Yet this great ally is wholly ignored in our self-sufficient attempts to deal with our problems. If we can develop the power to make contact in full consciousness with great earthly personalities who are living in the spiritual world, this would bring the real healing humanity needs.

Therefore in considering how we face change we must think how we open our consciousness to spiritual forces which can work creatively in us. This is the supreme challenge and hope. In our materialism we have wholly forgotten the existence of subtler worlds existing not far away but permeating the whole of everywhere on finer frequency rates to which our coarser senses are not tuned. The angelic kingdoms, the elemental beings of nature and our own friends who have left the body are all there to work with us in our risen thinking. And, since there is no death, the prospect of ever widening exploration of 'inner space' is infinite.

The expectation of imminent change means that the next twenty-five years are of great significance in human history. It is probably justifiable to take the apocalyptic passages in the Bible somewhat seriously as applying to our own age. Certainly very many are now filled with the supreme hope that the 'Revealer of the Word', the Christos, is in these years overlighting all mankind. The great Coming is already here on the invisible planes and we can prepare ourselves for this Event by lifting our understanding and learning to work and live into new human dimensions.

So to our question as to how we train ourselves to live into the new without succumbing to 'future shock' or losing psychic balance.

LIVING IN THE NOW

In considering 'living into change' we must first and foremost make good the oft repeated aphorism that only the present moment exists. The past is dead, the future may never come as we expect it. The Eternal Now is the one moment of which we have control and in which we can make changes and yet it is instantly past. It is a razor edge of moving experience. Like a surf rider we are poised on the surging crest of an advancing wave. If we lose balance we are thrown back to flounder in the back-log of memories and remorse for the past, or forward into a turmoil of anxieties about a future that may never come.

> Oh my Beloved fill the Cup that clears
> Today of past regrets and future fears.

FitzGerald's Rubaiyat is only superficially in praise of 'drinking and being merry for tomorrow we die'. Seen deeper, it is a profoundly allegorical statement of eternal value. It speaks of the wine of life and the Cup offered by Him who called Himself the True Vine. In that remarkable and inspired little book *God Calling*, one passage given from the High Source reads as follows:

> Regret nothing. Not even the sins and failures. Man is so made that he can carry the weight of twenty four hours, no more. Directly he weighs down with the years behind and the days ahead, his back breaks. I have promised to help you with the burden of today only; the past I have taken from you, and if you, foolish hearts, choose to gather again that burden and bear it, then, indeed, you mock Me to expect Me to share it.
>
> For weal or woe each day is ended. What remains to be lived, the coming twenty four hours you must face as you awake.
>
> A man on a march on earth carries only what he needs for that march. Would you pity him if you saw him bearing too the overwhelming weight of the worn-out boots and uniforms of past marches and years? And yet, in the mental and spiritual life, man does these things. Small wonder My poor world is heart sick and weary. Not so must you act.

We must admit if we are honest that the actual moment is rarely intolerable. Our agonies are nearly all involved with the regrets and remorse about the past or the worries as to what is going to happen in a week, a month, a year. 'One step enough for me' as Newman said. We are metaphorically crossing a morass on stepping stones in a fog. Always the next step is shown to us, but no further. Our fears arise from looking too far ahead. Once we implant in our soul the certainty that we are each of us being led by invisible guides who have the overall view above the fog, then we may boldly step forward.

Our spiritual world view does bring this certainty and it is essential to brave living into change. The invisible worlds do exist. Each man's destiny is guided by beneficent guides. There are angels who watch our faltering footsteps and are there to help and serve. Once we accept this, we can step forward with courage into the unknown and which is not unknown to our Higher Self, whereas if these invisible helpers did not exist then truly we are floundering in uncertainty and are driven to hang on to old fixed modes and habits and thought forms.

ACTING INTO THE HIGHER SELF

We have stressed that we are living in apocalyptic days. We must expect changes, social, psychological and even in the outer world. Many think that man's treatment of the living Earth has been such that this great sentient being will strike back in protest. This may be a fanciful way of putting it, but read Gordon Rattray Taylor's, *Doomsday Book*, written by a leading ecologist, to reveal what the scientists foresee as possibilities resulting from what we are doing to the living earth and to the delicate balance of the atmosphere. As he says, it reads like a horror story!

We are at times faced with human situations for which we have no precedent – what then do we do? Often we are helpless and revert to brain tracks or habits which lead us back into old reactions and an opportunity is missed. How often we kick ourselves for doing this! How then do we move forward into change? (It is said that in Chinese there is no word for 'crisis', the nearest definition being 'opportunity for important decisions'.)

Our world-view includes the postulate of the Higher Self. Each of us has this 'utterly trustworthy parental being' who is part of the super-conscious world and a counterpart to our subconscious mind. Psychology as yet only begins to recognise this all important factor in our being, though it appears to be the source of many of the creative impulses in our conduct previously explained through sublimation of the sexual drives. We are really working with higher 'drives' coming from the light filled plane of the super conscious, and the High Self is our

Higher Ego into which our lower ego must in time be dissolved. If we can take this postulate then we can act upon it. Literally 'act'. We can act into our higher self. Faced with a crisis situation without precedent, we can in a flash of lifted imagination conceive how our high self would react and then bravely act the part. This is a true and creative use of the inherent power of acting which is in all of us. It is not for nothing that the English are the greatest race of amateur actors. A new field opens up for the sublimated actor in each of us. We can move beyond the amateur drama club and carry the same talents into this new field of exploration, through conduct built on the imagination into the kingdom of the Higher Self. Then we might learn to move into change with the certainty that we are indeed being guided through totally new circumstances.

The trouble is that so frequently, when faced with a sudden call to action, we allow a preconception to flash into the mind as to our course of conduct. Once this has happened there is little hope for a new course, since the preconception must perforce throw us back into an already experienced habit. Thus we must learn to inhibit the instant reaction to the stimulus of the event and then calmly review the 'courses open', using the imagination to feel out the new. This is the ability that Keats called 'negative capability' – 'that is that a man is capable of being in uncertainties: mysteries and doubts, without any irritable reaching after fact and reason.' This he contends is the quality that goes to make a man of achievement.

The analogy of a fencing bout is a good one. We are faced with some challenge, which perhaps we take as an insult, arousing our anger. We hit back, parry and riposte, with bitter words. This is just what the devil wants and we are drawn down into painful emotion and mutual hurt. We can, if we choose, parry the attack but recognise that the true riposte is not at our opponent but at our own low-self reaction. Outer circumstances are so frequently the counterpart of our inner world. If we can 'inhibit' the hurtful reaction from ourselves and get our emotional rise into control, we are then free to choose a reaction which does not hurt.

Our inner world and outer world are so closely linked. We all have flaws in our character which actually draw us into situations and events (which are usually people) who present us with the temptation to fall again. So long as the weakness is not overcome, again and again we shall be drawn into the temptation. Through agony we at last recognise what is happening and by creative and imaginative conduct can learn to use such situations to overcome the flaw. John Vyvyan in his wonderful book *Shakespearean Ethic* develops this as the clue to Shakespeare's tragedies. The hero is faced by the temptation which is the counterpart of the flaw in his character, falls and is thrown into mental and emotional confusion, is hit again and if he falls again the situation deteriorates and the stage is littered with bodies. If the act of creative mercy can intervene there is hope for redemption.

WE ARE TOTAL CAUSE

As a result of materialistic philosophy in science we are too prone to assume that character is solely the product of heredity and enviroment. This gives us the outlet for transferring responsibility for how we behave to an outside cause – my parents were separated, I was an only child, we were too poor, our environment was impossible. The whole picture can be reversed. My 'I' is an eternal being. Therefore 'I' was already a developed soul before I was born. Indeed logically I must have used this earth plane many times in the long evolution of my soul. Therefore, in co-operation with my higher self and spiritual guides, I must have been given some form of pre-view of the destiny I was taking on in deciding to incarnate. In his remarkable poem called *Trial by Existence*, Robert Frost describes, from the heavenly viewpoint:

> ... the gathering of the souls for birth
> The trial by existence named,
> The obscuration upon earth,
> And none are taken but who will
> Having first heard the life read out
> That opens earthward, good or ill.
> Beyond the shadow of a doubt, ...
> But always God speaks at the end;

One thought in agony of strife
The bravest would have by for friend
The memory that he chose the life;
But the pure fate to which you go
Admits no memory of choice
Or the woe were not earthly woe
To which you give assenting voice ...

If we can take this view it brings a new courage and involves a shouldering of ultimate responsibility. It means that truly we are total cause of all that we are and all that happens to us. There are really no accidents because our higher self can very easily stage situations and experiences which are essential for our inner progress. Seen from the spiritual point of view we chose our heredity and environment as the outward setting for experiences which may develop the inner man. If we are really courageous we will act on the assumption that we took on the task of transmuting a difficult environment. The pioneer in the West took pride in tackling and taming wild forest land. So we may feel that we have taken on ourselves a task in descending into a difficult set of circumstances. They present a challenge for redemption and transformation. So we can serve the world.

Furthermore, let us face the implications of this heavenly pre-view of our destiny before descending to the 'obscuration upon earth'. We know that the next twenty-five years are critically important since mankind is approaching a great spiritual turning point. Very many souls must be crowding into incarnation so as to be on the planet to experience the great events in this generation. If we have woken up to the implications and have set our feet on the path to spiritual understanding, we may be sure that each of us, in our present incarnation, has a special task, however humble. We incarnated of intent and with a purpose, and probably in association with a group of souls with whom we had been together in previous earth lives. We have forgotten the task. Our High Self of course still knows it and waits patiently for us to awaken. When we do so, when we see and acknowledge what we are meant to fulfil before we leave this plane, a new meaning and sense of purpose will be given to our lives. We shall be able to go forward into battle with greater certainty and courage, working in ever greater consciousness with our high self. We may expect the 'spiritual movement' to develop with ever greater strength and purpose as individual souls thus learn to know the task which they undertook in coming to birth. Furthermore, as ever increasing numbers of workers for the spirit move over on to the higher planes, we may expect ever closer co-operation. The New Age groups are continually being strengthened by their members who, released from bodily limitation, can work in the subtle blending of thought from the etheric level.

We must have faith enough to see what it means to start absolutely from where we are now. We are where we are meant to be. This is axiomatic once we admit to our invisible guides. If we are striving for understanding of the spirit, then we must assume we are now where 'they' want us. We are all volunteers in an army which takes no conscripts. If higher command wish to post us somewhere else, our higher self would have no difficulty in staging events which throw us out of our present circumstances so as to bring about a new condition. Again we are called upon to act on this courageous view that we are in the right place now and the more consciously we can recognise the 'guidance' the more positive and remarkable will it become.

We float in our little canoe down a great river of events. If we fight against the current we court disaster. If with real trust, we let ourselves go with it, we can guide through the immediate wild water. We have no time to think about or be concerned with the rapids far ahead.

Remember that if it be true that we 'chose the life' and are being guided through experience on the earth plane of 'separation', then it is axiomatic that we must have built-in soul-powers to overcome all difficulties.

The spiritual pattern truly suggests that we must have latent reserves of strength on which we can to overcome any obstacle, and every overcoming strengthens the soul for the next step in the adventure through this training ground of soul.

Each man is truly an ambassador of God. We descend of intent into the chaos of the world and are each responsible for our personal area of growth and activity. Thus when we pray 'Thy kingdom come on earth…' we could see this as referring to our particular piece of 'earth', represented by all the ramifications of connection, responsibility and activity which constitute our life at the moment. In all these activities we are backed and supported by the invisible guides and nothing happens purely by chance. When life is considered from a broader viewpoint, it seems that there are really very few 'accidents'. The events which hit us as accidents may well be staged by our invisible guides to enable us to take a further step in development. 'To him that overcometh will be given the crown'. At any rate we must recognise that to act as if all accidents and untoward events are planned for us by or through our higher selves develops in us a strong and courageous view of our lives. We do not whine or complain if we shoulder full responsibility for all we are and all that happens. We are 'total cause'. Obviously our character and circumstances at the immediate moment are precisely the result of the cumulative past. History is us and now.

A most constructive change of attitude follows this sort of thinking. Less and less are we concerned with our own wills. If our plans go awry and we are prevented from doing what we would have enjoyed, the attitude is not 'How disappointed I am' but 'I wonder what He wants of me now and what new door will open since that one is closed?' Thus daily life would increasingly become an exploration into the ever new, with continuous opportunity for free choice and yet a knowledge of higher guidance. On earth we are learning to be free moral beings and to exercise creative initiative in the service of God. For this man has come into incarnation. We move out of the age of aggrandisement of the self-conscious ego into the New Age of transforming that ego into an instrument that can in freedom say 'Thy Kingdom come, Thy will be done on earth'. But man does not simply wait on Divine Grace. He is called on to become co-creator and take the initiative in forming a new society in co-operation with higher worlds of being. Hence 'living into change' is the great creative task for us all.

THE REFINING FIRE

Not in any way is this to belittle the pain of loss, the Soul-scarring of disappointment or remorse, the suffering in illness. Pain obviously is the great educator and here upon earth we experience it most poignantly.

Most of us have reached the stage of evolution when we are not liable to indulge in brutality arisen from animal passions. Most of the things we do which hurt others are errors of judgment which may have to be paid for by agonies of remorse. 'Seven times tried that judgment is – That did never choose amiss'. In other words our wrong-doing is usually more the mistakes of the reasoning middle self than the passions of the instinctual animal lower self.

Consider the passage in T.S. Eliot's *Little Gidding* where Dante speaks of 'the gifts reserved for age'.

> ... the rending pain of re-enactment
> Of all that you have done, and been; the shame
> Of motives late revealed, and the awareness
> Of things ill done and done to others harm
> Which once you took for exercise of virtue.
> Then fools' approval stings and honour stains.
> From wrong to wrong the exasperated spirit
> Proceeds, unless restored by that refining fire
> Where you must move in measure, like a dancer.

Indeed here is the secret, that the passage into the Now is like a dance and we can voluntarily give ourselves to the refining fire. The remorse, disappointment or agony of loss is this fire into which we can plunge until it purges us. It will leave us when the soul lesson is learned, for we are realizing that ultimately all loss on this plane is compensated for on the higher planes after death. There we shall meet again those whom we have 'lost', in conditions when we can blend much more closely than we ever could in embodiment. There we shall have the opportunity to do those things which our life on earth did not allow. So much do we have to forego in the limitation of a body and we move hereafter into realms of freer creative action. Thus this temporary parenthesis of life out of the eternal realms is the great schooling and the worst will pass. The blending of inner world and outer world makes our passage through events like a dance. We can let go into it and accept what comes in each day. We are to experience the metamorphosis of the soul through the refining fire, a burning of the dross as we move into the flame in conscious acceptance.

MEDITATION AND THE INNER CITADEL

Meditation is the channel for continuous reconstituting of the self to move into the new. Our low self is a creature of habit and will repeat brain tracks from the unconscious. These have frequently to be expunged so that we may allow new impulses from the high self. In the daily period of meditation we achieve an inner stillness and tranquillity. The entire nervous system and the vital processes rest as in deep sleep while there is a condition of alert attention in the mind, a listening to the world of being. We are then open to the qualities of the high self, which essentially are peace, love, gentleness, courage and joy.

While these fill the soul there is no room for the negative qualities of the low self which are remorse, regret, disappointment, anger, resentment for things past, and fear, anxiety and doubt about the future. These negative emotions cannot enter any more than darkness can remain in a room when we switch on the light.

When we pray 'forgive us our trespasses' we could read this as referring to our partnership of low self and conscious middle self personality. Forgive the silly things and blunders and hurts 'we' did yesterday. Let the mirror be wiped clean so that today we start quite fresh and try again. This the high self is always prepared to do. Indeed in a real sense the self is new each day. The self who thought itself insulted a week ago no longer exists. I now live afresh in a new day. Once I see this, I know not only that 'to understand all is to forgive all', but truly that 'there is nothing to forgive', since each day (once we see it) we can start anew. Polish the mirror afresh and reflect the positive high self qualities.

Realize too that we really are reflecting qualities: once admit the reality of higher worlds and you see that if you sound a quality such as courage or tranquillity it will resound upon higher subtler planes of spirit where Qualities are Beings. Up there in the Spirit Worlds they are planetary forces. As when you strike middle C on the piano it reverberates automatically on higher octaves, so the active sounding of soul qualities will react and draw down strengthening and living power. This, if rightly seen and used, becomes a creative and soul building technique.

Every time you allow yourself to express discouragement, criticism, cynicism, anger or fear you send out a jet of darkness into the already darkened psychic atmosphere of the world and are yourself dragged down. Conversely every time you take the initiative to build high-self positive qualities into the soul, you strengthen the bond with the planes of light. This is our human duty and purpose. It has been contended that we are the vocabulary we use. We are obviously free to choose to cut out all negative expressions. If we allow none to pass our lips, then in time we will cut them out also from our thoughts. We can learn to use what has been called 'the Perfect language'.

Our period of meditation teaches the low self to be still and tranquil. It gives it a taste of the joy and bliss of being in touch with the higher qualities. Then when we plunge into the day's activities all our doings will increasingly be coloured by the positive impulses. Each day they are strengthened and the citadel in the soul becomes more powerful. The low self is being trained to defend this citadel against attack by darker thoughts or impulses. We build this sanctuary of light in heart and mind which gradually can be held intact through the day's events. In time the whole day would become a continuous meditation – 'the yoga of action'. The citadel will become impregnable. If it could be filled with the Light of the Christ we should indeed have made our real contribution to the Coming of the Kingdom. The Christ said, 'If I be lifted up, all men will be lifted with me'. Each in his small way could work towards this end.

For, to carry the analogy of the defended citadel further, we are each involved in the war against the powers of darkness. Each is a spear-head or bridgehead point in the great battle now joined between Michael and his angels and the dragon of materialistic and negative thinking. The devil, Mephystopheles, described himself as 'I am the Spirit who always denies, negates. *Ich bin der Geist der stets verneint*' (Faust). He is the vitiator, the denier of the spirit, the eternal negative, and we fight him by positive thinking and acting; backed as we are by the Forces of Light which long through our initiative to take over and redeem the earth plane.

We are reminded of the Theban army in ancient Greece. It was made up of companions, lovers. In the front rank fought the young man immediately backed by his older friend, for it was certain that, through the love they felt for each other, neither would show cowardice. So we can feel ourselves backed and supported in the fight by the Invisible Lover, who is our Higher Self. To quote from that inspired book *Light on the Path* by Mabel Collins:

> Look for the Warrior and let him fight in thee. Obey him, for he is thyself, yet infinitely wiser than thyself .... Then thou canst go through the fight cool and unwearied, standing aside and letting him battle for thee. Then it will be impossible for you to strike one blow amiss. But if you look not to him, if you pass him by, then there is no safeguard for thee. Thy brain will reel and thy heart grow uncertain in the dust of the battlefield. He is thyself. Yet thou art but finite and liable to error; he is eternal and is sure. He is eternal truth. When once he has entered thee and become thy warrior, he will never utterly desert thee; and at the day of the great peace he will become one with thee.

If we could really make our inner citadel impregnable and so advance into battle, we would have achieved something of immeasurable importance. We would have created a seed point in the soul which we would carry through into the life between death and rebirth. Then when the time came for the ego to reincarnate it could with this strengthened seed draw to itself improved quality in the astral body or soul and enter earth life again with much bad karma expunged and erased. We are truly working for the future of our own souls and of the planet. We are involved in an endless process of metamorphosis of the soul as a creative deed which takes on ever greater interest and significance as we wake up to what it implies.

THE INNER TEACHER

Something like a new moral principle seems to be emerging in our age. No longer, as was assumed in Victorian days, is the issue clear for the following of conscience and 'doing the right thing'. 'Budge, says the fiend. Budge not, says my conscience.' It is now rarely so cut and dried. We seem constantly to be given a choice of ways each of which will lead to hurt or difficulty. We have deliberately to choose and take on ourselves the karmic consequences. As in the allegory of mountain climbing, two routes open and we choose one, putting the rejected alternative out of mind and not looking back with regret. Positive thinking often calls for selecting the boldest and most exciting course. For most of us, if we look back, the deepest regrets are for what we failed to do, for the opportunities missed. The gush of impulse in the heart suggests our course of action but then, ah, how often, we allow cold intellect to turn us away – it would cost too much, people would think me silly, I have an appointment on Tuesday, etc., etc.

> Thus conscience doth make cowards of us all
> And thus the native hue of resolution
> Is sicklied o'er with the pale cast of thought
> And enterprises of great pith and moment
> With this regard their currents turn away
> And lose the name of action.

We are all like Hamlet.

But when we acknowledge guidance and direction from the High Self we see that the way it speaks is precisely in the impulse of the heart, or the flash in the mind or the still small inner voice. So quiet are these hints that we too easily miss them and they are overlaid by our chattering mind or hard cold reason. Yet we could learn to work with this subtle co-operation. It is truly the key to 'living into change'. Self deception is of course easy. Obviously not all our heart impulses are to be trusted, but we can accept that we are learning to use a telepathic contact with High Self, our Guide, who must speak delicately. There is no constraint or enforcing. The technique for exploration into the New is clear.

We are indeed learning to work with our *Inner Teacher*. This may be of paramount importance for New Age education. Nowadays so much education is concerned with learning information given from outside. This may all have little relevance for wholly new conditions in the future. What we most need for living into change is a method of contacting the Inner Teacher. Let us quote from Browning's *Paracelsus*:

> Truth is within ourselves: it takes no rise
> From outward things, whate'er we may believe.
> There is an inmost centre in us all
> Where Truth abides in fullness: and around
> Wall upon wall, the gross flesh hems it in.
> That perfect clear perception – which is truth.
> A baffling and perverting carnal mesh
> Binds it, and makes all error: and, to *know*,
> Rather consists in opening out a way
> Whence the imprisoned splendour may escape,
> Than in effecting entry for a light
> Supposed to be without.

We need to devise forms of training for making this contact with the inner sources of truth. Then we shall with ever greater confidence find we can move through into the unknown. Presumably the greater the spiritual crisis the more certainly will the higher world offer its guidance and protection to those who are dedicated to its service. Therefore, in the ultimate apocalyptic challenge we must be prepared to commit ourselves wholly to the new.

THINK ABUNDANCE

We move into a New Age, which on inner planes is with us already. The Coming of the Kingdom means axiomatically that to God all things are possible. In Him is abundance. Here we touch a new economic law for a new society. He can obviously meet all needs. We however mostly spend our lives trying to satisfy wants and desires. This is a very different thing. If we could really learn to work for the doing of His Will, our needs would be supplied, miraculously. This has been proved in our time by many groups and individuals. It involves however an abandon of which most of us are incapable until extremity drives us to throw our lives wholly on Him. Then the 'miracles' can begin to happen. A kind of reckless reliance on God seems to be called for and, when achieved, it works. It is a surrender of self will, but does not mean becoming an ascetic. The saying 'Leave all and follow me' can mean a total casting away of the past with all its failures or successes, and a complete new start in the daily present. We must learn to 'think abundance' and to know that all things are possible through Him.

He is building a new world, right down into material society, and He wants nothing but the highest quality on all levels. We need not feel we are called to an arid puritanism, which is often associated with a readiness to accept the second-rate. Our Master and Lord is Cavalier enough to need the most beautiful and colourful and best. Cavalier and puritan represent the great cleavage in Britain's history and indeed character. We each of us carry this polarity in our very souls. That incomparable book *1066 and All That* declared that 'the Roundheads were right but repulsive and the Cavaliers were wrong but romantic'. A basic, if partial, truth! Puritanism knew that the new consciousness must rise above the sensual, but it seared the soul by its aridity. The Cavaliers, though falling at times into the licentious excesses of enjoyment of the senses, at the same time delighted in ritual and beauty. May it be that the New Age begins to resolve this basic cleavage in the national character! We lift above the lower sensual to a realization of the subtler senses which it is discovered brings a deeper and more refined delight and a demand for beauty in form and ritual living. We rediscover the romance and idealism in life, for never was there a more poetical and beautiful vision of new possibilities for transforming what is sordid in our lives. Thus the puritan in us rises above the downward drag of the coarser senses and unites with the true cavalier in our nature which longs for joy in life, beauty, and colour of ever new forms to delight the subtler senses to the Glory of God. God wants Quality in his Kingdom on Earth. Everything is to be the best on every level, but there is to be nothing beyond what is necessary. Thus we shall all be called on to simplify in our lives but at the same time to strive for beauty in His name, trusting absolutely that prayers will be answered which are offered up for the meeting of His needs.

Let us close with the enchanting little poem by T.E. Brown called *The Shell*. It summarises the whole issue in exquisite brevity.

> If thou couldn't empty all thyself of self
> Like to a shell dishabited
> Then might He find thee on an ocean shelf
> And say: 'This is not dead'
> And fill thee with Himself instead.
> But thou art so replete with very thou
> And hast such shrewd activity
> That when He comes He'll say 'It is enow
> Unto itself – t'were better let it be:
> It is so small and full
> And has no need of Me.

27

THE PURPOSE OF
MEDITATION NOW

THE PURPOSE of our conference is to talk about meditation, its practice, method and purpose. I want to start this second day by thinking a little more about its purpose. It is quite clear that in all the movements which are represented here, meditation is sensed as being of paramount importance at the present stage of our thinking. We represent a great many different lines of interest and we learn in each conference of this sort how to meet each other. That is our task because in the climbing of this mountain we have obviously each to choose our own route, and not every route is suitable to everybody. It must not discourage us that others of greater wisdom and skill are taking some other path. It maybe that our path is a very simple one but it is our path, 'a poor thing, an ill-favoured thing, but our own', and yet we must realise that we are all concerned with one great quest, which is the climbing of this mountain towards expanded consciousness, and a deeper understanding of the human and spiritual crisis which faces mankind today.

Our society really needs missionaries right in the heart of it to propagate the very idea of God once more. In this society of ours so many have lost God and have above all lost the sense of the super-sensible world, the reality of higher worlds. The world is divided into those who take the agnostic, atheist or materialistic view and those who realise that there exists a higher world, a world of beings, who are part of the living will of the Almighty and Eternal God and that the core of man belongs to this higher world. Many talk about the spirit and spiritual values, but implying by these words simply the human endeavour in the direction of art, music, altruism and the churches as opposed to politics, economics and money making. Spiritual values in this sense do not imply what we understand by the living spirit. This implies the dawning in our consciousness of the truth that we are in fact in touch with higher beings, that higher planes of consciousness exist and that we are destined to move on to these planes of consciousness because that kernel which exists in every human being is eternal and is part of the whole consciousness of the living God. The implications of the emerging view are obviously enormous. It is terrific news, if one might put it that way. It is the most important piece of information that anybody nowadays can get.

To put it another way, you are not your body; you are a spiritual being and eternal, seconded to a society on this earth plane for a limited spell of time in order that, when your task is done and your experience made, you may be released from the limitations and shackles of that fading body, that worn-out over-coat. Then you may move back again on to extended planes of consciousness but enriched in your understanding and through experience of self-will and self-hood, having attained something of the quality of a free moral being, who like the prodigal son, can find his way back towards the Father. We begin to see that this earth, as Keats so well called it, is not a vale of tears, so much as 'a vale of soul making'. We are all here for a very good purpose in order to undergo those experiences which can only be learned in the separation of the body and cut off from the direct experience of the Divine Worlds. It is as if the beneficent imagining of the world of absolute being, call it God or eternal consciousness, or what you will, has chosen to split itself up and to work down and down and down, until the original and archetypal ideas conceived and imagined are realised into physical form, in order that within the whole pattern of nature, there might evolve an organism which can carry the living spirit of man. This is the human body, this consummation of the design of nature, which is able to bear and house a spiritual being.

On whatever plane it may be living, a spiritual being obviously needs to be embodied so as to have the vehicle through which to work. Were we living on a flame planet we should have flame bodies; on a viscous planet we should have viscous or fish-like bodies. But living on this planet of which gravity is the chief force, we need a physical body in which the limbs are given over entirely to the world of gravity and the head is lifted so that it is open towards the heavenly world, and can think divine thoughts. Here is the perfect vehicle, in which the spiritual being can experience aloneness, isolation, cut-off-ness, shut inside himself. We are a world of lonely and separated people, cut off from the truth that we are part of the great living oneness of things. This is the truth which we apprehend with our thinking and with our imagination, that the whole of life is divine, and is all part of the Great Oneness which manifests on many different planes and gives on this plane the appearance of separation into a diversity of parts.

As far as we are concerned, this planet is relatively so huge that it needs the effort of constructive imagination to realise that it is a great living organism and we are the blood corpuscles as you might say, in that organism. Yet we have the illusion that we are just shut inside our skin. That of course is not so; we must recognise that on the higher plane we are our auras.

When we are released from the body, consciousness and sense of identity continues, though we have lost the physical sense organs and the brain. Obviously there is brain-free thinking on that plane. We don't need the brain. The whole of the universe is thought; it is thought that has made the convolutions of the brain and not the brain that makes thought. The brain on this plane is an organ of perception to perceive ideas and to experience thought in everyday contact in the sense world. We have to imagine the great spheres and spaces of thought, the whole of the cosmos shot through with living thought, of which we will be part, according to our faculties of perception, when we are freed from the body, and of which we can be part now in so far as we can develop true imagination and vision. Brain-free thinking can in fact be developed while we are here.

We are, I repeat, our auras, and the 'body' on the higher plane is the focal point of consciousness. The aura is not limited to the immediate surrounding of the body but is part of a vast radiating field of life which can extend indefinitely and contact everything else with which it has relationship and which has a kindred wave-length. This means that there is the possibility of infinitely wide experience. We must struggle to overcome the ridiculous limitation that has so riddled our consciousness in tacitly assuming that we are simply this little body. First of all we wipe out the idea that we are the body. It is nothing but the housing which we reject when its usefulness is over. We recognise that with every step of decaying or ageing of this organ, the spirit is gradually freeing itself in preparation for its final release. Next we must realise that we are our aura and that our consciousness can be in this wide field. It is from there that we think. We begin to see that there is nothing to stop us from being in consciousness anywhere. It will need practice. Some people obviously have the faculty highly developed; some of us get a glimmering of the width to which human experience can extend in exploring these higher worlds.

Now the great step in our thinking is to grasp that there are planes of consciousness, and by planes we mean different frequencies, different vibratory rates. A higher frequency can simply pass through lower rates unimpeded. These walls and our bodies are being passed through continuously by television and wireless, and there is no difficulty in our minds grasping that. So also it is perfectly possible for a fairy palace on a higher plane to be co-existent on this spot or there could be fields or a celestial river with higher beings walking along it. Space is an illusion. It is not that these wonderful realms are vastly far away. They are very close. The sense of distance is due simply to the degree of our lack of vision and the decaying of those organs of perception which exist in us all.

We must admit that this is a completely different idea from the more orthodox concept which is tacitly or overtly held all too often, that human consciousness starts at conception, the soul evolving through a life and then passing on perhaps to eternal life. The concept of the levels of consciousness means obviously, that we were there before we were born. Once we grasp the concept of pre-existence it ceases to be necessary to discuss whether there is survival of death. This becomes axiomatic. We are eternal, therefore we didn't start at conception. What started at conception was the beginning of this housing for the soul. We were there before birth as a spiritual being, as an aura which extended indefinitely. May I quote the wonderful passage from the seventeenth century poet, Traherne, whose work was rediscovered only in 1920. He had the faculty of perception into the womb and even beyond it. Many of his poems are concerned with this experience. He describes the experience of being in the womb and then says:

> I was within
> A house I knew not; newly cloath'd with Skin.
>
> Then was my Soul my only All to me,
> A living endless Ey,
> Scarce bounded with the Sky,
> Whose Power, and Act, and Essence was to see;
> I was an inward Sphere of Light,
> Or an interminable Orb of Sight,
> Exceeding that which makes the Days,
> A vital Sun that shed abroad its Rays:
> All Life, all Sense,
> A naked, simple, pure Intelligence.

That is what the embryo experiences, if we may take it from Traherne. He is looking through the gateway backwards to that oneness with the enormous plane of light, and then he narrows down into the grave of the body.

Birth into the body is indeed a form of death, and release from the body at what we call death is the great rebirth. That is the turn round in our thinking which our age has got to achieve. It is of vital importance because the world is teetering upon the edge of disaster.

It is perfectly obvious by the things that even the great scientists are saying that there is grave danger of our so polluting the world that life on this planet is threatened. We may even blow it up in our vast, wise ignorance. What we are doing is playing as children. With wonderful toys. This is not to belittle the fantastic achievement of mankind in making a moon rocket or atom bomb. It is an amazing example of creative group activity and it opens vistas of immense hope if man can only use his sense, but nevertheless it is like playing with toys, until we see that the universe is spiritual in essence. It is felt by so many scientists that the universe is essentially mechanical, physical and dead, and that this planet is nothing other than a dead speck of dust in the vast and indifferent universe, not, as is the truth, a living seed, so important that it is capable of evolving consciousness, and bearing the Lord of the Spiritual Sun, the entry of the Christos into this stream of consciousness. That is the highest compliment that the heavenly world could possibly pay to this tiny seed. We must learn to think of our solar system as an organism, a spiritual organism, and you cannot blow one small part off its orbit without damaging the whole any more than you can obliterate the pituitary gland of a man and think that this will do no harm to him because it is so small an organ. Man is playing with these toys in almost total ignorance that he is handling the physical image of spiritual forces and is watched by a spiritual world.

It is clearly of desperate concern to the higher world that man does not, in his folly, over-reach himself. This beautiful planet must be saved. It cannot be saved without our co-operation for the very simple reason that the Divine plan is that man should develop free will, and if free will is violated by an uninvited invasion of the forces of Michael and the Light, then the whole aeons of human development are negated as an experiment in free will. Yet it is not thinkable that the forces of the higher world will allow man to blow up his planet. This has got to be stopped somehow.

Many who have now left the body and moved on into the higher consciousness are certainly working, as scientists, doctors, musicians, artists or sociologists, to think into our thinking. They are seeking channels by means of which they can get into our hearts and into our thinking, and so by inspiration and intuition and flashes of new ideas build up the possibility of a new society. It is this co-operation within our thinking and within the flash of intuition in the heart, that needs to be made conscious. It is all very well for us to get good ideas and say 'wasn't that rather splendid; didn't I think of nice ideas'. What we should do is to give thanks in humility, for the ideas that we have produced and for the flash in the heart that guided us to take the right course. We must realise that we are in close co-operation and in the presence of guides and angelic powers and of our own friends who can in universal telepathy keep us in touch and guide us from the higher planes.

First, however, we have got to invoke and to invite. Here are the waiting forces of life which in co-operation with man can transform this world, can overcome the pollution, can rebuild society into the new Jerusalem, by flooding the hearts of man with love and joy and the intellect with understanding. Look down in imagination from the higher planes and see this darkened planet, obscured by hate and cruelty and all the disturbed emotions that the diabolical forces are creating and inflaming, and here in the fog and murk of this planet you may see visible points of light, points where it begins to glow. Porchester Hall and the gathering here may well be such a point, offering and dedicating its endeavour upward towards the light. Considering the urgency of the situation it is certain that such points will immediately be flooded with the light. We are like a resistance movement with invasion notified, and whenever the little signal light goes up secretly from the forest the paratroopers will drop. The invasion has certainly been notified by the forces of light and is imminent though we cannot tell when or how soon or in what form.

It is possible for us to rededicate our own wills, lives and actions towards the purposes of the higher world of God, thus co-operating in the forming of a new society. The world is in so critical a state that, to put it at the very lowest level, we might just as well put our last dollar on the spiritual world-picture. It is a picture full of peace, light and love, and above all joy and hope.

267

There is essentially nothing to be worried about once we grasp the fact that we are eternal beings, co-operating with an eternal plane. This is the most exciting adventure that human kind has ever undertaken, and it is the culminating point of aeons of evolution. Human consciousness has reached just that point when the huge step can be taken of opening itself to the higher world. This is the great breakthrough, the great home-coming. Nothing else matters. Whatever our own affairs or concerns or hopes, nothing is so exciting as this attempt to co-operate with the higher planes which we know to be watching and waiting, alerted for action. The difficulty for our friends on the higher plane is to devise ways of getting through to us without interfering with our freedom.

In our hearts and our minds we can create a centre of stillness and open it to the great vertical shaft of light pouring in from above. That light in the human heart can be transmuted into love which can be sent out on the horizontal beam and we create thereby the true form of the Easter resurrection cross. It is a way of seeing the six-pointed star three dimensionally. The great beam of light shoots from the zenith right through us into the depths and the cross form radiates out in love into the four directions of the compass. Surround this by the radiating aura and we have the majestic picture symbolised in the Celtic cross; but it is an eternal symbol for every religion representing the earthing of spirit and the transmuting of it in the heart. It is a marvellous image and this is the Easter image, no longer the agonised cross of suffering but the true Cross of Resurrection, which combines every religion in recognition of the one basic, spiritual fact that the higher worlds are alerted to co-operate with us as soon as we can make the gesture of invocation that opens us to their guidance.

In a bewildered world this is a picture of great joy and hope. This has been called the new Elizabethan age. We have entered into exploration, not merely round the world with Drake, but into the depths of space and not only physically but across the ranges of different vibratory rate into new spheres and dimensions of the universe so that we understand the living Cosmos for the first time and wake up to the enormous joy of this responsibility. It is almost as if we are reviving the Elizabethan picture of a Merry England forming a new society which is based on love and on joy and on the unshakable conviction that, as eternal beings, it does not matter if we are ill or broken or poverty-stricken or tortured by negative forces, because nothing can kill the inner core which is co-operating with the Christos and the Powers of Light, in bringing about the new Jerusalem. It is for this that we are meditating. We make our gesture towards the heaven world in order that they may come to the rescue and redemption of mankind. There is in the forces of Light a sense of urgency that their Commander-in-Chief has clearly demonstrated. This it seems to me is the purpose of meditation now and that is why we all, in our different ways and methods are concentrating on this way of making our breakthrough upwards towards those eternal worlds.

28

THE EMERGENCE OF
A NEW HUMANITY

DEAR FRIENDS. I have a feeling that a gathering like this is much more than just a lecturer holding forth with ideas to a captive audience ... but that we are together doing a deed. That to think together on such a theme as this – the Emergence of a New Humanity – should do something to the world itself. How can we put it? ... that the Earth should be spinning just a little faster by the time we finish. But the feeling that we are all increasingly getting is that man's role (and when I say 'man' of course I mean humanity ... male/female ... the role of the human species) is of paramount importance. There is an essential task that we are called upon to do ... and an essential step that it is incumbent on us to achieve.

Let me open with a little poem by a friend of ours, a modern poet, George Griffiths:

> Darkness would seem to be
> our chosen cloak
> whose very warp and weft's composed
> of suffering
> and death ...
> Yet he who knows the ebb and flow of tides
> within a tree,
> knows too the breath of planets
> in their pilgrimage.
> Also, in his compass, he would hold in view
> the rise and fall
> of circumstance

where man, as nexus of two worlds
stands poised at this mid-between
on razor's edge,
gifted beyond angels,
benisoned in light
and cast in the major role ...
could he but know it.

That little poem contains the lot. First the darkness of our world: 'Darkness would seem to be our chosen cloak whose very warp and weft's composed of suffering and death'. Seventy per cent of our news is about death in some form or another. And yet we are recovering the supreme knowledge that for the inner core of a man and a woman – for the 'I' in us – there can be no death because this is a droplet of divinity ... a spark of the eternal fire incarnated upon earth. Therefore we are recovering the realisation that death is the great educator to teach us the great and supreme fact that for the real being – the kernel of humanity, the man or woman – the 'I' within us is an immortal and imperishable being which never can die under any conditions. And it is only through the experience of death that we come to this supreme thought which will lift from us the terrible anxiety that rests upon our death-ridden culture.

And he goes on: 'Yet he who knows the ebb and flow of tides within a tree, knows too the breath of planets in their pilgrimage'. We are learning now to grasp this supreme fact that the whole of the Universe is alive ... is not a mechanism, but is mind. The holistic vision now takes hold of our consciousness. We realise that everything is life, everything is thought and guiding intelligence, and that matter is derivative from the world of creative idea. But yet we've gone through the experience of separation so that we stand over against that tree or these plants, separated from them, and have become observers – onlookers – to Nature, which enables us to control Nature – 'to conquer Nature' ... terrible phrase! – forgetting that we are Nature, that we are that point in Nature where evolution has become self-conscious ... integrally part of the Whole. And with that we then recover the knowledge that the Earth on which we tread, and of which we are part, is truly a living creature ... a being ... an organism; and that physical matter is only the external expression – the passing expression – of the life within it ... of the living idea behind it ... is a picture of the world of creative idea. And therefore we see that the etheric world – the world of vital forces present in all Nature – is the real being: invisible, but more real than the visible image. 'All that is transitory is but a parable', as Goethe says. Therefore 'he who knows the ebb and flow of tides within a tree'. *Well a tree stands still! Hard bark! You can't see it flowing!* But you can! Look into those roots! *But the roots are right underground – I can't see the roots!*

Yes, but you can! With the eye of the imagination you can look down and see the roots, and sense and experience the intelligence in the tips of the roots as they stretch down and grasp and lock themselves round the rock to take the strain of the moving branches in the storm. Of course you can see them ... with the realer eye of the imagination, though it's closed to the physical senses. And the rising of the sap: of course you can see it ... with the eye of the mind – this inner eye – that is one with the whole of the thought of the Universe. And there you can see the sap rising and you can realise what we normally don't see: that the whole of the tree is reaching out into a field of magnetic force ... reaching right to the very periphery – the far periphery – counter to gravity. The field of levity, lightness, light, which reaches out into ethereal space: that is the tree. So, once you know 'the ebb and flow of tides within a tree', you can also experience 'the breath of planets in their pilgrimage'. For we are seeing the wonderful thought that the whole Universe is Mind. That is the first of what are called the Hermetic Principles, the first Principle of the Hermetic Knowledge ... the ancient, ageless wisdom recovered in our age. We are in process, in the apprehending of holistic knowledge, of grasping once more the Hermetic Wisdom forgotten for these centuries, and it is both a scientific and a mystical concept. In this wisdom, mysticism and science meet again. And the first Principle is: the Universe is Mind. And the second Principle is the Law of Correspondences: as above, so below; as in the great, so in the small; as in the macrocosm, so in the microcosm – with the realisation that this microcosm, the human body, contains the entire Universe … that this is a microcosm reflecting the Whole. Outside the Temple of Delphi was carved: 'Man, know thyself, and thou shalt know the Universe'. A remark which can mean nothing to the mere rational, materialistic viewpoint … but it's the clue.

This microcosm is truly the temple, the outer picture of the divine archetype. The temple, in the sense of all temples, as the chamber – the structure – into which a spiritual being can descend in order to operate on a greater density … a heavier density; in this case on a solid rocky planet and therefore the temple has a hard skeleton but is truly the temple in which the spiritual being … the 'I' … the true higher ego, can inhabit and operate in this heavy density and heavy vibration of the physical Earth. So here we are: we're recovering this knowledge that what we are – each of us – is a spiritual being … a droplet of the great ocean of life and wisdom. Mind – our mind – therefore is a pulse of the eternal mind, which being so there is nothing, but nothing, except ourselves to stop that mind expanding into the whole ocean of mind. We are living in this appalling illusion that we're stuck – buried – in the sarcophagus of our five senses and the body. But the realisation is that we are perfectly free to expand and move out, overcoming self-consciousness and its drastic limitation, and moving out into cosmic consciousness … into oneness with the whole. And so Griffiths goes on: 'Also in his compass' … if once you've got the idea – if you're beginning to grasp – stretch the imagination out into the great whole:

> Also, in his compass, he would hold in view
> the rise and fall
> of circumstance
> where man, as nexus of two worlds
> stands poised at this mid-between
> on razor's edge,
> gifted beyond angels,
> benisoned in light
> and cast in the major role …
> could he but know it.

'Gifted beyond angels' ... now get this idea: that mankind – humanity – is the great experiment of God. The Earth is the great training ground for a hierarchy of spiritual beings. We can call it the Tenth Hierarchy, 'a little lower than the angels, but crowned with glory and honour'. 'Gifted beyond angels' because we have been given free will. Clue to the great experiment! It is as if the Almighty has sensed the need of having somewhere in His creation a being who can stand up to Him as a son and begin to create, himself. See what excitement if we dare have the impudence to look down with God's eyes at His creation. What a thrill to watch the part of His creation after aeons of evolution reaching the point when it can really begin in freedom to create, and in consciousness to overcome separation, egoism and desire ... and once more enter into its inheritance as a Son of God, and consciously come back as co-creator with God. Realise this: that the angelic world is part of the will of God. It doesn't need freedom in our sense of the word. It is already part of the Will of God, and the delight of the angel on all its levels is to work with, and for, God ... for the Divine Source. To obey It and serve It. But man, the Tenth Hierarchy, has been given the freedom.

Now we begin to see the marvellous, extraordinary gamble of the Heavens. Realise this: that a being which can see the angels – can see the elemental world working within Nature – cannot but respond and obey. If the Archangel Michael stood here and waved his sword, who wouldn't respond? Therefore the risk has to be taken of letting the Tenth Hierarchy go through the narrows – the difficult phase – of losing the spiritual worlds completely. It's part of the destiny, above all, of the West ... above all, of the Anglo Saxon race, to lose the spiritual world and gain the over-masculinated intellect and thereby explore the world of matter. It was not an accident. It was not a misfortune. But it is a gamble because it involves the dying – the atrophying – of the organs of subtler perception associated with the right hemisphere of the brain ... the feminine organs which can apprehend the Living Whole. We have in the last centuries overdeveloped the masculine left hemisphere of the brain and have achieved an extraordinary technology, but have lost the Living Whole and the World has died to us as a result. The result is that man has shrunk. Blake, that great seer, passionately speaking for the New Age (he's the real New Age prophet), saying among other things: 'Wake up, young men of the New Age!' Now listen to what he says:

> We have been the wrenching apart of the perceiving mind and what we perceive from their original indivisible unity to produce an externalised, fixed, dead nature and a shrinking of our humanity from the boundless being of the imagination into the mortal worm of sixty winters and seventy inches long.

That is what we've become. Shrinking from the 'boundless being of the imagination' which is really us. And the result is that we lose Nature. Listen:

> The Stars flee remote: the heaven is iron, the earth is sulphur,
> And all the mountains and hills shrink up like a withering
> gourd ...
> ... the Sun is shrunk: the Heavens are shrunk
> Away into the far remote: and the Trees & Mountains withered
> Into indefinite cloudy shadows.

We've lost the life in Nature ... it's gone dead to us. And a lovely quotation of Blake's:

> 'What', it will be questioned, 'When the sun rises, do you not see a round disc of fire somewhat like a Guinea?' 'O no, no, I see an Innumerable company of the Heavenly host crying, 'Holy, Holy, Holy is the Lord God Almighty'.

Blake could see right straight through into the Spiritual Sun. For remember, we are recovering the knowledge – and I'm asking you to take this now as a living idea – that within every visible form is spiritual being. And the spiritual being – the ocean of life – is primary. The secondary condition is the visible form. And it's that world of living being which is wholly lost to us because the five senses can't see it. The senses have become nothing more than filters to protect us from reality. As Eliot put it, 'Humankind cannot bear very much reality'. And Martin Armstrong in a poem called *The Cage* puts this brilliantly, the sense – very important to get – that the senses are really filters to protect us:

> Man, afraid to be alive
> Shuts his soul in senses five,
> From fields of uncreated light
> Into the crystal tower of sight,
> And from the roaring songs of space
> Into the small flesh-carven place
> Of the ear whose cave impounds
> Only small and broken sounds,
> And to his narrow sense of touch
> From strength that held the stars in clutch,
> And from the warm ambrosial spice
> Of flowers and fruits of paradise,
> Into the frail and fitful power
> Of scent and tasting, sweet and sour;
> And toiling for a sordid wage
> There in his self-created cage
> Ah, how safely barred is he
> From menace of Eternity.

Now will you take it? What is happening now ... now in our generation – in our time – is that we've reached the evolutionary point when we can take the step in consciousness beyond limited self-consciousness into all-consciousness ... into cosmic consciousness. From being an earth-bound creature man is becoming in all senses a universal creature: Homo Universalis. A new type of man is appearing. We have, you see, dissolved solid matter into energy by our intellects. We've arrived at the knowledge which is that the solidity of matter is mere illusion and everything is on the move the whole time ... everything is flowing ... nothing is still ... everything is interconnected ... everything is alive. And this is the point where the most advanced scientific thinking is bridging back into the mystical in realising that that energy – being alive – is also thought ... is part of the great ocean of intelligence pouring out from the Divine Source.

277

Therefore if you can enter (we've heard this earlier) into the etheric within the tree – 'the ebb and flow of tides' within the tree – you are instantly through into the Whole. Where does your vision end?

If I may dare, briefly, to throw in this rather amusing interlude: will you come with me now – I'm going to give you something which is quite childish – remembering that someone somewhere said that except ye become as little children you won't know what it's all about. Become as little children! A friend of mine, Douglas Harding – student of Zen – was hit by a wonderful thought: 'I haven't got a face! All these people I see here – human beings – all seem to have a lump on the top of their shoulders with hair on the top and seven holes in it. But I haven't got that. I am merely crystal space. Where does my face begin?' Now be childish! Don't let your intellect get in the way now. You may sometime have looked in the mirror, of course, and seen how many eyes you have, but forget that for the moment. Your real honest experience: how many eyes are you looking with? One? Or two? Or a thousand? As far as my face is concerned: outside here this is my green jersey thing... and then comes you ... and then comes the rest of the room. Where does it begin or end? Beyond that the clouds ... beyond that the stars. He suddenly saw that 'I am unique!' But so are you! As far as you're concerned, I have this lump on the top, but you – be honest – each of you begin there, but where do you end? He discovered that the Zen people said, 'Cut off your head!' and then roared with laughter because nobody understood. They also called it 'your original face'. Your original face encloses the lot, but all our culture and even our bringing-up of children is all forcing you to 'save face' ... to 'put a good face on it' ... to count: this is the nose, this is the eyes, this is the ears and all this.

But the real truth is that this incredible design has created an organ which enables a spiritual being to inhabit the Earth and to be in touch with the Whole, entirely unaware of the mechanism unless scientific intellect is concerning itself ... or unless you've got headache, eye-ache, earache ... then you're aware of your ears. It's a wonderful instrument. You see you know nothing – be honest – although the schoolchild will tell you about it: that light comes on, the image comes in as reversed and passes up into the mind through the retina. You can't experience that. If you're honest to your experience you have this crystal sphere through which you can look and which includes everything. Where does it end? It includes the stars … it's right for the tiny child to grope for the moon. Those lights above me could well be the Pleiades and they're just as much in my 'original face' if they're here, two feet away, or the Pleiades. In other words, I take from you today your faces and I give you the Universe, if you can but see it.

'Cast in the major role', that's what man is, 'could he but know it'. And this is what we are beginning to know. We're beginning to wake up to what our role is. Now what I'm talking about is of course not so much academic stuff … so much mere theory. This is burningly relevant to our time, especially to the young. The younger ones in this room, if I may do so, I would congratulate on having chosen to incarnate at this time. Because you know what happens: before the soul comes down to Earth it is given a pre-view of the destiny it is taking on and given the choice of withdrawing. No-one descends except who chooses. Now it is not thinkable that when you were given a pre-view of your particular destiny which you were taking on that you would not be shown also the setting for that destiny … the world situation. In other words, you would have been shown what the last twenty years of the twentieth century is bringing upon the World. The smashing-up of the old bottles in order to create new bottles which can receive the heady new wine poured out from the great tubs of Aquarius into the Earth. For we enter this period at the beginning of the Aquarian Age when the new energies – the powerful, cleansing energies which are ultimately Love – are being poured into the planet to cleanse it. You will certainly have been shown this extraordinary thing: that it is necessary to cleanse the planet of its evil and its pollution in order to make way for the in-flooding of the forces of Light which can cleanse it and bring about a new world.

This is the operation with which we are concerned. I may say that I wrote a book which I called *Operation Redemption* … if you want it that is my statement about it. But that appears to be what is happening. Now look at the scale of our time. The world looks awfully bad: 'Darkness would seem to be our chosen cloak whose very warp and weft's composed of suffering and death'. And, as we've said, the news spends all its time on talking about that breakdown. The breaking-down may well be, and I'm perfectly convinced is, the sweeping away of the products of our egoism in order to make way for a new humanity. Now we are recovering a tremendous concept ... no not recovering ... ours is the first generation which can see, through first hand experience, that humanity is one organism ... is one being. Stretch this Divine gift of imagination that Blake talks about, now. Wrap up the planet ... stand outside the planet and look at it ... you have no difficulty in doing so. Look at this beautiful orb of blue and silver ... and realise humanity – the noosphere – the human sphere, the human layer, covering the whole planet. Remember that Teilhard was so delighted at overpopulation. He said, 'Come on over-population! When we're jostling shoulder-to-shoulder over the whole planet we will wake up to the fact that we are one humanity'.

Now take that thought ... put your imagination into it. We are each of us a cell of the one organism that is humanity. Got that idea? Ours is the first generation that could grasp the concept of humanity as one. Now, cells in the body ... what happens when those cells choose not to work with the pro-grammed pattern, but to follow their own willful way? You get cancer. That is what cancer cells are. In the body of humanity many, if not most, of the human cells – because they've been given free will – are choosing to spend their time following egoism, desire, greed and all its outcomes, getting for self, fighting to get more power and get what they want, and ultimately war. In other words they are cancerous growths in the body of humanity. But now what is happening? We've been given free will. We're each of us free to choose and until now have felt that the purpose of life was to get more things, get more comfortable, get more what one wants, get more power, and so forth ... even fighting other egos ... bashing at each other like that! Now what

happens is that cell after cell stops and reorientates, and begins
to do what Teilhard called 'homing upon the Omega point';
pushes up through the obscure cloud of egoism around the
Earth and pushes its head out into the great dome of the
heavens ... and looks around and sees, 'My God! I belong! This
world of light is where I came from and what I belong to'. And
it sees the others that have pushed their heads up and recognises
them as brothers and sisters. One cell after another begins to do
that: to grasp what we call now 'the holistic world view'. And
may I just mention that wonderful word which has come into
common parlance in the last five years is spelt h-o-l-i-s-t-i-c
implying that the Whole is holy. And healing is restoring relationship to the Holy Whole.

Right! ... what happens when a cell sees that? It begins
consciously to align with the Divine programming once more.
So great is this concept that inevitably it must offer itself to be
worked through – to cooperate with – the Divine programming,
and ceases to be cancerous. This is the change that's now taking
place. Human clusters are coming together, dedicated to serving
the living Whole. It's an extraordinary process that is now
happening, for realise this: if once you see the holistic picture
and see what man is – if you can accept this picture – it is not
just academic knowledge. It becomes – to put it at its lowest –
wholly inappropriate to blow each others' brains out and all the
other nasty things we can do to each other. Do realise that we
are all cells in this one body of humanity, and as it's the same
divinity in me that is in you, I begin to see the meaning that those
who kill by the sword shall perish by the sword. And I begin to
see the real meaning of that great human maxim which is basic
to all the great religions, or rather the secret esoteric knowledge
in all the religions. Every one of them says in almost the same
words that the real human maxim which is the Law of the
Prophets is: 'Do unto others as you would have them do unto
you. Do not to others what you would not have them do to you.'
And every one of the religions has almost the same words. Look
at human history and think how much that has been put into
action. But this vision that we're getting – this new esoteric secret

knowledge ... this vision of holism ... this vision of what man really is – restores to us the necessity to live by that. Once you have seen what you really are and know that you are this immortal droplet of God – part of the whole – that is the first thing. Grasp the idea ... then apply it. You then have got to do something about it. And the emergence of the alternative lifestyle is what is happening now. The cluster of human cells coming together to live a lifestyle which truly serves the organic living being of Mother Earth ... Gaia, the Goddess of Earth. Inevitably this thinking – being alive – results in a change of living ... a new right livelihood ... a new way of living. And we are watching this form and we are taking part in it.

This is the great excitement of our time. And furthermore, the emergence of the alternative lifestyle, though it is only clusters appearing who may hardly have grasped the scale of the picture, is part of a great impulse that is pouring into us from the outside. It is not – I repeat this strongly – it is not just some-body's plan to improve society. That has been tried, intellectually, often enough with greater or less success. This is something much more, for the Universe is dynamic. Operation Redemption is launched, the planet is being cleansed by the in-flooding of this Light and Love as a creative power, breaking down the old forms, making way for the new. I remember a delightful little poem – a song – by Sidney Carter, the songwriter who wrote *Lord of the Dance* and so forth. It goes like this:

Dig Michelangelo,
Down in the marble,
A wonder is waiting
That no one can see.
Nowhere and never
And now and forever
I look for a thing
That is looking for me.
Over the water I
Sail like a fisherman,
Casting my nets in
The dark of the sea.

Nowhere and never
And now and forever
I look for a thing
That is looking for me.
Faith is a digger
And hope is a diver
And down in the marble
Or under the sea
Nowhere and never
And now and forever
I look for a thing
That is looking for me.

This is what we are doing ... this is the excitement. Now, the change that is coming is nothing less than the emergence of a new humanity. The emergence, dare one say, of what is virtually a new human species. Not a new race ... for the new species is composed of people from any walk of life, of the cancer cells which have reversed themselves and are joining together in bringing to birth the new. Notice that what tends to happen is that if a species gets obsolete it is pushed out onto a limb by Nature and evolution, and allowed to bow out ... and a stronger species takes over. This happened when Neanderthal Man, who was a fine fellow, met – what we call – Homo Sapiens who had developed the frontal lobe and was therefore able to organise in a way that Neanderthal couldn't do. So Neanderthal was pushed out and Sapiens took over and then developed his over-masculinated, patriarchal society: left hemisphere of the brain, unbalanced masculine, organising, controlling, developing the great culture that we have now. Unbalanced male/female: allow-ing the sensitive feminine right hemisphere organs, which can apprehend the living whole, to atrophy and go dormant.

Now in our time, with the holistic world view, with the way science has developed in discovering everything is alive and everything is on the move, a change is taking place and people are appearing who are really balanced male/female. It may turn out to be that actually there is a change within the subtle brain cells which creates the new balance. And it has been suggested

283

that it is no less than what is virtually a new species which could be called Mulier Homo Noeticus. Mulier – feminine, woman; Homo – woman/man (androgynous); Noeticus – consciousness directed. Mulier Homo Noeticus: woman/man of developing consciousness. This is nothing less than an evolutionary change of supreme importance.

Peter Russell is lecturing in a day or two's time on his book *The Awakening Earth* and has there powerfully put forward the concept that something is happening in evolution which has never happened before, which is that the drive of evolution – instead of just shaping forms – has turned inwards into that most advanced form in the evolutionary pattern, namely man – man/woman – and thereby given us choice to look ahead. We are free to choose the way they're going to go. Evolution, instead of just shaping us, turning in virtually says, 'Right, now what are you going to do about it?' We look out into the world: it's not insignificant that the impetus has launched in the world called Planetary Initiative for the World We Choose. We are beginning to be able to look into the future and plan the future. We are beginning to see as Barbara Marx Hubbard, the futurist from America who's written a magnificent book soon to be published here called *Evolutionary Journey* in which she sees really that we are ceasing to be merely Earth-bound creatures, but are becoming planetary creatures. I give you just a couple of lines from her:

> The evolutionaries believe there is a predictable, progressive patterning process in the Universe. Intelligent energy at the core of the designing system counteracting the increase of entropy and disorder, the death of the physical universe. A planetary species is at the historical point of transformation from Earth-only towards its universal phase of development. We are no longer an Earth-bound species. We are able to change and therefore take responsibility for the direction of change. The peak experience involves the crossing of the great divide between the basic needs motivation and chosen function or self-actualisation. We are to work to further the rise of humanness out of our humanity.

This is the most tremendous point. She develops first of all that we are becoming space men in the sense that we are pushing our technology out in space and there is no reason why we should not really take space as our field for exploration. But realise this: that to shoot our rockets up, marvellous though the achievement is, is still physical ... still gravity-bound. A more exciting thing that we are concerned with is the recovering of the lost knowledge that there is truly a polar opposite to gravity. But it's not a physical opposite. It's the passage through – into – what is rightly called ethereal space. This is what Blake knew and most succinctly put it. The task is:

> ... to open the Eternal Worlds, to open the Immortal Eyes of Man inward into the Realms of Thought ... into Eternity ever expanding in the Bosom of God the Human Imagination.

Now we're recovering what really imagination means: which is the faculty of moving into the world of life and light, and discovering that we can instantly be in the whole of this ethereal space. We're moving into the realm of thought which is instantaneous, and therefore all this worry about light years which dwarfs us, as Blake said, into a 'mortal worm of sixty winters and seventy inches long' is unnecessary. We rediscover that we are everywhere ... that light years don't hold good in ethereal space because it's the realm of thought. And we can move out instantly, which means again that it's possible for the human mind to apprehend all knowledge, and this is what the mystics, the visionaries, the great seers of the world, have succeeded in demonstrating. This concept of ethereal space out of Goethe ... through Steiner ... through Ernst Lehrs and George Adams ... is a scientific concept, but bridging the science of the spirit which therefore mechanistic science hasn't found. But it's the real polar opposite of gravity.

We discover that the levity pole is the life pole, lifting life, light – as opposed to the grave of gravity – until our consciousness can move through into it. And this is the true space exploration: inner space exploration which is indicated in the baroque churches – a lovely thought! Outside you look up into the blue sky; inwards you move and look up, not at the ceiling, but you look through the painted ceiling and there are all the beings sitting upon clouds. Of course they've entered the world of levity, and there is some saint in apotheosis, and there is Jesus sitting on the rainbow, and the cross is disappearing into golden heights of the highest light. That is the real experience that Dante went through and that is opening to all of us in this counterpart to the physical space exploration. So we are really becoming – in a double sense – the space beings.

Right! I draw towards an end and I want to give you here a passage from Aurobindo, that great seer from India:

> The future belongs to the young.
> It is a young and new world which is now in process of development and it is the young (or the young in spirit) who must create it.

Let me hasten to say to those of you in the audience, like myself, who are getting on in years: this does not exclude you. For youth is not a time in life – a number of years – but it's a condition of mind. And I would interpolate here Yeats' lovely sentence that:

> An aged man is but a paltry thing,
> A tattered coat upon a stick, unless
> Soul clap its hands and sing, and louder sing
> For every tatter in its mortal dress,
> Nor is there singing school but studying
> Monuments of its own magnificence; ...

Well! There you are, all of you who are getting on, let 'Soul clap its hands and sing, and louder sing for every tatter in its mortal dress'. We discover that we are young. I'm speaking for the old ones now ... all these young people think they are their body (identify with it more or less). We with the body beginning to fade discover that our immortal being, housed in that body temporarily, is eternally young. It doesn't age ... it's lifted out of age. So all of you: not only have I taken your face away and given you the Universe, but also to the older ones I restore you to youth because you realise that the 'I' in you is ageless or simply your choice. Don't identify yourself with the aches of your body ....

THE EMERGENCE OF A NEW HUMANITY

and then the aches themselves may fade if once you get that attitude. But that was all in brackets in the middle of my quotation!

> But it is also a world of truth, courage, justice, lofty aspirations and straightforward fulfilment which we seek to create.
>
> Our ideal is a new birth of humanity into the spirit; our life must be a spiritually inspired effort to create a body of action for the great new birth and creation.
> ... Our ideal is not the spirituality that withdraws from life, but the conquest of life by the power of the Spirit. It is to accept the world as an effort of manifestation of the Divine, but also to transform humanity by a greater effort of manifestation than has yet been accomplished, one in which the veil between man and God shall be removed, the divine manhood of which we are capable should come to birth and our life should be remoulded in the truth and the light and power of the spirit.
> ... It is the young ... who are free in mind and heart to accept a completer truth and labour for a greater ideal. They must be men (and women) who will dedicate themselves not to the past or the present, but to the future. They will need to consecrate their lives to an exceeding of their lower self, to the realisation of God in themselves and in all human beings and to a whole-hearted and indefatigable labour for the nation and for humanity. This ideal can be as yet only a little seed and the life that embodies it is a small nucleus, but it is our fixed hope that the seed will grow into a tree and the nucleus be the heart of an ever-extending formation. It is with a confident trust in the spirit that inspires us that we take our place among the standard-bearers of the new humanity that is struggling to be born ...

There! That is what we are about, dear friends. Hold this pause ... Realise that we are part of the great organism of humanity ... a human cluster. Realise that a gathering like this is not only two hundred people. It is first of all one mind, part of the Divine Mind, and secondly that many, many beings from the invisible worlds will join in to help us and take part. Both the angelic world and also our friends out of the body who are deeply concerned with the spiritual awakening that is now taking on. In this moment of silence let us open our hearts and our minds with thanks – with gratitude – to all in the invisible world with whom we are now in touch. And having collected this power and ethereal light, let us send it out into the darkened world to be taken up by the angelic beings and used for the healing of humanity and the tormented Earth. This is the deed that such a gathering can achieve … Glory be! …

THE WREKIN TRUST TODAY

THE LECTURES in this book are amongst those Sir George Trevelyan gave between the 1960s and 1980s, mostly under the auspices of the Wrekin Trust which he founded in 1971 as an education charity to provide adult learning opportunities on these great themes. During this time the Trust provided conferences, courses and programmes that enabled up to ten thousand people a year from diverse disciplines and viewpoints to explore leading-edge topics in a non-sectarian way.

In 1982 the Trust received a Right Livelihood Award for its work 'forming an essential contribution to making life more whole, healing our planet and uplifting humanity'.

Sir George died in 1996 and two years later the Trust entered a new phase. Whilst continuing to provide a modest programme of learning events it now emphasised its purpose to 'awaken and revitalise a spiritual dimension in society by empowering and supporting a deeper connection between visionary organisations and individuals whose approach is based on holistic, spiritual and ecological principles'. The Wrekin Forum was established in 2000 and now has one hundred and seventy associate organisations and individuals. Since 2000 the Wrekin Forum has held annual Round Tables and seeded several projects. In 2006, to honour the centenary of Sir George's birth, a major conference was held in London on 'The Emerging Spirituality Revolution: Embodying the Spiritual Imperative of our Time'. With over four hundred people affirming the urgent need today to provide deeper spiritual connections for those developing as conscious instruments for creative change, a framework of connections is being established across the British Isles.

A series of regional Round Tables, participative spiritual inquiries, Quest group and 'Cafés Spirituels' are underway, as well as projects for spirituality in youth work and in schools and also adult education.

A Co-Creative Circle brings together those associates holding a focus of some kind in the sense that Sir George envisioned, 'Out of a crumbling society will emerge individuals who are touched by higher guidance. These will inevitably flow together with others of like inspiration and a new quality of society will begin to form'. The Wrekin Forum promotes collaboration and sees this as the way forward offering those individuals and organisations who would like to participate actively in the 'adventure of our time', as Sir George Trevelyan envisaged, to support our work by becoming associates of the Wrekin Forum.

JANICE DOLLEY

For further details and a warm response from the Wrekin Trust please contact:

Janice Dolley
Development Director
Wrekin Trust
Courtyard Lodge
Mellow Farm
Hawcross Lane
Redmarley D'Abitot
Gloucestershire GL19 3JQ

T: 00 44 (0)1452 840033
E: info@wrekintrust.org
W: www.wrekintrust.org
or www.wrekinforum.org

Registered Charity No. 262303

For further details on the life and work of Sir George Trevelyan, see www.sirgeorgetrevelyan.org.uk or read *Sir George Trevelyan and the new spiritual awakening* by Frances Farrer (ISBN 0-86315-377-1) available from most libraries (copies can be purchased direct from the Wrekin Trust at the above address for £20.00 inc p&p).

GODSTOW PRESS

Because philosophy arises from awe, a philosopher is bound in his way to be a lover of myths and poetic fables. Poets and philosophers are alike in being big with wonder. ST THOMAS AQUINAS

THE SONG OF ORPHEUS, the music that charms stones, wild animals and even the King of Hades, is the song of poets who have a sense of the divine at heart. For the forces of greed and evil to succeed, that song must be drowned out by noise.

What is today if not noisy? Not only in our society but within ourselves there is the clamour of many distractions. Just living life we forget ourselves and the song that we heard as children is heard but rarely if at all.

The aim of Godstow Press is to sing the Orphic song, through books of fiction, poetry and non-fiction, as well as through CDs. Besides publishing first editions we shall include on our list works which have been privately produced by writers and musicians who have thought, perhaps, that they sing alone.

Together, artist and audience, we shall form a choir.

We have no plans at the moment to make our books generally available through the trade and we depend entirely on personal contact with readers. For more information and inclusion in our database, please get in touch with us.

Godstow Press
60 Godstow Road
Wolvercote
Oxford
OX2 8NY
UK

www.godstowpress.co.uk
info@godstowpress.co.uk
tel +44 (0)1865 556215